For Mischa,
and innocence recollected

Before we begin, you must all be warned:
Nothing here is vegetarian.

Bon appétit.

—HANNIBAL LECTER, MD

Praise for *Hannibal Lecter and Philosophy*

"The eighteen essays in this smart and playful anthology address, among other subjects, the connections between psychiatry and empathy, aesthetics and haute cuisine, *friendship, art, and the nature of desire. Get to know Hannibal Lecter, this book suggests, and you get to know what it means to live a life of the mind, as well as the flesh."*

> —MIKITA BROTTMAN, Author of *Meat Is Murder! An Illustrated Guide to Cannibal Culture*

"Hannibal Lecter and Philosophy is a smorgasbord of dark delights. The menu offers a seared entree of our own empathetic responses as manipulated by facial close-ups, as well as an exploration of the morality of people-eating; main courses featured include a steamy analysis of sociopathic feelings of divinity and a chilled look at horror-pleasure. In servings that ponder the films, television series, and novels, this book will help anyone with a taste for intellectual blood sharpen her thoughts on the refined, sophisticated, and delicious Dr. Lecter."

> —SARA WALLER, Editor of *Serial Killers: Being and Killing*

"Hannibal Lecter refuses to be categorized and his multiple incarnations make any attempt nearly impossible, as well as dangerous (just remember the poor census taker). Thankfully, the contributors to this volume have not attempted to analyze Hannibal, as he cannot be reduced to a set of check marks, but instead have focused on what Hannibal reveals about various aspects and ideas ranging from aesthetics to friendship to the morality of cannibalism. More importantly, these essays explicitly and implicitly focus on why we are fascinated with Hannibal and what that fascination reveals about human nature. No matter which version of Hannibal the reader prefers, he or she will find all of the essays illuminating, perhaps frighteningly so."

> —MICHELLE GOMPF, Author of *Thomas Harris and William Blake: Allusions in the Hannibal Lecter Novels*

"On very rare occasions, an author will dream up a fictional character who steps from the book that first brought him to life and enters the realm of pop myth. Bram Stoker did it with Dracula, Arthur Conan Doyle with Sherlock Holmes, Edgar Rice Burroughs with Tarzan. And in a pair of now-classic horror-thrillers from the 1980s—RED DRAGON and THE SILENCE OF THE LAMBS—Thomas Harris did it with Hannibal Lecter. Though Dr. Lecter informs Clarice Starling that he is a phenomenon that resists explanation, this rich and provocative collection proves otherwise. With penetrating insight and a sophisticated wit that the good doctor himself would surely appreciate, these essays shed consistently sharp light on the moral, psychological, and philosophical complexities of America's most beloved cannibal killer."

> —HAROLD SCHECHTER, Author of *Man-Eater: The Life and Legend of an American Cannibal*

"Hannibal Lecter is suave, cultured, brilliant—and profoundly evil. Who is Hannibal, really—vampire, psychopath, artist, devil? Drawing upon philosophers from Plato to Foucault, and Augustine to Nietzsche, this book will engage any reader interested in this villain's multiple incarnations on page and screen. By examining Hannibal in relation to numerous philosophical issues, including revenge, justice, evil, forgiveness, autonomy, empathy, and even humor, the authors in this collection provide subtle insights into one of our most fascinating fictional monsters."

> —CYNTHIA FREELAND, Author of *The Naked and the Undead: Evil and the Appeal of Horror* and co-editor of *Philosophy and Film*

"Like a savory multi-course meal prepared by chef cuisinier / serial killer Dr. Lecter himself, Hannibal Lecter and Philosophy stimulates the intellectual appetite, provides variety, cleanses the palate between courses, and concludes leaving the reader both satiated and wanting more. Within these pages will be found a sumptuous, complexly layered reading experience, covering in relation to the fiction, film, and television incarnations of Dr. Lecter philosophical topics as varied as the cosmopolitanism and classifications of cannibalism; natural law; moral virtues and professional ethics; the existence and nature of God; moral dualism and pluralism; corruption and incorruptibility; psychopathology, psychiatry, and psychology; neuroscience; the pitfalls of friendship, love, and empathy; the aesthetics of the culinary arts, the fine arts, and murder; behaviorism versus transcendental evil; the cruelty of wit and humor; and monstrosity and horror. All of this makes for a heady meal, to be sure; yet as is typical of the Popular Culture and Philosophy series, both the general and academic reader alike will find something to please one's taste here. Come, let these writers show you to Dr. Lecter's table, where pity has no place but which can be far more engaging than theater. Prepare for a dark but illuminating feast."

> —PHILIP L. SIMPSON, Author of *Making Murder: The Fiction of Thomas Harris*

"Poor Clarice—up against the greatest screen villain of all time! Poor Will— knowing the truth is not enough! Poor Hannibal—searching for his equal! . . . Or is it his next meal? This delectable six-course banquet cuts, peels, pulls, and savors every morsel at the table Hannibal has set before us. Chewing on the deeper meanings of the books, films, and TV series, the chefs . . . um, writers . . . in this book revel in a range of tastes that can help us better sample the world around us."

> —JOSEF STEIFF, Editor of *Sherlock Holmes and Philosophy*

"Psychopath. Vampire. Devil. Monster. Hannibal Lecter's truly phenomenal popularity, homicidal though he may be, raises complex ethical and socio-philosophical issues, explored in this addition to the Popular Culture and Philosophy series."

> —ROBERT CETTL, Author of *Serial Killer Cinema*

Popular Culture and Philosophy®

Hannibal Lecter and Philosophy

The Heart of the Matter

Edited by

JOSEPH WESTFALL

OPEN COURT
Chicago

Volume 96 in the series, Popular Culture and Philosophy ®, edited by George A. Reisch

To find out more about Open Court books, call toll-free 1-800-815-2280, or visit our website at www.opencourtbooks.com.

Open Court Publishing Company is a division of Carus Publishing Company, dba Cricket Media.

Copyright © 2016 by Carus Publishing Company, dba Cricket Media

First printing 2016

Printed and bound in the United States of America.

ISBN: 978-0-8126-9904-3

Library of Congress Control Number: 2015949856

Le Menu

Savoureux

Fromage

Dessert

Café

Hello, Dr. Lecter

JOSEPH WESTFALL

Hannibal Lecter . . . is . . . our most recent version of Mephistopheles—erudite, omniscient, satanic, and out to seduce Starling's very being with the promise of knowledge.

> —NOËL CARROLL, "Enjoying Horror Fictions"

If Hannibal Lecter isn't a Count Dracula for the computer-and-cellphone age, then we don't have one.

> —STEPHEN KING, "Hannibal the Cannibal"

In fact, there is no consensus in the psychiatric community that Dr. Lecter should be termed a man. He has long been regarded by his professional peers in psychiatry, many of whom fear his acid pen in the professional journals, as something entirely Other. For convenience they term him a "monster."

> —THOMAS HARRIS, *Hannibal*

Hannibal Lecter.

"A brief silence follows the name, always, in any civilized gathering" (Harris, *Silence*, p. 4). Dr. Lecter hates to be discourteous, but he is busy with a patient just now—apparently, he has something rather meaty to work through. You may await him in the waiting room. He'll be but two shakes of a (silent) lamb's tail—not a moment more. But while you wait . . .

Stephen King calls him "the great fictional monster of our time," and it is a difficult point to dispute. With his suave appeal, his charm, his wit and intelligence, his vast memory and encyclopedic knowledge, his ability to excel in apparently any field of endeavor, and his immaculate taste in clothes, wine, music, art, architecture, literature, and most of all *food*—it would be difficult to deny him greatness. And why would we? Denying the greatness of Hannibal Lecter is usually the first step in the direction of appearing at his next dinner party. Dr. Lecter does so appreciate having the willfully blind, the ignorant, and the rude for dinner.

Of course, in our denial, then, we would discover the monster. He can be seen from two sides, as Clarice Starling noted: "one showed his charm, the other his scales" (Harris, *Hannibal*, p. 302). Charm and scales, a cocktail suited only to the boldest of palates.

First Principles, Clarice

He is described as "a small, lithe man . . . Very neat" (Harris, *Dragon*, p. 58), with "a wiry strength" (Harris, *Silence*, p. 14). Until he amputates it himself, he has "six fingers on his left hand" (Harris, *Silence*, p. 13)—a perfect duplicate of his middle finger, described more than once as "the rarest form of polydactyly" (Harris, *Silence*, p. 20). His "cultured voice has a slight metallic rasp beneath it" (Harris, *Silence*, p. 14). Looking a little more closely, we see he has "small white teeth," and perhaps most remarkably of all, his "eyes are maroon and they reflect the light redly in tiny points" (Harris, *Dragon*, pp. 58–59). He is regularly described as being characterized by an extraordinary stillness, and "His ego, like his intelligence . . . and the degree of his rationality, is not measurable by conventional means" (Harris, *Hannibal*, p. 136). He is an acute observer, and of his physical senses, his sense of smell is perhaps the most acute: "He could smell everything" (Harris, *Silence*, p. 22).

Dr. Lecter has appeared in several guises over the past forty years or so, in different contexts, and at different stages (not always chronologically ordered) along his life's way. He has appeared as a character in four novels by Thomas Harris: in the first of these, he is but a brief, daring interlude (*Red Dragon*, 1981); in the last two, his is the triumphal melody that overtakes all (*Hannibal*, 1999; *Hannibal Rising*, 2006); and in the middle, in *Silence* . . . he is the countermelody in a minor key that haunts us long after we've left the symphony hall (*The Silence of the Lambs*, 1988). And if Hannibal Lecter reminds us of music, we would be remiss not to mention the performers who have brought that music to life—the incarnations of Harris's literary specter, as it were. Brian Cox, Anthony Hopkins (yes, of course, Anthony Hopkins!), Aaran Thomas (if only briefly), Gaspard Ulliel, and, most recently, Mads Mikkelsen. In each case, a different take on our old familiar cannibal—who somehow, even as he ages, never grows old. Of course, not every Lecter is to every Fannibal's liking. But even when we find ourselves disappointed with one (or more) of his incarnations and interpretations, we never find ourselves thinking that Hannibal Lecter *himself* is not great, nor that Hannibal Lecter is *not* a monster. Somehow, Dr. Lecter survives even his many presentations, interpretations, and performances. The disappointing presentations are betrayals, we think, not only of the fans, but of Lecter himself. Somehow, despite the fact that he is a work of fiction, there is a "Lecter himself." Hannibal Lecter has a life of his own. Even Thomas Harris notes that, when writing *Red Dragon* and getting to know his characters in that novel, "I was not comfortable in the presence of Dr. Lecter, not sure at all that the doctor could not see me" (Harris, "Foreword" to *Red Dragon*, p. xi).

One thing every version of Hannibal Lecter shares, besides the cannibalism, is a capacity for driving us—his readers, his viewers, his witnesses, his fans—to think. We find in Lecter an unsettling combination of things we would like to be and things that horrify, if not utterly disgust, us. We like this man whom we do not, should not, like. And this raises a whole host of questions about human existence which, in the manner of a good psychiatrist, Dr. Lecter poses but never resolves. Like Socrates, he goads us to ask them—*What is the good life? What are our responsibilities to others, and to ourselves? What must we risk in order to live well? What must we preserve? What can we allow ourselves to become? What are we already?*—but he has no answers for us. Which is not to say that he has not answered these questions for himself, just that he cannot make his answers our own. If we're going to learn something from Dr. Lecter, we must—like Will Graham, like Clarice Starling—discover the lesson for ourselves. He can give us that rare gift, but we have to want it. We have to take it.

It is generally considered rude to question the motives of a man offering a gift, and I would not want anyone—least of all, our dear doctor—to suspect me of *this* offense against courtesy. But it is impossible to encounter Hannibal Lecter without wondering who—and what—he is. How to classify the extraordinary, perhaps unique, individual who presents himself so well-attired (in a "very well-tailored person suit," perhaps) to the world? Naturally, I hesitate to make the census taker's mistake—to "quantify" Dr. Lecter, to "reduce [him] to a set of influences" (Harris, *Silence*, pp. 19–20). No, Hannibal Lecter is infinitely more interesting when he is unquantified, unquantifiable, immeasurable, mysterious. We shouldn't try to understand him too much, to know him too well, to get too close to him. "We can," after all, "only learn so much and live" (Harris, *Hannibal*, p. 484). But still . . . we can hazard some perhaps amateurish, admittedly incomplete, undeniably discourteous, but nevertheless well-meaning attempts at finding Lecter's place in the world.

Certainly, the philosophical issues raised in the different chapters of this book weave through these various depictions, sometimes preferring one to the others, sometimes working two or more of them together. Hannibal Lecter prompts us to reflection, and the first thing he prompts us to reflect upon is himself. "First principles, Clarice. Simplicity. Read Marcus Aurelius. Of each particular thing ask: what is it in itself? What is its nature? What does he do, this man you seek?" (Demme, *Silence*).

The Psychopath

As we are told more than once, Dr. Lecter is considered—at least after his incarceration, at least by Dr. Frederick Chilton—a "pure sociopath" or a "pure psychopath," although Will Graham cautions us that these terms don't apply to Hannibal Lecter, strictly speaking. Strictly speaking, we don't have a word for what Lecter is. In any case, one of the most common presentations of Hannibal Lecter is as a psychopathic killer, in the fictional tradition of Norman Bates, and the real-life tradition of Ted Bundy and others. There was for many years much speculation about who might have served as the basis for Thomas Harris's creation, and Harris fed this speculation when, in his rare interviews, he would mention one or another serial killer as having inspired one or more of Lecter's attributes.

Only recently, however, did Harris reveal the primary source of his inspiration—a doctor whom Harris had met in a prison in Mexico while working as a crime reporter. The doctor "was a small, lithe man" who "stood very still and there was a certain elegance about him." His "eyes were maroon with grainy sparks like sunstones." Harris did not know the doctor was in fact a prisoner at first, but the prison warden reveals, shortly after Harris's conversation with the doctor, that, "The doctor is a murderer. As a surgeon, he could package his victim in a surprisingly small box. He will never leave this place. He is insane" (Harris, "Author's Note" in *Silence*, 25th Anniversary Edition, pp. xi–xiii). When Harris questions the warden's diagnosis of insanity, noting that poor people from the local community come to the prison freely and are treated by the doctor for their ailments, the warden responds, "He is not insane with the poor." Throughout his discussion of the doctor, Harris refers to him as "Dr. Salazar." It is a pseudonym, perhaps because, contrary to the warden's prediction, the doctor did get out of prison, eventually. "Dr. Salazar served twenty years in prison. When he was released he went to the poorest barrio in Monterrey to serve the aged and the poor. His name is not Salazar. I leave him in peace" (p. xiv).

Of course, journalism being what journalism is, journalists did not leave "Dr. Salazar" in peace. He was later identified as Dr. Alfredo Ballí Treviño, a Mexican physician who served twenty years in prison for murder, and died in 2009. He apparently knew he was the basis for Harris's character, and was teased by those close to him as a result thereof. Despite the man's crimes, one cannot help but recoil at such *rudeness*.

In any case, one presentation of Hannibal Lecter is as a psychopath, or something like a psychopath, in the manner and style of Dr. Treviño, and this deeply informs Brian Cox's performance as Hannibal "Lecktor" (as it is spelled somewhat inexplicably in the film) in *Manhunter*, Michael Mann's 1986 adaptation of *Red Dragon*. Cox played Lecktor as a synthesis, he has noted, of the infamous Scottish serial killer, Peter Manuel, and Cox's own son (a teenager at the time; now an actor himself), Alan Cox. What comes through are a profound intelligence married to a sense of entitlement, a kind of merciless arrogance and unwillingness (or inability) to consider other people's needs or desires in making his own choices:

classic signs of psychopathy. Beyond this, the limited portrayal of Hannibal Lecktor in *Manhunter* does not allow us to go.

The Anti-Hero

Another, much later, depiction of Hannibal Lecter has its origins in the novel, *Hannibal*, although it only comes to full fruition in *Hannibal Rising*. There, Lecter is no longer simply killing and eating his victims for the pleasure it gives, or out of some deeply rooted psychological urge, but instead as a means of accomplishing his otherwise sympathetic goals—in *Hannibal*, to overcome his psychological fixation on the murder and cannibalization of his sister, Mischa, and to win Clarice Starling's heart, and in *Hannibal Rising*, to avenge Mischa's death. Like Frank Castle ("the Punisher") or Batman, in his anti-heroic presentation Hannibal Lecter appears as something of a superhero, but one willing to do what more traditionally heroic individuals are not: to kill in order to get what he understands to be justice. While this interpretation of Lecter dominates in *Hannibal Rising*, and as one might expect, Gaspard Ulliel's performance as the Young Hannibal in the film version, it characterizes only the last third of *Hannibal*. That said, it's this anti-heroic take on Lecter that comes through most in Anthony Hopkins's performance in Ridley Scott's film adaptation of *Hannibal*.

The shift from villain to anti-hero seems to have come as something of a surprise to fans of the Hannibal Lecter franchise, and thus it's unsurprising that *Hannibal Rising* (book and film) and *Hannibal* (film) are the most controversial presentations of Lecter among Fannibals. While we take an inexplicable and morbid pleasure in giving witness to Dr. Lecter's criminal activities and culinary crimes, we don't want to root for him, exactly. Or, if we *do* want to root for him, we still want to feel like it's wrong to do so. *Hannibal Rising* and, to a lesser extent, *Hannibal*, make Dr. Lecter seem like he's basically a good guy—and this is not, generally speaking, his appeal.

The Vampire

Probably the most famous and well-loved presentation of Hannibal Lecter yet is Anthony Hopkins's performance in *The*

Silence of the Lambs, and later, in the film, *Red Dragon*. This is the Lecter—specifically, from *Silence*—that the American Film Institute ranked as the greatest screen villain of all time. This is the Lecter we see in the first two novels, as well, and he's incredible: not a psychopath, exactly, since psychopaths can be explained and understood; not an anti-hero, as he acts unequivocally on his own, twisted behalf without any sense of the rightness of his actions. He is evil, and mysterious, and powerful (despite the limitations of his imprisonment)—and a cannibal—and in these ways, he has a clear resonance with that cannibalistic arch-villain of old, Dracula. Like the vampire, Lecter bides his time, hiding among human beings as one of the most cultured and best educated of their number, awaiting his opportunity to strike—and then, brutally, bestially, killing and eating his victims. Hopkins captures this duality well, in the way he makes that sucking noise after mentioning the census taker's liver ("with some fava beans and a nice Chianti"), or in his brutal murder of the two guards in Tennessee (displaying the eviscerated body of one as a macabre angel of *liberté*), in *Silence*; and in the scenes with Edward Norton's Will Graham in Lecter's study (where Lecter tries to disembowel and murder Graham) and in the asylum exercise room (where he strains at his bonds like a wild animal) in *Red Dragon*.

Unlike an "ordinary" psychopath, however, a vampire isn't motivated by traumas and psychotic urges. A vampire is motivated by hunger. And his hunger is coupled with an understanding of himself as inherently superior to the human beings upon whom he feeds. It is not quite that he thinks of people as pigs—contrary to Will Graham's assessment in the early episodes of the television series, *Hannibal*—but, rather, that he thinks of himself as being as far above ordinary human beings as pigs are below them. (To use Nietzsche's language, he conceives of himself—and this goes for Dracula as well as Lecter—as an *Übermensch*, an overman or superman.) He kills and eats because he wants to, because he likes to, and because no objections anyone could provide—in the form of ordinary human law, or ordinary human morality—apply to one as great as he is. The presentation of Hannibal Lecter as a sort of vampire is the presentation of an individual of immense power—but also of inexplicable and extraordinary weaknesses: garlic and crucifixes and holy water and wooden stakes for the one in Transylvania; the memory of Mischa and the fascination with Clarice and the potential for friendship with Will for the one in Baltimore.

The Devil

The vampire is not the most powerful being to whom Hannibal Lecter forms an unholy analogy, however, and if we look to the first two-thirds of the novel, *Hannibal*, as well as to the performance of Mads Mikkelsen as Lecter in the television series of the same name, we see something even more sinister than Dracula: we see Hannibal Lecter as the devil. Mikkelsen seems in fact to have won the role, at least in part, thanks to his interpretation of the character along such satanic lines. As Bryan Fuller has noted on a number of occasions, Mikkelsen interprets "Hannibal Lecter as a fallen angel. He sees him not as a cannibal psychiatrist but as the devil, who is enamored with man, and . . . living out his temptations in concert with Will Graham" (Stephenson, "This Is My Design"). We see this characterization of Lecter frequently in the television show, although often quite subtly (fire in the background of a shot focused on Mikkelsen's Lecter, for example), but sometimes quite directly: as the serial killer Abel Gideon notes in conversation with fellow asylum inmate Will Graham, "He's the devil, Mr. Graham. He is smoke" (*Hannibal*, Season 2, "Mikōzuke").

But we needn't look to the television series to see the devil in Dr. Lecter. He is depicted very much in this way in the novel, *Hannibal*, and again—as with Dr. Gideon's comment to Will— quite explicitly. Romula, the woman in Florence whom Rinaldo Pazzi has extorted into assisting him in getting a fingerprint from Dr. Lecter (who is masquerading, at this point in the story, as Dr. Fell), nearly accomplishes her task when, looking Lecter in the face, she runs away. When interrogated by Pazzi about her failure, Romula explains, "That is the Devil . . . Shaitan, Son of the Morning. I've seen him now" (Harris, *Hannibal*, p. 156). And even prior to that, in *Red Dragon* and *Silence*, one of the marks of Satan as he appears in human form—an asymmetry on the left (usually a misshapen left foot, or even a hoof in the left foot's place) from which we get our English word "sinister" (meaning, quite straightforwardly, "on the left")—

makes its appearance on Lecter's person. In addition to his red and illuminated eyes, Dr. Lecter has that extra finger on his left hand.

Presenting Hannibal Lecter as the devil, however, is more than simply finding elements of the mythology surrounding the Prince of Darkness in the mythos surrounding the Chesapeake Ripper. More than this, this last presentation is one of power: Hannibal Lecter as (nearly) omniscient, as (nearly) omnipotent, as in control of almost every event in which he has any stake at all, as setting himself up as a rival to God—which he does, again and again, in comparing his own work as a killer, and an eater, and a sower-of-death-and-destruction in general, to God's. (Lecter's collection of church collapses springs to mind—a collection of news items by way of which he often means to show that God is a murderer, enjoys killing, and insofar as we are created in His image, we should enjoy it, too. That's a devilish argument, if ever there was one.)

Hannibal Lecter observes ordinary human beings like us from on high; he figures us out, determines what makes us tick; and then he presents us with temptations tailored specifically to us. He does this to Will Graham, to Margot Verger, to Alana Bloom, to Abigail Hobbs, to Randall Tier, to Donald Sutcliffe, to Abel Gideon, to Francis Dolarhyde, to Clarice Starling, to Frederick Chilton . . . whether it's the books or the movies or the television series we're talking about, Hannibal Lecter is never simply a serial-killing cannibal psychiatrist. He is always also the mirror in which we see our darkest desires reflected, the tincture of evil (and sometimes more than a tincture) in every soul. To the extent that he sees our darkest parts, he can manipulate them—and us—to arrange the world as he likes, without ever even having to lift a finger (or eleven). He does it, not by corrupting us, exactly, but by something far more destructive: by pointing us out to ourselves. It's especially appropriate, then, that this devil has made psychiatry his profession. And equally appropriate—*proper*, we might add, for the doctor's urbane benefit—that we have a group of philosophers, those savants of self-reflection, gathered here to ask of him as of themselves, *who—and what—are you?*

• • •

As Inspector Popil notes, "The little boy Hannibal died in 1945 out there in the snow trying to save his sister. His heart died with Mischa. What is he now? There's not a word for it yet. For lack of a better word, we'll call him a monster" (Harris, *Rising*, p. 283). We don't always see the monster in Dr. Lecter, however, despite the fact that the monster is always there. Sometimes, if we find ourselves unadvisedly peering a trifle too deeply into those maroon eyes, we see something of ourselves lurking in the darkness behind those pinpoints of light. Like Will Graham and Clarice Starling before us, we come to know ourselves in our conversations with the monster. And Hannibal Lecter is the best and scariest monster we've got, because of all our monsters he's the most like us, even if he remains on some level always and forever more a mystery. Socrates once noted of himself, "I investigate not these things, but myself, to know whether I am a monster more complicated and more furious than Typhon or a gentler and simpler creature" (Plato, *Phaedrus* 230a). And, according to Nietzsche, "A foreigner who knew about faces once passed through Athens and told Socrates that he was a *monster*." Socrates replied, simply, "You know me, sir!" (Nietzsche, *Twilight* §3). As Socrates knew, we all seem sometimes monstrous, and monsters are not always ugly. Charm *and* scales: monstrosity and mystery can, in their union, seem to us sometimes like beauty.

As a monster, of course, Lecter will eventually attack us; eventually, he will try to kill us and consume us, if we let him. But be warned: he will not merely attack us from the outside. He will come to understand us, slowly, one morsel at a time, and his assault will take us whole, both inside and out, like eating an ortolan—a debauched delicacy, bones and all.

Each of us is, in some ways, deeply and darkly a mystery. None of us is known fully to ourselves. Philosophy and self-reflection can shine a light in some of the dark corners, but "this we share with the doctor: In the vaults of our hearts and brains, danger waits. All the chambers are not lovely, light and high. There are holes in the floor of the mind" (Harris, *Hannibal*, p. 253).

Dr. Lecter will see you now.

I.

Having an Old Friend
for Dinner

1
Cosmopolitan Cannibal

Mandy-Suzanne Wong

You just came here to look at me. Just to get the old scent again, didn't you?
Why don't you just smell yourself?

— Hannibal Lecter in *Red Dragon* by Thomas Harris

A gourmet magazine invites me of all people to interview Dr. Hannibal Lecter, epicurean connoisseur and culinary artiste. Naturally we meet in Copenhagen. City of Mads Mikkelsen, Hans Christian Andersen, and the great philosopher Søren Kierkegaard. Home of Noma, the world's greatest restaurant, and its superstar chef René Redzepi, who serves live insects on purpose.

I propose Nyhavn, a row of sun-colored buildings along a canal. Except the world-renowned ice cream parlor that makes its own waffle cones, each building is a cozy restaurant with a snug little bar. Wooden boats in the canal, a Flamenco guitarist on the sidewalk. The smell of Danish beer and the summertime crowd and the new waffles. I can't think why he agreed.

And then he says (I'm looking the wrong way), "You've been at Andersen's for breakfast on Bernstorffsgade. You came from there on foot. Quite the little tourist, aren't you?" He gives me the details of the shampoo they put out at my hotel, the detergent they use on the sheets, and the hotel's shameful location next to an amusement park and a big Metro station.

I haven't told him where I'm staying. He smells it on me.

He says, "Someone with your skin tone oughtn't to wear so much gray. You should use committed hues, not try to look like you've stood under the chimney."

His eyes are reddish with black pupils. The tilt of his head is clinical. *The better to see you with, my dear.* "Your mother must be very beautiful," he says. "You can't abide it at all."

That's why he agreed. Not because I'm anything to look at. Nor because I write about eating from philosophical points of view.

"A philosopher," says Dr. Lecter. "That means you want to talk about anthropophagy."

Eating human flesh. Also known as cannibalism.

I almost say: *That's something we philosophers could really sink our teeth into.* I refrain.

The doctor says, "Your great German predecessor, Arthur Schopenhauer, called anthropophagy a form of supreme error. I wonder if you believe, as he did, that I am worse than the common murderer who lets his victim's sweetbreads go to waste, more heinous than a slaughterer of millions. Or if you think you're another Michel de Montaigne, a magnanimous French brain, who'd want to see me as some kind of noble savage."

Don't lie to Dr. Lecter. He will know. He responds to courtesy, not flattery. I mustn't grovel or try to cloak my terror in indignant silence.

"Neither," I say.

I won't forget the small white teeth in Dr. Lecter's smile. This is why he agreed to talk to me: because he thinks it would be fun to show me some painful truth about myself, about philosophers who dare to peel away the masks we wear, and the awful things they often find.

Are you ready for that?

The Saw

Sometimes philosophers and scholars summon the courage for brutal honesty. We call it critique. This is not what a restaurant reviewer does. It's worse, way worse. And dangerous. Critique is thinking with no holds barred. It's a thoughtful perspective that finally makes you realize all the implications of what you believe.

I mean all of them, not just those that make you look good. Critique will devour your illusions. A nice chopped salad made of everything you thought you knew. You'll emerge with the certainty that you're a schmuck, a tool, a meaningless bunch of carbons, or worse.

Not that philosophers are pessimistic or (when sober) cruel. Critique is an honest search for answers. But it's an honesty as sharp as a new autopsy saw, and that kind of honesty never tells you what you want to hear. It reveals that many popular beliefs, even those on which our society is founded, are based on unfair or just plain inaccurate assumptions. Critique is a popular tool in philosophers' *batterie de cuisine*. We use it to think about political systems and other systems of belief, often to reveal how people actually relate to one another and the world—which is usually very different from how people *think* they relate to one another and the world. Different enough to leave scars.

This sort of honesty is Dr. Lecter's favorite, most damaging weapon. (Just ask Clarice Starling.) He thinks I'm a little child who wants to play with this deadly tool. That's why he's giving me the time of day.

Monstrously Good Taste

For a while we talk food, the selection and preparation of ingredients. It comes down to quality over quantity. Because cooking and enjoying food are cultivated arts for refined sensibilities. At the same time, Copenhagen's Chef Redzepi says that cooking must be honest. To be honest about eating, you must accept that it is killing. That's why the shrimps are moving in Redzepi's appetizers.

"*Gourmandise*," says Dr. Lecter, "*good taste* 'unites an Attic elegance with Roman luxury and French subtlety, the kind which chooses wisely . . . savors with vigor, and sums up the whole with profundity: it is a rare quality, which might easily be named a virtue'. You recognize the words of Brillat-Savarin" (Brillat-Savarin, p. 95).

Or not. Dr. Lecter is better informed than everyone he talks to.

"Dumas tells us that Brillat-Savarin was a gourmand of exquisite taste," he continues. "*Le grand dictionnaire.*"

That one I do remember. Alexandre Dumas's *Great Dictionary of Cuisine*, a favorite of Dr. Lecter's that remained his companion throughout his incarceration. In all the discordance between the doctor and various legal authorities, only Starling recognized good taste as one of his defining characteristics.

"Taste in all things was a constant between Dr. Lecter's lives in America and Europe, between his life as a successful medical practitioner and fugitive monster" (Harris, *Hannibal*, p. 225).

At the mention of Dumas, I wonder if *The Man in the Iron Mask* was another favorite. I take a seat opposite the doctor and envision the mask from the asylum, the metallic guard over his man-eating mandible.

We're in a traditional restaurant at the end of Nyhavn. It is cozy and smells of the sea, very Danish. When I see the menu I fear it's too inexpensive to suit Dr. Lecter's tastes. But he is gracious, and we decide on caviar with an assortment of herring. The atmosphere is congenial. I find myself saying, perhaps unwisely, "Dumas also says that cannibalism is a form of gluttony."

"He's referring to the Roman god who devoured his own children. So ravenous that he overlooked his son Jupiter, whom the Greeks call Zeus."

Sigh of relief: references to cannibalism in ancient art and myths fascinate Dr. Lecter, who once served as a curator at the Uffizi Museum in Florence. He reminds me of the lecture he delivered there, where he reviewed anthropophagy as a theme in Dante's poetry. "For Dante, as for the Greeks and Romans, it was a symbol of terrible, almost unimaginable betrayal," he says. "A figure for the worst possible thing that could ever happen to anyone or that anyone could ever dream of doing."

We still have that ancient outlook. Eating human flesh remains unthinkable. Inhuman. Monstrous.

"Wherever I go, that word echoes after me," sighs the doctor, "often trailing a thoughtful and respectful silence."

He means the word *monster*. It's what people say when they can't think of any way to describe him that stands a chance of being accurate. Will Graham used that word; Jack Crawford used it. The popular press. Even to his so-called "peers in psychiatry, many of whom fear his acid pen," Dr. Lecter was "something entirely Other" (Harris, *Hannibal*, p. 137). They too called him *monster*. It gave people an excuse to hunt him down like an animal, believing they could do to him whatever they wanted. *"Our freedom is worth more than the monster's life. Our happiness is more important than his suffering"* (Harris,

Hannibal, p. 174). Thus proclaimed Rinaldo Pazzi as he stormed the Uffizi. Such a bad idea.

Well, Dr. Lecter may have cooked eleven people (that we know of), but he did it in style, the kind of style that anyone would envy. Sure, he's a man-eating beast, and maybe *monster* looks good on him. But he's also unmistakably civilized, a man of impeccable taste. The eminent Frederick Chilton called him "sophisticated," "perceptive," "not insensitive" (Harris, *Dragon*, p. 57). I have it on good authority that Dr. Lecter is "known for the excellence of his table" (Harris, *Silence*, p. 25). An "extraordinarily charming man, absolutely singular," said a reputable lady who once knew him well: "Sort of made a girl's *fur crackle*, if you know what I mean" (Harris, *Hannibal*, p. 300).

Dr. Lecter is an inhuman monster. But at the same time, if you pretend he's not just the kind of human being you want to be, you're probably lying to yourself. And I promise it will hurt when the doctor shows you the truth. He's everything we fear and everything we want to be. Human and inhuman and the shifting face of the shadowy threshold in between. He is both and neither, Us and Them.

I say, "How in the world do you manage?"

Inhuman Humans

Strictly speaking, a monster isn't human. (Can you imagine Godzilla and Smaug garnishing bantam egg pizza with arugula?) The word *monster* is also a metaphor for people who conduct themselves like wild beasts. Mothers-in-law. Serial killers like "the monster of Florence." Frankenstein's monster is a tricky one. Looks sort of human, acts not quite human. The press enjoys linking Dr. Lecter to Frankenstein's creature.

"Can you really be human and not human at the same time?"

He replies, "Why didn't you visit when I lived in Baltimore?"

Meaning he won't answer my question.

Meaning the answer's really yes, and Dr. Lecter thinks it should be obvious.

We all have animals inside us. Monkeys' genes, fishes' genes. We have *things* inside us too, blunt objects like kidneys, livers, brains, which may be separated from the rest and eaten. A philosopher might propose that the nature of humanity is *duality,* two-sided: every human is both human and nonhuman. Not all philosophers believe this. Some find it hard to swallow. Others realize that being has way more than two sides to it. Like Dr. Lecter. He believes in chaos.

He's a perfect example of a nonhuman human. One side of him is a man-eating beast who follows his nose, listens like a bat, and pounces in silence. The other side is the civilized, disarming human being of boundless talent and epicurean taste. Dr. Lecter lives on the threshold of both sides: he is neither one of them, yet he exceeds the sum of both. This earns him several adoring fans. It also makes a lot of people want to lock him up and throw away the key.

Those who hate him envy his extreme humanity. Or they find his inhumanity too bright a mirror.

Elaborations of Carbon

With the herring we have chopped red onions, pork rinds, and baby potatoes, and we plan on aquavit.

"When the Renaissance explorers discussed anthropophagy," says Dr. Lecter, "they saw in it a sort of threshold between the civilized and the beastly. They also made a distinction between sacrificial and nutritious flesh-eating. Once you start making distinctions, you find it hard to stop, you see. Just look at Aristotle."

I will spare you our debate on whether Aristotle thought up too many categories to describe reality. Suffice it to say that Dr. Lecter wins.

Having creamed Aristotle, Dr. Lecter expounds on Renaissance thinkers' distinction between eating human flesh as part of some religious ritual and adding it to the dinner menu.

"The sacramental decapitation and some might say *quasi-Eucharistic* ingestion of a sacrificial victim is one thing, frying someone's brain in crumbs of brioche quite another. What you give your god is valuable. If it wasn't, it wouldn't be a sacrifice. The ingredients of an entrée, things you buy at the store— flour, butter, watercress—such things have no greater value than anything else. The worthy *cuisinier* can create a delectable experience out of whatever he happens to find in the nearest pantry."

A person eaten for dinner amounts to a chicken or a fava bean. The human being served with fava beans has no greater value than the fava beans. At least, consumed in sacrifice, we'd preserve the dignity of a well-intentioned gift. On Dr. Lecter's table in tiny pieces with croutons, well . . .

Do you hear that sound? Like a giant, angry bee next to your ear, dissonant enough to make you ill? That's the sound of the philosophical autopsy saw. "We are nothing but elaborations of carbon," says the doctor, and his tone implies that it doesn't bother him in the slightest.

Of course it doesn't. He wrote it. *"We are elaborations of carbon, Clarice. You and the skillet and Daddy dead in the ground, cold as the skillet"* (Harris, *Hannibal*, p. 31).

He means that we are nothing more. For now we're alive and human, but all that is temporary, and anyway it's nothing special. Genetically speaking, our bodies are almost indistinguishable from plants and animals. Humans' contribution to our world is no more valuable than that of invasive weeds. The ability to recognize this humiliating fact is central to Dr. Lecter's outlook. It's what enables him to eat people with the same lack of concern with which the rest of us sink our teeth into cows and artichokes.

The Red Dragon knew. "Lecter was capable of understanding that blood and breath were only . . . fuel," he believed (Harris, *Dragon*, p. 89).

Philosophers call it de-anthropocentrism: the idea that the human species is not—and never was—the central, most important species on earth.

This idea is gaining popularity but not without resistance, for the last thing anyone wants to be is one of those pathetic, comatose, shriveled *batteries* that all humans become in the *Matrix* films. *Things* that are technically alive but relate to the world as nothing more than lifeless ingredients and tools. In Dr. Lecter's kitchen, that's precisely what we are . . . right alongside the cucumbers. Being killed for food is an unsacred, meaningless death; which means that being fattened up for someone's skillet is a meaningless life. For many people, meaningless death and enslavement are worse than death itself.

"People hate you because you proved that dignity is meaningless."

"No one needs to prove it. Everyone knows already. They just pretend not to."

The blade of the saw offers bright and sharp reflections. Dr. Lecter is frightening because he's everything we'd love to be and the face of the worst thing that could happen to anyone. As I sit with him, thinking, savoring the eggs of Scandinavian trout, I realize that the worst possible thing is happening everywhere. We are all cannibals and the bare life at the mercy of other cannibals.

Bare Life

Bare life is a philosopher's term for a living thing that's been abandoned by the group (or society) that it was supposed to depend on. The killing of bare life is never a crime or a sacrifice.

Think of a horse living out its life in a slaughterhouse, unable to graze but fattened up on slops. She doesn't have a name, she's an ingredient for glue. Think of a human body, brain-dead, kept breathing till the doctors can harvest its organs. Or a prisoner at Guantánamo, stripped of his human rights.

Anyone who killed such a being wouldn't be punished. These things are alive, but their lives are forfeit. Physically, they live, but they lack the trappings that would make their lives worth fighting for (such as "human rights"). They are *stripped bare* of everything except their bodies, which anyone may treat as though they were soulless things—mere elaborations of carbon—maybe even turn them into some kind of fuel.

For Dr. Lecter, Paul Krendler was bare life. Donnie Barber, Benjamin Raspail. This is how the rest of us treat all our food sources. In fact, in everyday human life, all nonhuman beings—as well as humans who are deemed unworthy of the species—are treated as bare life.

A Philosophical Problem

"Allow me to pose a philosophical conundrum," Dr. Lecter says over smoked herring and raw yolk. "It's a true story. British sailors lost at sea run out of food. They kill and eat one another. Substitute the sailors for American prospectors stranded in the mountains, and the story remains true. These people acquire the taste for man-flesh. They feel entitled to it. And when those who are left find their way back to civilization, not a single one of them is convicted of murder. If anyone stands trial, he is instantly acquitted. Why? Don't look to the law, which is nothing but a colander. Only think of what we have discussed."

"That was an exception," I say.

"They were not savages. Their victims were people they knew. They were Christians. There was no sacrificial altar. Just a campfire if they were lucky . . . and whatever they could do for seasoning. By the way, the prospector discovered that the breasts of his male companions came with their own sweet tang, no marinade required."

"The situation was exceptional."

"Was it? These people weren't insane."

"As I said, this was an extreme situation."

"And who made that decision, hmmm? Who decided that certain lives were worth more than certain others? Who decides when to strip a man down to his animal body so that he has no more worth than a tomato?"

"Well, I mean . . . how do *you* decide?"

Retorts don't trouble Dr. Lecter. He's not excited, simply laying out a problem like a lecturer at the front of a class.

"Convenience," he replies. "If someone is uncivil, I might do the world a favor. Then again, I may not. The world has never been so courteous to me."

In other words (I keep this to myself), his decision's arbitrary.

The point is Dr. Lecter's "conundrum" has no morally good answer. Who does get to decide when a living thing is just a thing? Anyone. Anytime. Most of the time, our reasoning is far from airtight.

You'd like to think you're above that sort of behavior, wouldn't you? Hmmm?

But Dr. Lecter murmurs, "Upon such dread foundations reposes life as we know it."

I look at my herring and potatoes. The fishes' little eyes are black and frozen open. The potatoes are only baby ones.

Sovereign Foundations

There's a philosopher at work in Italy. His name is Giorgio Agamben, and I bring his name into our conversation because he studies political arrangements throughout history—all the different ways that earthlings try to coexist and preserve their favorite ways of life—and everywhere he looks, he finds someone who's placed another in the position of *bare life*.

The ones in the position of power: Agamben calls them *sovereign*. This word doesn't just apply to kings and queens. Sovereigns are people who take it on themselves to decide that their own lives and perspectives are worth more than those of others. In other words, the term *sovereign* applies to anyone who decides that another living being is just bare life, something that it's not a crime or a sacrifice to kill. For every bare life, there's a sovereign that has made it so.

Cosmopolitan Cannibals

A man decides to kill a cow for food, kill a weed because it's ugly, or kill a marlin for fun. The man is sovereign. So is the society that condones killing animals and plants. The animals and plants are just *things*: bare life.

A group of people called "the justice system" decides that if one man kills another, the killer forfeits his life. Those who kill him can't be punished. The condemned is bare life.

A man named Hitler decides he only likes Christians. Jewish people are rounded up and shot, marched to the gas chamber, and variously tortured. All of it is legal. Hitler and the Nazis are sovereign, Jews bare life.

The US military deploys drones to the Middle East, killing thousands of civilians while aiming at a few people who just might wish harm to the United States. No one will be punished for the deaths of those civilians. Compared to the belief that someone among them just might wish harm to the United States, those people's lives have the value of ants'.

When Dr. Lecter devours a man or woman, the doctor is sovereign, the victim bare life. In fact, from his point of view, everyone is bare life. That's why he can eat people without (in his own auspicious opinion) endangering his good taste or entirely sane notions of right and wrong. But the rest of society has other ideas. Most people think Raspail and Krendler are worth more than mere ingredients, so whoever deprives them of their valuable existence deserves to be punished. *That* individual is the one who legally counts as bare life. No one would go to jail for killing Hannibal the Cannibal.

Agamben finds this distinction in almost every political structure: wherever there are human beings interacting with other beings, there's someone who's decided that he, she, or they are sovereign and everything else bare life. Sovereigns consider themselves civilized, cultured, *human*—worthy of survival. Bare life is the opposite: monstrous, ignorant, *inhuman*—unworthy of the protection that society promises to those who live in it.

Anyone can be a sovereign. Any sovereign can become bare life on the turn of a whim. Just because the wind changes.

The Black Diamond

Agamben says that the distinction between *bare life*, whose death is not a crime, and *sovereigns*, who decide when it's all right for things to die that way, amounts to the distinction between the nonhuman and the human. That distinction is the foundation of contemporary politics. We choose random places in the sand and draw the line over and over. *This* side needs protection, so the *Other* side will have to die. Humans are always on *This* side. Nonhumans are always on the *Other.* Unworthy humans get thrown in with the nonhumans, with the rats and invasive bugs.

But didn't we just figure out—you and I, here in Copenhagen's bright, chill noon—didn't we just learn that the difference between human and nonhuman is *never* guaranteed? Didn't Dr. Lecter show us that *every* human being is also and already nonhuman?

Being human means being both human and nonhuman—in constant battle with oneself. Each of us takes that battle out into the world. We take it out on other people. The battle between the human and the inhuman *within ourselves* is the foundation of our relationships with other people, other species, and things on small and massive scales alike.

You're not up for dessert, are you? I'm not either. The aquavit and then we walk. We come to the ocean.

We stand before the Black Diamond, the black-granite extension to Copenhagen's Royal Library. It is a giant, gleaming mirror with sharp angles, black as death. Inside are the manuscripts of some of the world's greatest philosophers.

Dr. Lecter seems at first to enjoy our discussion of Agamben (who, by the way, writes most intelligently on werewolves).

"And what do you think?" he says.

"I think people like watching you going through the same struggle."

"Because we all secretly want to eat each other? How refreshing."

"No. Well. I can't speak for other people."

"This Italian. You find his ideas humbling, even humiliating. You think that is somehow good for you. How magnanimous," he says and loses interest altogether.

Muzzled and strapped to a dolly like furniture or a crate of potatoes, Dr. Lecter may be nothing but bare life to agents of "the law"—but here, free and relaxed in this vibrant city, there's no doubt that he is sovereign. So I'd just as soon not press him. It wouldn't do to try his patience.

2
I, Cannibal

JOSEPH WESTFALL

Every moving thing that liveth shall be meat for you; even as the green herb have I given you all things.

—GENESIS 9:3

If you know nothing else about Hannibal Lecter, you know at the very least his rhyming nickname. And knowing his nickname, you know this, as well, that "Hannibal the Cannibal" *eats people.* You don't have to dig much deeper into the Hannibal Lecter mythos to recall that indelible line in Anthony Hopkins's unforgettable performance in *The Silence of the Lambs*: "A census taker tried to test me once. I ate his liver with some fava beans and a nice Chianti"—and then that awful sucking noise that remains, so many years later, so intimately associated with the horror of Lecter's cannibalism. Right at the very heart of Thomas Harris's character—and brought to the center of his various screen incarnations—is the fact that, unlike most people, even unlike most serial killers, Hannibal Lecter is a cannibal.

Obviously, murder is wrong, and there is no ethics in the world that seriously questions that point. (This is different from saying, of course, that "killing is wrong," since there are numerous forms of killing that most ethical systems and many people see as justified—including killing someone in self-defense, if not also killing enemy combatants in time of war, and for some, euthanasia or "mercy killing," as well as capital punishment.) One need not even broach the topic of cannibal-

15

ism in order to see something wrong with the way in which Dr. Lecter conducts his affairs, and cannibalism is not even included in the criminal charges against him. In fact, cannibalism is not, in itself and as such, a criminal offense under United States federal law, nor in forty-nine of the fifty states or Europe—although murder and the desecration of corpses certainly are. The only exception in the United States is Idaho, where in 1990 cannibalism (except when "the action was taken under extreme life-threatening conditions as the only apparent means of survival") was specifically outlawed as a class of "mayhem." If convicted of cannibalism in Idaho, one can be sentenced to a maximum of fourteen years in prison (*Idaho Code 18-5003*).

Yet, as we learn from Thomas Harris, Lecter is found not guilty—by reason of insanity, although that was not his defense—and it seems that the only basis one might have had for judging Dr. Lecter insane (rather than merely murderous) is, in fact, his cannibalism. So, even though cannibalism is not in itself a crime, cannibals do seem to be treated differently in the courtroom—and in the court of public opinion—than other murderers. At the very least, the Chesapeake Ripper was.

Thus, in addition to sorting out just what sort of a serial killer Hannibal Lecter is, and whether or not he is a psychopath, we must try to engage the question of cannibalism in order to come to a deeper understanding of Hannibal the Cannibal. What is it, to eat other human beings? Why would one do such a (disgusting) thing? And is it—should it be considered—unethical to do so? Despite the fact that eating human flesh is profoundly taboo in our culture and the great majority of world cultures, philosophy often asks us to reconsider our basic beliefs to see if they have a rational basis. In the case of cannibalism, Hannibal Lecter would ask us to reconsider, too—and, generally speaking, it is wise to do what Dr. Lecter asks.

The Cannibal Within

The word *cannibal* appears to have its origin in the writings of none other than Christopher Columbus, who used the Spanish term *Canibales* to refer to the native inhabitants of the New World. The word is itself a reference to the Carib peoples (after whom their native region, the Caribbean, is named), and has no necessary or automatic connection to the eating of human flesh. There were rumors and legends in Europe during this period, of course, that the "savages" of the Americas were primitive in every way, including that they were *anthropophagi* (the word at the time for eaters of other human beings), and there is some evidence that cannibalism was practiced by some cultures in the precolonial period. The French philosopher, Michel de Montaigne, discusses one such cannibalistic culture in 1580 in his famous essay, "On the Cannibals," which describes a people who roasted and ate the flesh of their prisoners of war— after they had been executed, of course. (Montaigne compares this practice favorably with the French practice at the time of torturing their prisoners of war—since the victims of torture were still alive when the French cut flesh from their bodies; the victims of the cannibals were not.)

Cannibalism was almost certainly not as widespread as Europeans feared it was, although their fears were stoked by the reports of the returning explorers—who were given freer rein in massacring and conquering these peoples by their European patrons when those patrons believed the indigenous people were unrepentant and atheistic savages. In fact, some European powers came to believe that it was their religious duty and divine right to convert (and enslave) the "cannibals," to "liberate" them from their evil, irreligious, unchristian ways (Avramescu, pp. 106–12). Columbus himself seems to have been skeptical of claims that the *Canibales* were cannibals— but the truth was less useful to the project of European colonialization than was horrific hyperbole, and the name stuck. It was useful to European interests at the time that indigenous Americans be seen as both savage and, specifically, unchristian or atheistic, and charges of cannibalism were useful for that purpose. And *cannibal* is a far less cumbersome term than *anthropophagus*, in any case.

Historically, cannibalism has been levied as a charge against others, typically without evidence, as a means of demonizing a culture, ethnicity, religion, or country that one wishes to conquer or destroy. European colonialists accused both indigenous Africans and Americans of cannibalism; Christians accused Jews of cannibalism; Protestants accused Catholics of cannibalism; and so on. The world's first real cannibals were the Neanderthals, however, and there is physical evidence at numerous sites of the attacking, murder, and cannibalization of groups of both Neanderthals (*Homo neanderthalensis*) and humans (*Homo sapiens*). In fact, according to the paleobiologist Antonio Rosas, "this practice . . . was general among Neanderthal populations" (Thompson). Which is simply to say that, although they may not have enjoyed it, or wanted to do it, and may even not have done it with a high degree of frequency, Neanderthals were as a species cannibalistically inclined. Evidence exists of cannibalism in early human communities, as well, and of the human eating of Neanderthal flesh. Worth noting in this context, of course, is that most human beings today have some Neanderthal DNA (in addition to eating each other, *Homo neanderthalensis* and *Homo sapiens* interbred, as well). Some of our earliest ancestors dined at least occasionally on *other* of our earliest ancestors. All of us spring from cannibal stock. We are the cannibals we've been looking for.

The anthropological evidence of early human cannibalism was only relatively recently discovered, however. For most of recorded history, cannibalism was primarily a product of the mythmaking and imaginative arts—that is, there was an idea of cannibalism with very little evidence thereof. While that idea was alive and well in European myths and legends, the first case of cannibalism for which there are multiple historical accounts didn't occur until the Middle Ages, during the First Crusade. In December 1098, after having sieged the Syrian city of Ma'arra, European crusaders discovered the city was poorer than they had imagined—there was very little to loot, and almost no food. Starving, but wishing still to push on toward Jerusalem, the Christian warriors reportedly cooked and ate the bodies of the Muslims they had massacred. (One source tells of crusaders boiling bodies in large pots, and roasting the bodies of dead children on spits. Another tells of starving crusaders eating chunks of the flesh of their conquered enemies raw.) While most ancient and medieval accounts of cannibalism accuse other people—the enemies, the "savages"—of such grotesque behavior, the story of the Siege of Ma'arra sees European Christians making this accusation against themselves. Despite the starvation conditions,the crusaders willfully defiled the bodies of their Muslim enemies, but in a way they would not have done their Christian comrades.

Of course, today we are all familiar with two other sorts of stories about cannibalism from history. Stories of starvation cannibalism recur in our culture every few years or so; perhaps the most famous are the story of the Donner Party in the Sierra Nevada mountains in the winter of 1846-47, and the case of the Uruguayan rugby team whose plane crash-landed in the Andes in 1972 (later documented in a book which was the basis of the 1993 film, *Alive*). In both of these cases, the accounts of cannibalism were of already deceased members of the groups in question. A slightly different tale of starvation cannibalism is the story of Alfred "Alferd" Packer, who in the winter of 1873-74 attempted a mountain crossing in Colorado with five other men. After returning to civilization, Packer confessed to having murdered and eaten some of his fellow prospectors in order to survive. He was tried for murder, convicted, and sentenced to death (legend and a local newspaper at the time have the judge poetically addressing Packer with the line, "Stand up yah voracious man-eatin' sonofabitch and receive yir sintince"—but the judge actually said no such thing). He later received a new trial, was convicted of the lesser charge of manslaughter, and sentenced to forty years in prison.

Finally, and perhaps most like our dear Dr. Lecter's *gourmanderie*, are those cases of psychopathic serial killers who take edible trophies from their victims—perhaps most famously in recent times, Jeffrey Dahmer. Numerous such cases—sometimes proven, sometimes merely suspected—appear in Christopher Berry-Dee's chronicle, *Cannibal Serial Killers*. The specific details of these men's crimes are mostly irrelevant and grisly enough not to go into here, but one trait does stand out: in apparently every case, cannibalism is linked to sexual gratification. While Hannibal the Cannibal does share these real-life murderers' culinary interest, in his total lack of sexual interest in his victims, Dr. Lecter is nothing like them. He is, then, as he might well agree, a cannibal apart.

That said, we are fascinated by Lecter's cannibalism, however horrifying we find it to be, in some of the same ways we are fascinated by real-life cannibals, whether prehistoric, ancient, medieval, modern, or contemporary. And in our fascination, in our willingness to buy books like Berry-Dee's and pore over the stomach-churning details, although we are not complicit in their acts, we find ourselves drawn to these flesh-eaters (if only ultimately to be repulsed by them). As Mads Mikkelsen has said about cannibalism, "There's something we can't understand, we can't comprehend it. And the things we can't understand tend to intrigue us and make us very curious. And I guess Hannibal is the icon of all the cannibals" (Stephenson, "A Taste for Killing"). The icon of *all* the cannibals. Face it, Fannibals: we take some (non-gustatory) pleasure in cannibalism.

Three Kinds of Cannibals

In that same interview, Mikkelsen makes an important distinction. He notes, "People eating other people has been scaring people since the beginning of days, right? We've got gruesome stories of people doing it out of need, out of ritual. And then we also have people doing it for fun." Thus, we can see in Mikkelsen's remark, and we also find in the history and study of cannibalism, three distinct kinds of cannibals, whom for ease of reference we might dub: (1) starvation cannibals, (2) cultural cannibals, and (3) hedonistic cannibals. Starvation cannibals eat human beings because they fear that, if they do not, they will starve to death. Cultural cannibals engage in some culturally or socially sanctioned form of cannibalism, whether religious, political, or otherwise. And hedonistic cannibals eat other people because it gives them pleasure to do so.

(1) Starvation Cannibalism

Of all the kinds of cannibalism, starvation cannibalism is probably the easiest for most of us to understand and to justify. Pushed to the limit by the possibility of death, many of us are willing to do whatever it takes to survive. And the instinct for survival certainly can push us to do things we would never have considered doing under ordinary circumstances, things in fact that we might have considered disgusting or wrong in any other situation. This is how we feel especially about cases such as those of the Donner Party and the Uruguayan rugby team. Caroline Logan describes a more recent example in "Cannibal Warlords of Liberia" where, in the post–civil war squalor in which many citizens of Liberia live, cannibalism is a last resort for survival for many people. Perhaps it is harder for us to feel the actions of Alferd Packer were justified, but even so, I think many of us would have to think long and hard about whether

Congo, as a part of a strategy of massacring an̶
one's enemies, including feeding parts of the b̶
prisoners to others—cannibalism as a weap̶
were, alongside rape, torture, and other h̶
tions (Griswold). As Frederick Chilton n̶
an act of dominance" (*Hannibal*, Seaso̶
need only study the civil wars in Lib̶
how devastating and gruesome suc̶
when sanctioned—explicitly or o̶
the military, or by the state.
The last kind of cultural̶
call nutritional cannibali̶
to supplement an othe̶
speaking, nutritiona̶
times—although n̶
sort of cannibal̶
ancestors. Alt̶
time, it app̶
some of th̶
when o̶
Near̶
att̶

gion of which ma̶n̶d̶
consumption of human flesh—in t̶h̶e̶
with and feed the sun. A modern example is ritual ca̶n̶n̶i̶
conducted in the belief that killing and eating one's (typically
political) opponents will grant one supernatural powers (as, for
example, once again in Liberia; see "Liberia's Elections, Ritual
Killings and Cannibalism" by Schmall and Williams). For a fascinating philosophical account of religious and ritual cannibalism as the basis for understanding cannibalism itself as a
cultural system, see *Divine Hunger* by Peggy Sanday.

Political or military cannibalism is another form of cultural
cannibalism, which is generally more about degrading and
demoralizing one's enemies than it is about nutrition or ritual
power. The cannibals discussed by Montaigne are of this sort;
they eat their enemies as a way of demonstrating to them that
their power is unquestionable. And cannibalism is among the
atrocities that occurred in the Democratic Republic of the

degrading

dies of some

n of war, as it

man rights viola-

tes, "Cannibalism is

n 2, "Futamono"). One

eria and the DRC to see

acts of dominance become

herwise—by rebel factions, by

cannibalism to consider is what I

m—which is the use of human flesh

wise non-cannibalistic diet. Generally

cannibalism is a response to hard

t the extremity of starvation—and it is the

sm most likely practiced by our prehistoric

ough they did not eat other people most of the

ears to have been perfectly acceptable in at least

ose prehistoric communities to resort to cannibalism

her food sources were less plentiful. In the case of the

derthals, this seems to have meant at least sometimes

acking and murdering large groups of people in order to use

their corpses for food. We might also include in this category the widespread practice of "medicinal cannibalism," primarily in Europe and Asia, which reached its height in the Middle Ages and early modernity. During this period, physicians often instructed their patients to eat human body parts—often, but not always, taken from mummies and other ancient dead—in the treatment of various ailments. This practice was not uncommon; as the scholar Richard Sugg notes in *Mummies, Cannibals and Vampires*, "The question was not, 'Should you eat human flesh?' but, 'What sort of flesh should you eat?'" (see also Dolan). Hannibal Lecter, acting intentionally and oh-so-independently of the mores of his culture, is not what we would call a cultural cannibal. A *cultured* cannibal, perhaps, but that's different.

(3) Hedonistic Cannibalism

The third kind of cannibalism, after starvation cannibalism and cultural cannibalism, is hedonistic cannibalism—and it's in this category that we'll undoubtedly find Dr. Lecter. A hedonist is just a pleasure-seeker, and so a hedonistic cannibal is someone who eats people because he or she enjoys it—not for some other reason. Although people are very different, and thus their pleasures also differ, there seem to be three basic categories of hedonistic cannibal: (a) paraphilic cannibals, (b) sadistic cannibals, and (c) recreational cannibals.

Paraphilia is the modern scientific word for what we used to call "sexual perversions," and psychologists have a long list of paraphilias that they've identified in their patients. Paraphilias are what we might call abnormal sexual desires, and they are often characterized by extreme behaviors. One paraphilia is—as you might have guessed—anthropophagy. And as we've seen with most of the real-life cannibal serial killers who've been identified and studied—think again of Jeffrey Dahmer, or perhaps Albert Fish, "the Werewolf of Wysteria"—hedonistic cannibalism typically presents itself as related in some way to sexual desire or gratification. Cannibals like Dahmer and Fish eat their victims as part of consummating their sexual desire for those victims. Despite the fact that most of the known contemporary cannibals are of this sort, there are no paraphilic cannibals in the works of Thomas Harris—least of all Hannibal Lecter, from whom sexuality is almost entirely absent (until the end of the novel, *Hannibal*, at least, when he makes his romantic getaway with Clarice Starling).[1]

Related in some ways to paraphilic cannibalism, but not identical with it, is sadistic cannibalism. A sadist is someone who derives pleasure from inflicting pain on others, and at least as often as not, the pleasure sadists feel is a sexual pleasure. In such cases—and, again, I would include both Dahmer and Fish in this category—cannibalism is undertaken as a means of further degrading the cannibal's victim. Which is to say that such cannibals do not torture and kill their victims in order to eat them, but eat them as a way of further demonstrating the contempt they feel for them, which contempt inspired them to attack their victims in the first place. In these

---

[1] For more on Dr. Lecter's sexuality, and how it might influence his actions, see Chapter 18 of this volume.—Ed.

cases, then, sadism *is* the paraphilia and cannibalism is merely the means by way of which the killer derives his pleasure. But we can imagine a different sort of cannibalism, one that is not related to sexual pleasure, but the pain and suffering caused by which are pleasant to the cannibal—who practices cannibalism precisely in order to bring about that pain and suffering. I think many of us who are familiar with Hannibal Lecter see something of this sadism in him; certainly, those closest to him—Clarice Starling, Will Graham, Jack Crawford, Lady Murasaki, Bedelia du Maurier, and so on—see something of the sadist in him, and sometimes diagnose him as such. And to be fair, there is more than one instance of Dr. Lecter engaging in what seems to be purely sadistic behavior—the coerced self-disfigurement of Mason Verger, for example, or the murders of the five men who killed and ate his sister in *Hannibal Rising*. Yet . . . he does not cannibalize Verger, just tortures (and eventually causes the death of) him. Nor does he cannibalize Rinaldo Pazzi, although he kills him and uses his death to produce a tableau worthy of Renaissance Italian art. Although he does eat the cheeks of Grutas and his crew, he does not kill them *in order to* eat their cheeks—he kills them to get revenge for the death of Mischa. Which is to say that, in these instances, Hannibal Lecter isn't really acting as "Hannibal the Cannibal." He's exacting revenge, acting in a genuinely aggrieved albeit sadistic way.

This leaves us with the very last category within the very last kind of cannibalism: recreational cannibalism. Recreational cannibalism is just what it sounds like: consuming the flesh of other human beings for no reason other than that one enjoys it. Sometimes we eat the things we eat because we're hungry and they're all that's available; sometimes, we eat what we eat because we think it's good for us; sometimes what we eat is determined by familial or social expectations. But sometimes we choose to eat the foods we eat solely because we like how they taste. And this is precisely what is going on for the recreational—or, we might say, "culinary"—cannibal. Recreational cannibals do not especially require the nutrition that human flesh provides, nor do they participate in cultures where such tastes are encouraged or expected. In addition, recreational cannibals do not derive sexual or sadistic pleasure from cannibalism. They are not, in our somewhat antiquated sense of the term, "perverts." The pleasure they derive is purely gustatory: they're foodies. They love to eat.

The thing about recreational cannibalism in this sense of the term, however, is that there don't seem actually ever to have been any such cannibals. Recreational cannibalism may be exclusively present in myth (the Cyclops in Homer's *Odyssey*), legend (the witch in "Hansel and Gretel"), and fiction (the family in *The Texas Chainsaw Massacre*). Even if there is no evidence that recreational cannibals actually exist, the idea of human *haute cuisine* fascinates and repels us in a way little else can—and one such cannibal stands head and shoulders above the rest. Once again, as Mads Mikkelsen notes, Hannibal Lecter is "the icon of all the cannibals." Whereas paraphilic and sadistic cannibals appear to act on forces and motivations that are psychologically out of their control—they are mentally ill, and require treatment—Thomas Harris always presents Lecter to us as far more lucid, far saner, than those other (perhaps more realistic) cannibals ever are. Whatever Dr. Lecter's ailments, his passion for human flesh is never presented to us as satisfying any need—just a desire. Hannibal Lecter may kill people because he is a psychopath possessed of an irrepressible urge, but that isn't why he eats people, too. He eats them because he likes it.

Is Cannibalism Morally Wrong?

It is almost certainly our gut instinct to say, without delay and without question, that cannibalism is morally wrong. Certainly everyone who learns of Dr. Lecter's cannibalistic proclivities dubs them evil—if not also evidence of insanity. But as we've seen, cannibalism is a far larger and more complex phenomenon throughout human history (and prehistory) than many of us realize. And that complexity should give us pause, if only for a moment, during which time we can reconsider our thinking about one of our greatest taboos. Is every instance of cannibalism morally wrong—or is it just that we find the thought of eating other human beings to be so revolting that we refuse to allow ourselves to consider the possibility of a morally permissible cannibalism?

Central to many philosophical discussions of the ethics of cannibalism is a distinction borrowed from the ethical discourse about euthanasia, and first employed in the examination of the ethics of cannibalism by the philosopher William B. Irvine in "Cannibalism, Vegetarianism and Narcissism": the distinction between *active cannibalism* and *passive cannibalism*. Generally speaking, active cannibalism is the killing of other human beings in order to eat them; passive cannibalism is the consumption of human flesh from already deceased individuals whom one did not kill for food (p. 12). Since every instance of active cannibalism is an instance of murder, and no one really wants to question the moral wrongness of murder, we can say right off the bat that every instance of active cannibalism is morally wrong. Of the kinds of cannibalism delineated in the previous section, it seems that most of them can occur in either active or passive forms. Only sadistic cannibalism—one of the subtypes of hedonistic cannibalism—seems not to admit of a passive variety.

Passive cannibalism, on the other hand, is more complicated, morally speaking, since it's really about the ethics of corpse disposal, really. Does a corpse have the right not to be eaten? Almost certainly not, since a corpse is no different in kind from any other dead body, and dead bodies don't seem to be able to have rights. There are of course numerous non-philosophical arguments against corpse desecration—that it is sacrilegious, or obscene, forbidden by God or the gods. These arguments are interesting, for what they're worth, but they fail to compel us precisely because they require us, in advance, to subscribe to a single religious or cultural system of beliefs—and we don't all have the same religious or cultural backgrounds. We might also of course argue that allowing people to butcher, cook, and eat the bodies of their dead fellows, while not itself murder, might encourage many people in our society to become more comfortable with causing harm to living human bodies, too, by way of a kind of desensitization and a gradual loss of respect for humanity as such. But, as Irvine notes, "there are documented cases in which people have practiced passive cannibalism for generations and have nevertheless maintained respect for their fellow humans" (p. 12). Montaigne, in his conversations with a South American cannibal who had traveled to France, certainly found him to be no less human or humane than his fellow Frenchmen (in fact, as we've already seen, Montaigne believed the French could learn a thing or two from the cannibals—although not about fine cuisine, one imagines). And while one might wish to raise all sorts of objections to cannibalism on nutritional or sanitary grounds, it remains the case that these are not *moral* objections. Many things that are bad for our bodies (such as eating raw eggs or getting no exercise) are not for that reason *evil*.

Thus, beginning again at the beginning, with starvation cannibalism, we see immediately that there is a huge moral difference between passive starvation cannibalism and active starvation cannibalism. An active starvation cannibal is really starving, but—like Alferd Packer or Vladis Grutas—kills to eat. While we might sympathize with their hunger, as well as their willingness to do anything to avoid painfully starving to death, we cannot condone murder, and Packer and Grutas are murderers. At the same time, however, this seems to give us grounds for suggesting that passive starvation cannibalism, however disgusting, is nevertheless not morally wrong. If you are starving to death, and if the only nutritious food source available to you is corpse flesh, I think you are on safe moral grounds preparing yourself a meal.

As for cultural cannibalism, we can again say right away that all *active* forms of cultural cannibalism—the religious cannibalism of the Aztecs, the political/military cannibalism in Liberia and the DRC, the nutritional cannibalism of the Neanderthals—are morally wrong, at least on any moral belief system that prohibits murder. The passive forms of cultural cannibalism are, however, more difficult to judge. Some religions encourage what anthropologists call "endocannibalism," the eating of the bodies of deceased members of one's own community, as the preferred funerary ceremony. While the Greek historian Herodotus noted that there was no amount of money so great that you could pay a Greek to eat the bodies of his dead parents, he also noted that the Callatiae (an ancient tribe from India, who practiced funerary cannibalism) could not stomach the thought of burying or cremating their dead in the manner of the Greek religion (Herodotus, *Histories* III.38). While it is more difficult to make sense of a passive form of political or military cannibalism (what is sometimes called "exocannibalism," exclusively eating the bodies of members of other communities), we might return to the example of Montaigne's South American cannibals, who do not kill their prisoners of war in order to eat them (they execute them for engaging in war against them), but who do eat their bodies after they've been executed—which isn't to say that the practice is morally right, just that it's not the *cannibalistic* aspect of the practice that makes it wrong. And one might have a more sympathetic understanding of Neanderthal cannibalism if the Neanderthals had only resorted to eating corpses. All indications are, however, that they killed whole families for food—and this, one probably doesn't need to add, is wrong.

Perhaps the most difficult form of cannibalism to adjudge with any degree of confidence, however, is hedonistic cannibalism—despite the fact that we do live in a culture that would seem to teach us that doing anything solely for our own pleasure is at the very least selfish, if not outright wrong. As we've already seen, all forms of sadistic cannibalism require that the person being eaten be tortured while they're alive—and, thus, are morally impermissible. Paraphilic cannibalism is in most known cases so closely associated with sadism that it is difficult to imagine someone whose anthropophagic paraphilia did not also involve physical (including sexual) abuse, as well as murder. In fact, it seems most known cases of paraphilic cannibalism are in fact instances of anthropophagolagnia, a sexual desire to both rape and cannibalize the object of one's desire. This was certainly the case for Dahmer and Fish. But we are all aware of another paraphilia—necrophilia, the desire to have sex with corpses—and there is no necessary connection between necrophilia and rape, sadism, or murder (we might say that most known cases are in fact of "passive necrophilia"). And it doesn't require a great feat of the imagination to conceive of a comparable sort of paraphilic cannibalism—one that took sexual gratification in the eating of corpses (whether associated with necrophilic desires or not), but was not engaged in murder. Thus, we can say that, *if it exists*, passive paraphilic cannibalism is morally comparable to necrophilia—which may be illegal and sacrilegious (insofar as it typically constitutes corpse desecration), but is not clearly immoral (since no one is actually being harmed).

By the same token, passive recreational cannibalism—simply taking pleasure in eating corpses, or parts of corpses, and eating them for the pleasure it gives—is not immoral, at least not insofar as it's cannibalism. If corpses are someone's property, then passive recreational cannibalism might be wrong insofar as it's stealing; if it's wrong to desecrate corpses, of course, then passive recreational cannibalism would be wrong on those grounds—but, again, the *eating* is not what would make it wrong. (For an interesting counterargument that rests upon conceiving of cannibalism as a sort of disrespect, see Lu's "Explaining the Wrongness of Cannibalism.")

Active recreational cannibalism of the sort conducted by Dr. Lecter is decidedly evil, however; there's no two ways about it. While some kinds of killing—self-defense, war, capital punishment—might be morally justifiable in at least some instances, they are justified in every case by the fact that the good brought about by the act of killing justifies the use of lethal force. That one prefers the livers of census takers to the livers of calves is no such good.

One last note of interest: perhaps the most horrifying contribution to the discourse of cannibalism made by the Hannibal Lecter series is not, in fact, Lecter's recreational cannibalism itself—but the fact, noted in passing in the Thomas Harris novels, depicted only once in the films (in the prologue to *Red Dragon*), but ubiquitous in the television series, that Dr. Lecter not only eats human beings: he butchers them, cooks them, and serves the meat to other (typically unsuspecting) people. Hannibal Lecter is renowned for his wonderful dinner parties in the world of the Baltimore elite, and he seems regularly to serve "long pork" in more traditionally consumed meats' stead. While Lecter himself is engaged at these dinner parties—as he is elsewhere—in active cannibalism, his dinner guests are cannibals too, just unwitting ones. In *Dinner with a Cannibal*, author Carole Travis-Henikoff calls this "benign" cannibalism, "because the diner has no knowledge of what kind of meat he is eating . . . or has already eaten" (p. 25). So long as one is unaware of what one is eating, and has reasonable justification in leaving the source of one's meal unquestioned (one has no reason to distrust the chef, for example), then benign cannibalism—as horrifying and disgusting as it might be—is perfectly morally acceptable. But ignorance is only an excuse to a certain point . . .

Once Will Graham and Jack Crawford become suspicious of Dr. Lecter, and specifically, begin to suspect he is a cannibal, then they have every reason to believe that he might be serving them human meat when they join him at table. Over the course of the series, Jack and Will make the transition from benign cannibals to passive cannibals—perhaps passive political cannibals (who eat people as a means of seeking justice), or perhaps it's some new sort of utilitarian or instrumental cannibalism, but cannibals they are. Once they know that they might be eating human flesh—and the flesh of murder victims, no less—they become morally responsible for what they eat. Their purpose may be noble (capturing the elusive and destructive Chesapeake Ripper), and their intentions good, but they are eating people in full knowledge of the fact (in Will's case, at least) that they are eating people. That kind of a meal has moral consequences.

And this, perhaps, is Hannibal Lecter's ultimate goal: he would, were he given the opportunity, make cannibals—or canapés—of us all.

3
What's So Bad about Eating People?

BENJAMIN MCCRAW

Part of the enduring interest in the Hannibal Lecter character across the novels, movies, and television series involves the tension of the contrast between his highly educated approach to life and the more typical low-class serial killer found behind bars and stalking victims. Lecter's diet neatly brings both tendencies together: high culinary skill and imagination paired with the knowledge that . . . *it's people!* We tend to associate cannibalism with either faraway tropical tribes living outside the Western world or with clumsy, psychotic serial killers easily seen as sub-human monsters. But Lecter's different: he's high-class *human* plus low-class murderer: finally, a cannibal we can get behind.

We often take Lecter's monstrosity for granted. He's a bad guy and all—he kills people and eats them—but we quickly move past this to consider why he's so engaging, how he reflects us and our society, and so forth. But I want to pause on the moral question too often taken as a given: that he's a moral monster in his cannibalism. If Lecter were to make a case for his actions, how could he go about it (assuming that he *would* go about it)? And how should we think about his cannibalism in light of his self-defense? Can we make good on our moral reaction of horror at his cannibalism?

Throughout the films and television series, we can count about ten of Lecter's victims that he cannibalizes. We're going to focus on them even though Lecter kills many more for various reasons: escaping capture, avoiding detection, derailing investigations, and so forth. But we can group the people he eats into three main groups: those he kills early in his life (primarily in the *Hannibal Rising* movie), those he kills only as dinner (mostly in the series), and a handful of major characters from the movies he kills for reasons in addition to a desire to eat them. I propose that we put on our "Hannibal Lecter hats" to consider each of these groups and how he might justify their ultimate end (in his stomach).

An Eye for an Eye . . . On the Dinner Plate

Lecter's first instances of murder and cannibalism occur early in his psychological development (emphasizing the *"psycho"*). In *Hannibal Rising*, we see the horrors Lecter encounters in WWII—his flight from his home during the Nazi invasion, the death of his parents, and the murder and cannibalization of his favorite little sister, Mischa, by the soldiers holding them prisoner. After leaving the orphanage into which he's been placed—and where he's learned to defend himself and others with violence—he travels to France, to live with his uncle and his aunt. His love for his aunt sets the scene for his first murder and act of cannibalism.

The local butcher—Paul Momund—crudely insults Lecter's aunt. Now, it's generally a bad idea to insult the love interest of a serial-killing-cannibal-in-training, and Lecter doesn't respond with a socially and morally acceptable ass-kicking. Instead, he decapitates Momund for his insult and prepares his cheeks in a way indicative of high culinary skill, refinement, and appreciation. Lecter's treatment of Momund would be overkill (pun definitely intended) for pretty much any non-Lecter person but it fits the sort of actions we'd expect of him later on. This action foreshadows the "ruthlessness plus culinary sophistication" that makes Lecter so intriguing.

Lecter's second act of cannibalism occurs after he's left France and his aunt behind. After learning that the troops responsible for the death of Mischa are alive, he travels home to Lithuania to track them down. At the scene of her murder and his torture, one of the soldiers finds him with an eye towards killing Lecter before he can exact his revenge on the group. But, as many come to find out, it's far easier to think you'll kill Lecter than to succeed. The soldier out to kill

Lecter—Enrikas Dortlich—ends up like Momund. Lecter kills him and eats his cheeks.

So, we've got the first two cases of Lecter's murder and cannibalism. How could one possibly think about these actions as morally justified? Well, the details of their deaths and actions in Lecter's story suggest a defense that such an intellectually capable person might give. "Consider," we can imagine Lecter saying, "the ancient tradition of the *lex talionis*—the law of the talon." (Whether you choose to hear this via Brian Cox's, Anthony Hopkins's, or Mads Mikkelsen's distinctive voice is up to you.) "Indeed, Nature sets down her own laws and we, as part of Nature itself, must obey her. Even the word of God recognizes the balancing Nature exacts from us: 'life for life, eye for eye, tooth for tooth, hand for hand, foot for foot'. My treatment of Momund and Dortlich simply recognizes these laws and respects them." Lecter's hypothetical defense blends what philosophers call Natural Law Theory with a *lex talionis* perspective on punishment.

According to Natural Law Theory, there is a set of moral laws or codes that derive from nature (generally speaking). There are certain natural goods or rules that determine morality. For instance, life is a crucial part of nature and, thus, we should expect to find moral codes making certain kinds of killing—like murder most obviously—wrong, and certain kinds of aiding life—like protecting the innocent or self-defense— morally correct. Depending on the particular version of the theory, we might find a fairly extensive list of the goods and actions promoted by nature: procreation, community, and so on. Lecter's imagined defense above appeals to "Nature" as the source of morality for the actions in question. The actions he has done ultimately are right *because* they are sanctioned by Nature. How exactly? That's where the law of the talon comes in.

The *lex talionis* is an influential approach to the justification of punishment or, in fancy philosophical lingo, retributive justice. Lecter appeals to this law as a law of Nature: it's part of the "natural order of things" that we should meet actions in kind. Someone assaults you, then you are either obligated or permitted (depending on the strength of the theory in question) to assault them back. Someone steals your property: you may take from them in equal proportion. The law of satisfaction reigns here: do that which makes the crime against you satisfied. Now, the *lex talionis* isn't necessarily connected to the Natural Law Theory, but Lecter can use it to rationalize his deeds.

What does this tell us about the death and cannibalization of Momund and Dortlich? Lecter views his actions simply as satisfaction or returning like for like. Dortlich is obvious: he murdered and ate Mischa. The law of retribution cries out that Dortlich should be killed and eaten himself. Lecter simply obliges the natural law demanding that Dortlich pays back what he's done. What of Momund? He's no killer and he's no cannibal. But use a bit of Lecter's own intellectual creativity. Momund treats Lecter's aunt simply as the meat he sells by treating her so crudely. She's not really some person to be respected but a mere thing to be used and insulted. Lecter, in turn, views Momund as he views her: as a piece of meat. His viewing is just more literal than Momund's, but the attitudes seem to match. Lecter simply treats Momund as he treats people (especially Lecter's aunt). The *lex talionis* is in effect here: Momund's dehumanizing attitude towards others results in his (literal) dehumanization into dinner.

It's important here to realize that the *lex talionis* doesn't merely work to justify his killing but his eating as well. Even if someone else had murdered Momund and Dortlich, Lecter could use the *lex talionis* to defend eating them: he treats Momund as Momund treats others and returns Dortlich's treatment of Mischa back to him *even if we separate out the fact that Lecter killed them*. So, the *lex talionis* in Lecter's hands can justify the cannibalism itself; even if separated from the act of murder providing him with the corpses to eat.

The Lecter of *Hannibal Rising* shows the vengeance exacted against those who do him wrong and the ways he treats those victims reinforce a kind of "eye for an eye" attitude in returning to those *exactly* what they've done to you. When someone eats you (or your sister), you eat them back. When someone treats you like meat, you owe it to them to treat them the same—as meat—and eat them.

The Ickiest Dinner Party EVER

Another way to categorize Lecter's post-vengeance victims would be by their overall role in his story. Lecter selects both minor and major characters to serve and the reasoning behind each category can be different. How might Lecter consider the minor characters killed and eaten? First off, we can think about the famous, unnamed Census Taker that Lecter eats with a nice Chianti and fava beans. The TV series features a dinner party Lecter throws composed of various characters from the show: Andrew Caldwell, Michelle Vocalson, Darrell Ledgerwood, Christopher Ward, and probably unnamed others. Andrew Caldwell is a doctor killed in the "Sorbet" episode. While drawing blood from Lecter, he suggests that Lecter would probably lie about his health, but that such lies would be useless given that the blood will speak to Lecter's true conditions. Later on, Lecter comes upon Caldwell on the road as a result of a broken down car—a coincidence, I'm sure. The police later find Caldwell's corpse as we see Lecter packing his fridge with organ meat.

Lecter finds Caldwell's name via his business card in a Rolodex. In the same episode, we see the same Rolodex Lecter uses to select other characters he kills and cooks for his party. He finds Vocalson, a customer service representative; Ledgerwood, general manager of a book store; and Ward, an IT consultant, in the list of cards. After selecting each person's card, we see Lecter preparing meat in the artful ways we come to expect from him: implying the specific end of each person. Throughout the show, we can suspect many of the fine culinary triumphs Lecter eats and feeds to his guests contain the remains of some unnamed victims that serve only to be served.

What does Lecter think of these minor characters and the ethics of his actions towards them? The kill/dinner list from "Sorbet" is important and crucial to understanding how Lecter sees his actions. In the same episode he speaks of his own eating. "The feast is life. You put the life in your belly and you live." I seriously doubt Lecter's giving us a grand metaphysical theory that "you must consume life to live." If that were true, Lecter wouldn't have to take so much joy in the presentation, eating, and appreciation in consuming. No—the point is how Lecter thinks of the parts of the feast: simply as lives to be consumed. The show's hero, Will Graham, comes up with the same view of Lecter's attitude towards the people he kills and eats. In speaking of the Chesapeake Ripper (Lecter), Graham claims "that's how he sees his victims. Not as people, not as prey. Pigs" (*Hannibal*, Season 1, "Sorbet").

This seems to be how Lecter views the minor characters; simply as food to be consumed. How can this be? Well, Lecter might offer the following: "Philosophers have engaged for millennia in the debate about human nature and, more importantly, its role in morality," Lecter begins, "but consider the moral role of the community in living a *human* life. Humans are social animals. But what of those animals among us who aren't social? The ones that either can't or won't abide the merest of social rules? Well, they just can't be all that human now, can they? The obstinately rude animals around us lack the social community needed to distinguish man from beast. By rejecting communal or social rules in their rudeness, they are rejecting *us* and rejecting the part of them that makes them like us. In the end, they just aren't human in any meaningful sense."

Lecter invokes humanity as the standard for morality here: those that are human are moral beings worthy of treatment as such but non-human beings just aren't moral beings at all. In this, Lecter offers a variant of a theory given by the philosopher Immanuel Kant. For him, humans are defined by their rationality and our reason is what determines morality. The moral law is nothing more nor less than the fully *rational* law. Since laws are universal in scope, the moral law simply becomes the obligation to act in ways that are universally applicable without exception. Only beings capable of conceiving and acting in accordance with laws, then, are moral. Lecter adopts the same attitude substituting social politeness for rationality and rudeness for irrationality.

And, as with the *lex talionis* above, Lecter's hypothetical rationalization can work on his cannibalism even if we leave his murdering aside. If morality comes down to respecting humanity as Kant famously claims, then corpses have no moral standing. They aren't human and, thus, eating them isn't disrespecting anyone. Lecter can morally justify his cannibalism, therefore, just as easily as his murder of these minor characters with no change in the Kantian reasoning provided.

Lecter's Rolodex of names supports the hypothetical, tweaked Kantianism here. The Rolodex isn't a hit list. If so, then he would just kill them straightaway. They aren't a list of grudges. He doesn't seem to view the people named in it with malice or take a sadistic pleasure in killing them. In reality, they are simply a grocery list. Lecter lists those who, by being rude, fail to meet his standards for humanity. They are simply non-human animals fit to be slaughtered, cooked, and eaten. They are simply pigs to Lecter, as Graham notes. And there's nothing immoral, on Lecter's view (or Kant's for that matter), about killing and eating a pig.

Some People Just Need Some Killing?

We've looked at the early vengeance-based kills in *Hannibal Rising* and the less-than-famous kills for a dinner party in the series *Hannibal*. Other movies have more memorable victims/dinners than these two. Paul Krendler from *Hannibal*, and Benjamin Raspail and Frederick Chilton from *Silence of the Lambs*, are well-known characters Lecter kills and eats. Or, at least in the case of Chilton, he very heavily hints at Chilton's imminent demise.

Having kidnapped Clarice Starling, Lecter holds her at Krendler's house until it's time to kill and serve the owner. Probably Krendler's death is the most interesting we see in the films: Lecter opens his skull, fries a bit of his brains, and eats that part while Krendler is alive and conscious. That scene sticks with you. Raspail's death, however, is unseen but something to which Lecter confesses: the police find his corpse in a church missing a few organs. And, finally, Chilton's end is not seen and not even accomplished in the films. Instead, we are led to believe he's dead (he's missing in *Hannibal*) but the end of *Silence of the Lambs* assures us: Lecter has tracked him down and tells Clarice that he's "having an old friend for dinner." It's the film's version of *To Serve Chilton*. What drives Lecter to kill and eat these characters?

Krendler taunts and plagues Clarice throughout the film. He's lewd, abuses his authority, and accepts a bribe to harm Clarice, providing a character that the audience actual *wants* to be killed. So, we have several items that make him an excellent candidate for Lecter's expertise: he's tremendously rude (and we know what Lecter thinks should befall the rude), he antagonizes Lecter's friend in Clarice, and he's generally incompetent as a law enforcement official. Any one of these makes him suitable for being on Lecter's kill list but the trio makes him suitable for Lecter's *grocery* list. Killing Krendler makes Clarice's life better and probably improves the lives of anyone who knows him.

Lecter kills Raspail for incompetence. When Raspail, a musician, performs with the Baltimore symphony, Lecter hears his playing as a serious detriment to the overall quality of the music. In fact, Raspail is so bad that Lecter thinks he's even ruined an entire work just by his poor playing on its own. Lecter feels no ill will towards Raspail but his death serves to enhance the aesthetic quality of the symphony. In killing Raspail, Lecter has improved the lives of anyone listening.

Finally, it seems very plausible that Lecter kills Chilton out of equal parts revenge and, again, incompetence. Lecter disapproves of Chilton the person as well as Chilton the psychologist. By killing Chilton, Lecter can satisfy his own desires for vengeance as well as remove a therapist he considers woefully inadequate in one fell swoop. Ultimately, in each person's death, Lecter thinks he's improving some segment of the world. Killing Krendler improves the life of Clarice, offing Raspail helps the listening experience of anyone attending the Baltimore Symphony, and dispatching Chilton improves his life as well as psychotherapy in general.

This suggests a response from Lecter justifying his actions by the benefits they have. We can imagine Lecter: "every rudimentary chef knows that you must break some eggs to make an omelet. Just consider these people some bad eggs that must be broken to make a fabulous frittata out of life. No one could miss Krendler: his rude and atrocious character worsens everyone around him. And I should receive an ovation for Raspail's fate. I saved the symphony from something worse than death: his playing. Frederick's death is no loss to anyone except the patients he tortures and the discipline of psychology he has trampled. Indeed, each of these actions was a great boon to humanity: morally, musically, and psychologically. By killing these men, I've made the world better than I found it."

In these words, Lecter justifies his actions with an appeal to consequentialism. A consequentialist views the morality of any action as dependent on its consequences. If an action has good consequences, then the action is good; if it has bad effects, then the action is bad. Of course, killing someone is generally bad. It leads to pain for the victim's family and friends, and it removes a person and their life from the value of the world. But, Lecter asks us to reconsider killing Krendler, Raspail, and Chilton with the specific consequences or effects those actions have.

Slaying Krendler removes a significant problem for Clarice in both her personal and professional lives. He's dirty: Mason Verger is able to buy him off and bribery makes for a seriously flawed law enforcement official. His incompetence and his awfulness to Clarice mean that Lecter thinks of the world without Krendler as better than the world with him in it. Killing may be bad in general but not *this* killing. The same sort of defense could apply to Raspail. Lecter lives life in search of beauty: in food, music, art, and so forth. Raspail's awful playing in the symphony makes the world less beautiful. In his death, Lecter promotes the music the symphony should have been playing all along and, in eating him, Lecter transforms Raspail's ugly music into beautiful food. Lecter moves from the unattractive experience of hearing him play to the beautiful experience of him on the plate. Chilton's death, in the same way, removes a hack from the lives of potential patients as well as a thorn in Lecter's own side. The death of each leaves no black mark on the world, but in their dying they contribute to the improvement and beauty of the world. Though killing is bad in most cases, each death turns out for the good. Cracking these eggs makes for a tasty omelet.

But it's not just their deaths that fit his hypothetical consequentialism. He isn't just removing something bad but also creating something good—the high culinary dinner made from each victim. Here is where the cannibalism and his particular height of gustatory accomplishment become important. By killing, Lecter has made the world less bad but, by making them into aesthetically and culinary pleasing dinners, he's added goodness to it through the happiness of his dinner guests. So, as with the other moral theories used, we can separate Lecter's murder of his victims from his eating them and find consequentialism here justifying his high-end cannibalism separately from murder. At the end of the day, we have a double whammy: Lecter's murders remove badness from the world and Lecter's dinner parties contribute goodness to it.

What Is So Bad about Eating People?

So far, Lecter can muster some justification from ethics for killing and eating his victims. Different sorts of victims require different sorts of moral defenses: his early victims fit an "eye for an eye" sort of theory, his dinner party ingredients fit a tweaked Kantianism denying their humanity, and his more infamous victims have a consequentialist justification. Does this mean that it's actually okay for Lecter to have murdered and cannibalized these people? Unsurprisingly, the answer is "um . . . *no.*"

There's one significant moral theory he hasn't used, and the neglect is telling. Historically, virtue ethics occupies a significant role in philosophical thinking about morality. On this kind of theory, we should focus on a person's virtues or character. If a person acts out of good character traits—AKA virtues—then that person's actions are good. Likewise, if a person acts out of bad character traits—AKA vices—then that person's actions are bad. Often, virtue ethicists associate virtues with living a flourishing human life. We should be kind, courageous, honest, self-controlled, and so forth because these sorts of traits lead to living a good human life; that is, living well. Meanwhile, liars, cowards, and mean-spirited folks tend to lead less-than-pleasant lives on the whole by actually being unpleasant themselves.

In justifying his actions above, Lecter focuses on what he's done; thinking of their consequences or how they relate to moral rules. But a virtue ethicist would focus on the character Lecter displays in killing and eating his victims as well as the kind of life his character leads him to live. So far, we've seen that it's fairly easy to distort these other theories into forms that seem to make cannibalism okay. Can we use virtue ethics—even a perversion of it—to justify Lecter's actions? That seems impossible. What sort of person is Lecter: does he display positive character traits? Does he live well? I think the clear answer is "no." What sort of person does Lecter's killing and cannibalism uncover? Not a very good one: he's cold, callous, manipulative, disrespectful, (excessively) proud, and so on. His personality doesn't contain the sorts of traits that we associate with decent human beings—just the opposite, these are the traits we think of when we consider morally heinous people.

What about the kind of life Lecter lives? On first glance, the Lecter of the TV series seems to do well. He seems happy: he has friends, a fulfilling job, successful hobbies, and so on. Even the Lecter of the movies often gets away with murder. There are speed bumps when the cops get close but he manages to escape. But is this true: does Lecter live well? No. He has people in his life but those aren't really friends in any significant way. If they get close, they learn what he is and then they must die. He has only acquaintances. Further, he must live on the run. Even if he remains out of prison, he has to live his life constantly on guard against the authorities. It's an isolated and paranoid existence. If humans really are social animals, then it's *Lecter* who leads an inhuman life. And that's just not living well. The way he lives his life and the actions he takes constantly prevent him from leading a decent life.

Virtue ethics, then, gives us a way to think about the morality of Lecter's actions that's hard to twist into a distorted rationalization. Eating people really is a bad thing to do, because there's just no way to think of a morally good person who cannibalizes in the way Lecter does. And this seems to hold even if we take murder out of the equation. Typically—life-boat or stranded-in-the-Andes situations aside—we don't view acts of cannibalism grounded in virtue or the good life. Viewing people as potential dinner or proto-meat doesn't express what we'd associate with a *good* character and the form of life involved in harvesting human corpses for supper fails to reflect what we'd reasonably call the "good life." The traits his actions uncover belong to the person who seems fully inhuman and one leading a life unrecognizable to anyone living a decent human existence. Finding a way to justify Lecter's actions from the perspective of virtue ethics requires more than a distortion or perversion—it requires a direct inversion: taking those traits we think are virtues for vices (and vice versa). To use virtue ethics to defend his actions would be to undo the theory at its very core and the theory would merely collapse. Lecter can manipulate his actions to make them seem to fit various ethical theories but he can't manipulate *himself* to fit the sort of person we admire. Even if Lecter thinks he can justify his actions, there's no way he can justify himself. And so, virtue ethics gives us the condemnation of Lecter we find so natural and forceful when thinking about his acts of murder and cannibalism.

II.

What Does
He Do, This Man
You Seek?

4
Acts of God

TRIP MCCROSSIN

"Oh, Officer Starling, do you think you can dissect me with this blunt little tool?," Hannibal Lecter quips in *The Silence of the Lambs*, sporting his best Southern drawl, reviewing with disdain the questionnaire she's just presented to him. As we watch, she's able to get but a few words out in her defense before he cuts her off with a humiliating tirade. "You look like a rube," he chides, in the film as in the novel, "a well-scrubbed, hustling rube with a little taste," and carries on in this vein for a long and merciless minute, until she's visibly shaken (Harris, *Silence*, p. 20). In the novel, though, several hundred words of provocative dialogue intervene.

Their exchange begins with Starling's attempt to entice him with his own curiosity about, as she says, "what happened" to him. "Nothing happened to me, Officer Starling," he replies, "*I* happened. You can't reduce me to a set of influences" (Harris, *Silence*, p. 19). Readers of *Red Dragon,* and viewers of the first film version of it, *Manhunter*, recall Lecter communicating this already to Starling's predecessor, Will Graham. "We don't invent our natures," he'd urged, "they're given to us along with our lungs and pancreas and everything else. Why fight it?" (Harris, *Dragon*, p. 259).

In both cases Lecter then ruminates, eloquently as always, on the nature of good and evil generally, and on the "problem of evil" in particular, in such a way as to offer himself as a kind of solution. As Graham and Starling struggle with Lecter—to elicit his help in understanding and capturing more mundane "monsters," and also eventually Lecter himself—they struggle

45

in the first place to offer an alternative to Lecter's solution. As we naturally identify with Graham and Starling, but just as naturally are captivated by Lecter, we're reminded that *we* struggle similarly.

There is much in their complex storyline that helps us in this, as it's developed over many years now, in four novels, five films, and a television series. Here we make a modest beginning, exploring a provocative contrast that emerges as the storyline unfolds, in what we come to learn about Lecter's past that may qualify his early assertion that we "don't invent our natures." In the process, we make out an additional source of our enduring fascination with the storyline, over and above the sheer talent of the writers, actors, and filmmakers who've brought it to life.

What Feels Good to God?

The problem of evil, commonly phrased as the question, "why do bad things happen to good people, and good things to bad?" began as a theological problem, as far back as the Old Testament's Book of Job. How, according to Milton's turn of phrase in *Paradise Lost*, do we "justify the ways of God" to humanity, if this means somehow reconciling faith in God's wisdom, power, and benevolence with the misery we regularly suffer nonetheless?

The problem is also a modern *secular* one—as Susan Neiman has argued in her book, *Evil in Modern Thought*—which poses a threat not to God's standing, but to human reason. How, that is, can we make *reasonable* sense of the world, if we can't make sense of it teeming with suffering that *defies* human reason?

Interestingly, Graham's, Starling's, and Lecter's storylines address neither version of the problem exclusively, or perhaps even primarily.

The theological version we find, for example, in Lecter's challenge to Graham and Starling that they draw the lesson he does from his parable of "church collapses." Fans of the television series will recall that Lecter's challenge arises first (following the storyline's internal chronology, rather than that of the novels, films, and television series as they've appeared) in the therapy session that concludes Episode 2 of Season 1 ("Amuse-Bouche"), and again in their third session in Episode

9 of Season 2 ("Shiizakana"), back when Lecter was, of all things, Graham's therapist. Readers of *Red Dragon* find Lecter invoking the parable again some years later, once captured and imprisoned at the Baltimore State Hospital for the Criminally Insane, in his "brief note" to Graham, which, in light of the series, we can imagine easily enough is meant to remind him of the earlier therapy conversations. Later still (assuming order of appearance now), Lecter includes it in his phone call to Graham, in *Manhunter*, and in the second film version of *Red Dragon* in their last in-hospital meeting. Readers of *The Silence of the Lambs* will recall the parable from the missing dialogue cited above. And readers of *Hannibal*, finally, will recall that when Starling is called upon to explain to Jack Crawford Lecter's enduring fascination with her, what she reaches for most naturally is again the parable.

"It wasn't the *act* that got you down," Lecter challenges in his note, referring to Graham's killing of Garret Jacob Hobbs, whom he'd pursued before pursuing Lecter. "Really," he goes on, "didn't you feel bad *because killing him felt so good?*" And "why shouldn't it feel good? It must feel good to God—He does it all the time, and are we not made in His image?" "God dropped a church roof on thirty-four of His worshipers in Texas" not long ago, he continues, "just as they were groveling through a hymn. Don't you think that felt good?" Why else would God do such a thing, he's asking, or let it happen, which has to feel really just the same, especially to the likes of the *thirty-four*? And so, feeling good as it does, surely God "won't begrudge you one measly murder," Lecter concludes, the measly murder of Hobbs that is. And if so, why should Graham begrudge himself?

"You'd be so much more comfortable," he urges, "if you relaxed with yourself," with your "given" nature—"why fight it?" (Harris, *Dragon*, p. 259). *Lecter* doesn't. *He* embraces *his* given, and he believes *God-like*, nature. And so, he's urging, should Graham—and likewise, by extension, should the rest of us.

What's in a Phone Call?

Lecter's phone call in *Manhunter*, if we imagine it follows up on the note in *Red Dragon*, revisits and interestingly extends an idea from the conversation in "Amuse-Bouche," the idea of *power*.

In the conversation, Lecter having described the Texas church collapse, Graham asks, "did God feel good about that?" "He felt powerful," Lecter answers. And in the later therapy sessions, with Lecter's guidance, Graham becomes more comfortable admitting that in killing Hobbs he'd felt a "quiet sense of power." But now, in *Manhunter*'s phone call, Lecter's going deeper still. Killing "feels good," he says, "because God has power, and if one does what God does enough times, one will become as God is."

Lecter's God is Saint-Fond's God, from the Marquis de Sade's *History of Juliette*: "Why did you stray into the paths of virtue?" God asks. "The perpetual miseries with which I've blanketed the universe, should they not have convinced you that I love only disorder, and that you had to imitate me in order to please me?" (my translation). Lecter's solution to the problem of evil is, in effect, that he's just doing God's work.

All the more provocative, when Lecter talks of God, as he often does, most recently in the television series, he's not doing so as an intellectual or otherwise insincere sleight of hand. As portrayed in *Hannibal Rising*, the younger Lecter was without faith, as a result perhaps of losing his sister, Mischa. "We take comfort," he says as he's burying her, "in knowing there is no God" (Harris, *Rising*, p. 222). By the time we meet up with him in the television series, though, clearly this has changed. However unusual his conception of God—as *mal*evolent, that is—he leaves little doubt that he *believes*.

Lecter's talk of God is meant to convince Graham and Starling, and by implication the rest of us, to think and do as he thinks and does. Both resist, and in the process help us to. Starling's resistance, though, is more successful and so more provocative.

Typhoid and Swans

"You've given up good and evil for behaviorism, Officer Starling," or rather, he insinuates, *tried* to. "You've got everybody in moral dignity pants," he challenges, "nothing is ever anybody's fault. Look at me, Officer Starling. Can you stand to say I'm evil? Am I evil, Officer Starling?" What he wants is to provoke her to admit that she can't "give up" the idea in his case, even if perhaps only in his. But she resists, admitting that she understands him to be "destructive," yes, but insisting in turn that for her "it's the same thing." "Then *storms* are evil, if it's that simple," he mocks, and "we have *fire*, and then there's *hail*. Underwriters lump it all under 'Acts of God'." Surely, he's urging, she can't want to treat him *this* reductively.

She tries to correct her mistake, indicating that she'd meant to say that he'd been *deliberately* destructive. But, as if to say that it's simply irrelevant, he cuts her off with a Sicily church collapse. "The facade fell on sixty-five grandmothers at a special Mass," he describes. "Was that evil? If so, who did it? If He's up there, He just loves it, Officer Starling. Typhoid and swans—it all comes from the same place" (Harris, *Silence*, p. 19).

For fans of the television series, this will all seem naturally, though also a bit oddly, to ring a bell. In keeping still with the storyline's internal chronology, that is, Lecter seems again to be channeling earlier conversations with Graham, in Episodes 9 and 10 of Season 2.

"What do you think about when you think about killing?" Graham asks, in the third of their therapy sessions in Episode 9 ("Shiizakana"). Consistently with what we've heard him say already, Lecter answers that he thinks "about God." "Good and evil?" Graham asks in turn. "Good and evil has nothing to do with God," he answers, and proceeds to explain this with what he'll reprise in the above conversation with Starling, which is the version of the parable involving the Sicily church collapse and the common source of typhoid and swans. The distinction between good and evil, if it has nothing to do with God, must then be useful only to *us*, especially if we resist Lecter's understanding of God as malevolent. And also, if it helps to keep open, as he believes it does, the possibility of fundamental evil, immune to behaviorist reduction.

And it's precisely this that's at stake in the dinner conversation, between Graham and Lecter, which concludes Episode 10 ("Naka-Choko"). The conversation is key to Graham's plan to convince Lecter that the two of them are finally "just alike," by convincing him that he's now a killer in Lecter's image, in order to lure him into revelation and capture. This he does by intimating, ever so coyly, that the meat he's provided for their dinner is from a recent victim. As Lecter later tussles with Starling, he would naturally remember a particular portion of the conversation, and see it as paving the way for confronting her as he does. "You can't reduce me to a set of influences,"

Graham says, describing himself as he imagines Lecter would describe *him*self, "I'm not the product of anything." And so, when later slighted by Starling's "what happened to you," Lecter has Graham to thank for knowing just what she'd expect to hear.

But here's what's odd. Graham goes on to say of himself, continuing the pretense, that "he's given up good and evil for behaviorism," which is what Lecter later takes to be the source of Starling's dismissive attitude toward good and evil. Lecter doesn't note the tension. And so what he later accuses Starling of would have to be different from what he takes Graham to be attributing to himself, so far unaware of the pretense. And Graham must indeed mean something different, because behaviorism is based on precisely the contrary assumption that none of us is meaningfully irreducible to this or that set of influences. What's important to Lecter at this point, it seems, is to *educate* Graham, as he would later try to educate Starling, as to the sheer folly of "giving up good and evil," whatever may be its philosophical, psychological, forensic, or other motivations. "Then you can't say that I'm evil," Lecter challenges Graham, as he will later challenge Starling. "You're destructive," Graham replies, "same thing," just as Starling will eventually say, leading in both cases to storms, fire, hail, and other acts of God. "Is this meal an act of God," he asks, rhetorically— urging Graham to concede, as he'll later urge Starling to, that it's surely unwise to be *this* reductive.

Similarly confronted, Starling's motivated to defend herself, invoking *deliberation* as what sets Lecter's destructiveness apart, which provokes the parable. But Graham remains silent. In the spirit of the parable, which he's heard only recently, and assuming the pretense, the meal *is* an act of God, and a *deliberate* one at that. Graham's responding as he imagines Lecter would. It makes sense, then, that Starling's response is importantly different.

What More Fit or Complex Subject

Within the first few minutes of the pilot episode of the television series, before Graham's encounters with either Hobbs or Lecter, we find him lecturing at the FBI Academy about a recent crime scene, the killing of Mr. and Mrs. Marlow.

"Everyone has thought about killing someone, one way or another," he concludes, "be it your own hand, or the hand of God." He's equating the two hands in a way that he might well think back on when Lecter confronts him with the parable. What he asks them in closing, though, suggests something else.

"Now *think* about *killing* Mrs. Marlow," he challenges them, as he projects eerily onto the screen behind him the image of her lying dead in a pool of her own blood, and ask yourself, "Why did she *deserve* this? Tell me *your* design. Tell me who *you* are" (*Hannibal*, Season 1, "Apéritif"). Whoever killed Mrs. Marlow, and however they may think about their acts in relation to God, what most of us naturally do, and Graham is asking his students to do more carefully, is to think of them in relation to *us*. We tend to think that we can explain such acts, that is, if we can explain them at all, not because God's capable of the same, but because we're perfectly capable in the first place.

And Starling is reaching in just this same direction in her own response to Lecter's parable, later on, in *The Silence of the Lambs*. "I can't explain you," Starling interjects, seemingly anxious to redirect the conversation, "but I know who can" (Harris, *Silence*, p. 19). She's daring to reject the answer Lecter's implying, which is that God, or more precisely God's behavior, can. But he's already rejected her appeal to behavioral science. And she's also already ruled herself out. So what precisely is on her mind here? What she eventually proposes, of course, is that *he*'s on her mind.

Lecter stops her curtly, though, with "upraised hand," before she can say so. He's newly offended, it seems, by her continuing insinuation that he can be reduced "to a set of influences." "You'd like to quantify me," he objects, offended in particular that she's "so ambitious" as to be blind to his being not derivatively, but fundamentally evil, and as such, no conventionally recognized sort of evil at all. He takes himself not to be, on the one hand, a *moral* evil. "You sensed who I was" we hear him say to Graham, for example, in the second of their three meetings in the second film version of *Red Dragon*, "back when I was committing what you *call* my *crimes*." Nor does he take himself to be merely a *physical* evil, on the other hand, as he's made clear to Graham and Starling, some altogether material phenomenon from which we suffer, such as storms, fire, hail, and other acts of God. He's surely too much fun, his taste too refined, for him to be but that. And so, by process of elimination, what he is must ultimately defy reason in any interestingly conventional sense.

He's offended by Starling's ambition, yes, but anxious to teach her nonetheless—to think differently about good and evil, about God's relation to such things, about his own in relation to God, and in the end, just as importantly, about *her* own. For now, though, he finds her unprepared, and so he proceeds to humiliate her, as if to reassert in anger his preferred status.

Once on the other side of his humiliation, while Starling admits that his various observations are "hard to face," she's also undeterred. "You see a lot," Dr. Lecter," she admits, "but here's the question you're answering for me right now, whether you mean to or not: Are you strong enough to point that high-powered perception at yourself?" "Look at yourself," she goads him, "and write down the truth. What more fit or complex subject could you find?" (Harris, *Silence*, p. 20).

Lecter has offered himself as a response to the problem of evil, and Starling has rallied with what she believes is a reasonable alternative.

Looking and Seeing

The modern history of the problem of evil gives us not only a secular in addition to a theological problem. It has also given us, as Neiman has argued, two competing traditions of response, beginning midway through the eighteenth century. One tradition, inspired by Jean-Jacques Rousseau, insists, as she puts it, that "morality demands that we make evil intelligible." The other, inspired by Voltaire, insists instead that "morality demands that we don't" (Neiman 2002, p. 8). In which of these two traditions does Starling live most comfortably?

"*All* is well leaving the hands of the author of things," Rousseau famously tells us at the outset of *Émile*, "but degenerates in human hands" (my translation). We're not naturally corrupt, that is, only socially. The good news, then, is that however bad we've managed to muck things up, making them better again, and so redeeming ourselves is pretty much entirely *up to us*. It's just a matter of understanding better how, time and again, we've unwittingly crafted for ourselves circumstances that have deepened our corruption. And the better we understand this, the less likely it is we'll carry on mucking things up. Good news, yes, but also no small task, especially given that, as both an effect and a cause of our deepening corruption, our natural instinct to preserve and promote *ourselves* has steadily overwhelmed our equally natural instinct to act compassionately toward *others*. And if we want to get serious finally, though, we've options. We can accept ourselves as we are, but make laws as they ought to be, in order to rein in our inclination to evildoing, even while leaving the inclination otherwise intact. We can also keep laws as they are, but educate ourselves to be as we ought to be. Preferably, we do both at the same time.

Even Rousseau's biggest fans will admit that it's a heavy lift, though, and all the more so as time's gone on, the various behaviors that "shock nature and outrage reason" growing ever worse through the ages. So maybe Starling's better off following instead the lead that Voltaire provides in his satirical novella, *Candide*. The main character, Candide, famously suffers page after page of trial and tribulation, alternatively heartened and appalled by the constant refrain of his mentor, Dr. Pangloss, that in spite of it all reason compels us to view our world as nonetheless the best of all possible ones. And so, the good doctor insists, our various misfortunes, however unpleasant, are contributions to this greater good, and so not so bad after all. In the end, though, Candide's fed up. It's our *experience* that compels us finally to assert that it's *not* reason, but rather *work* that distances us from the "three great evils, boredom, vice, and need" (my translation).

Is Starling in one camp or the other? And what about Graham? On the face of it, they both seem pretty clearly to be on Rousseau's side rather than Voltaire's. Confronting and understanding evil, sweating the endless details, is hard work, and it does relieve boredom and need, but it's clearly the work of *reason*. Oddly enough, Lecter seems to agree. "You look," Lecter exhorts Graham, in the second film version of *Red Dragon*, "but you don't *see*." And in *The Silence of the Lambs* he exhorts Starling similarly, insisting that all she needs to identify the killer she's after, Jame Gumb (better known as "Buffalo Bill"), is all already there in her case files, if only she'd "pay attention."

But Graham and Starling are bound to admit, as are we, that there may be limits. There's the one at least, it seems, which is *Lecter himself*.

As we know from *Hannibal Rising*, before Lecter was busy being Lecter on this side of the Atlantic, he was busy being Lecter throughout Europe, avenging his sister Mischa, pursued in the process by Inspector Popil. "There's not a word for it yet," Popil admits, speaking of what makes Lecter *Lecter*. "For lack of a better" one, he adds, "we'll call him a monster" (Harris, *Rising*, p. 283). When Graham comes later to consult with Lecter, in *Red Dragon*, he doesn't resist Dr. Chilton's echo of Popil, in his disappointed appraisal of Lecter as "impenetrable . . . an enigma" (Harris, *Dragon*, p. 57). Later still, in *The Silence of the Lambs*, Crawford too echoes Popil, in warning Starling to beware of "what he is." Lecter's a "monster," he tells her, but otherwise, "nobody can say for sure" (Harris, *Silence*, p. 6). "Maybe you'll find out," he adds, at least a little hopefully, but this isn't to be. Starling's reason does allow her, with Lecter's guidance, a greater understanding of Gumb. And this greater understanding allows her to apprehend and kill him. But in the process, she only comes to enough of an understanding of Lecter *himself* to trust that he's no threat to her once he's escaped.

So the situation's complicated. Graham and Starling respond to the problem of evil in the spirit of Rousseau—except when it comes to *Lecter*. In the presence of an evil as inscrutable as it is terrible, don't we at some point just throw up our hands? Granted, we carry on *working* to thwart, or at least mitigate it—working very hard indeed. But as we do, don't we also sometimes quietly resign ourselves to allowing it to defy reason? Graham and Starling do. Why shouldn't we? Perhaps because there's something that we know that Graham and Starling don't.

A Place for Mischa

There is an important split in the Lecter canon, with *Hannibal* (the novel) and *Hannibal Rising* (the novel and the film) standing against the rest on at least one important point. Portions of these three works break with what came before, and in a crucial way—because these portions not only reveal to us Lecter's origins, but in the process *revise*, and revise *radically* a key idea of Lecter's that we read about in *Red Dragon* and *The Silence of the Lambs* and hear about in *Manhunter*. "We don't invent our natures," on the one hand, "they're given to us along with our lungs and pancreas and everything else." "Nothing happened to me," in the same spirit, "*I* happened." But, as we read in *Hannibal* and read and see in *Hannibal Rising*, something *did* happen to him.

Hannibal Rising readers will recall that beginning in the summer of 1941, as Lithuania became a battleground on World War Two's Eastern Front, and for most of the remainder of the war, the Lecter family hid from military forces in their generations-old "forest retreat." As the Front collapsed in the winter of 1944-45, and as Russian forces moved West, Lecter and his sister Mischa were orphaned, and later captured by former mercenaries turned looters, led by the loathsome Vladis Grutas. "We have to eat or die," Lecter hears them resolve, his "last conscious memory" of the lodge as, starving and desperate, they kill and eat Mischa. When we meet him next, Lecter's a "child coming out of the brush," scooped up by Russian troops, and deposited at the orphanage that Lecter Castle's become, to begin the long road that is the rest of his life (Harris, *Rising*, p. 45).

What we come to learn about the rest of Lecter's life, from the pages of *Hannibal* and *Hannibal Rising* and from the film version of the latter, is that Mischa's horrific death becomes, not surprisingly, its guiding force. The remainder of *Hannibal Rising* is animated by Lecter avenging Mischa, as he pursues and kills Grutas and his crew one by one. *Hannibal* readers will recall that even after many years, Lecter's focus is more intellectually, but no less passionately, focused on her. He's become an avid fan of astrophysicist Stephen Hawking's work, and his early speculation in particular, later disavowed, that eventually "the universe would stop expanding and would shrink again, and entropy might reverse itself." Lecter wants more than anything for Hawking to have been right originally, for "the expanding universe to stop, for entropy to mend itself, for Mischa, eaten, to be whole again." In language memorable for fans of the television series, Lecter's hope is that "should the universe contract, should time reverse and [broken] teacups come [back] together, a place could be made for Mischa in the world" (Harris, *Hannibal*, pp. 363–64). And the idea remains pivotal right up to the novel's final pages, though sadly not the film's final frames.

For eighteen years—from the publication of *Red Dragon* up to that of *Hannibal*—we were happily captivated by Lecter's charms, secure in the knowledge that the object of our fascination was a basic, fundamental evil. He was altogether different, we'd been told, and believed, from Hobbs, Dolarhyde, Gumb, and their real-life counterparts—a provocative counterpoint, however fictional, to the ever-growing conviction that all evil is ultimately reducible to this or that "set of influences." And then, suddenly, with Mischa, it seems we were wrong.

Or were we?

In both instances in which Lecter tells us that in his case at least, *evil's born, not made*, he's telling us something else too. He's telling us that, while he may be in this sense fundamentally evil, his actions enjoy a kind of justification nonetheless. He's imitating God, after all, at least as *he* understands God, and believes the rest of us should also. And isn't it God, after all, who, from Lecter's mature perspective, would have subjected Mischa to Grutas and company's horror? Or allowed it to happen to her, but how much better is *that*? And does he not believe that "if one does what God does enough times, one will become as God is"? And if he becomes "as God is," then if entropy doesn't "reverse itself" of its own accord, Lecter himself can make it happen anyway—can find, that is, a place for Mischa.

Hannibal readers find Starling and Lecter struggling again, as they had years earlier in *The Silence of the Lambs*. As the novel comes to its conclusion, they struggle around this idea in particular, *where* in the world to make a place for Mischa, and struggle once and for all. "Mischa could have Starling's place in the world," he'd considered, but she counters: "If a prime place in the world is required for Mischa," she proposes, "what's the matter with *your* place?" (Harris, *Hannibal*, p. 476). With Starling's help, Lecter comes to realize that Mischa can indeed find a place in the world, but that this needn't be at Starling's expense. Mischa's place in the world, it turns out, she convinces him, is in Lecter *and* Starling *together*. Cut from Rousseau's mold to the end, it's Starling's *reason* that helps her resist being consumed by evil, though the threat to her identity is now hypnotic, rather than culinary. Reason *saves* her, literally, though how unscathed we don't know. And, interestingly, it does so by helping evil, in the person of Lecter, better understand itself. Again, how unscathed we don't know.[1]

What begins in the horror and thriller genres, ends as something of a love story, however odd this may seem. When we last visit them, we read that Lecter and Starling are living incognito in Buenos Aires, a happy couple now, dancing on their terrace, seemingly without a care as to whether or not Lecter's being hunted still. Does Starling remain under Lecter's earlier hypnotic influence, or is she with him now of her own accord in some meaningful sense? She may "come to some unwilled awakening," we learn, but only "if indeed she even sleeps." We're left to wonder. And if for "many months now, he has not seen Mischa in his dreams," has Lecter given up his evil culinary ways? Again, we are left to wonder. But we should beware. As the narrator warns us in parting, we "can only learn so much and live" (Harris, *Hannibal*, p. 484). And yet, it seems we can't help ourselves. We do wonder, about both of them.

And we're still wondering when the narrator returns to us in *Hannibal Rising*, and we read that in establishing Lecter's "vital statistics" now, from his uncle's recently discovered correspondence, we "may watch as the beast within turns from the teat and, working upwind, enters the world" (Harris, *Rising*, p. 2). And as to this beast *within*, we're naturally fascinated by what we're told in turn, in the transition between the first and second of the novel's three parts. Lecter has escaped capture for his preparatory murder of Paul Momund, and set his sights on Grutas and company. He is, we're told, "growing and changing, or perhaps emerging as what he has ever been" (Harris, *Rising*, p. 159). Perhaps also, then, as we watch him dancing with Starling, unable to heed the narrator's warning to look away, Lecter's emerging *still* as he's ever been. If so, thanks are due to Starling, and so we also naturally wonder whether *she too* is emerging as *she*'s ever been.

In the uncertainty the narrator's left us with, we can't help but let our thoughts linger on the dancing couple, wondering

---

[1] For more on the consequences—for Hannibal Lecter, as well as for the Lecter mythos—of the culmination of his relationship with Starling in *Hannibal*, see Chapter 18 of this volume.—Ed.

what will become of them—or, more precisely, what they will *become*, together and each in their own right. But with their competing responses to the problem of evil seemingly reconciled, for the time being at least, we also can't help but hope—for them, and for us.[2]

---

[2] I'd like to thank my son Sean for my copy of *Hannibal*, which he gave me on Father's Day the year of its publication, helping to set me on this particular path, and for all of the other paths we've shared since that best of all possible days when he was born. Thanks also to his mom for helping him in the process.

5
Office Hours Are for Patients

DANIEL MALLOY

There are moral principles that apply to all of us all the time. Dr. Hannibal Lecter regularly violates many of these—they forbid us, for example, from killing other people, from desecrating corpses, and from lying. Dr. Lecter obviously has very little problem breaking these rules.

There are other codes of ethics, however, which apply to only some of us and only some of the time. Many professions, for example, have codes of ethics specific to themselves. The principles included in these codes are sometimes just explanations of how the more general moral principles apply to members of this profession; and they are sometimes specific principles to the profession that have little to no connection to broader moral principles.

Professional codes of ethics are just one example, however, of the moral principles that govern particular kinds of relationships. For virtually any sort of relationship among humans, there is an implicit or explicit set of governing moral principles. Parents have duties to their children that no one else does, and vice versa. Coworkers have certain duties that they owe exclusively to one another. Friendships, similarly, have an implicit ethical code that governs them.

Before Dr. Lecter was revealed to be Hannibal the Cannibal (or the Chesapeake Ripper), he was a well thought-of psychiatrist. In fact, it is that reputation that first brought him into contact with the FBI and Will Graham, and it was at least in part responsible for the continued consultations with him after his capture. But aside from using his psychological insight to aid FBI investigations, he also served as a therapist for Will Graham and others connected with him. We know Hannibal Lecter is not a good person, but is Dr. Lecter an ethical therapist?

This question requires explaining what is involved in being an ethical therapist, and, in turn, the basics of professional ethics for any field. This chapter argues that, just as Dr. Lecter wears a "person suit" to hide his less savory activities as the Chesapeake Ripper, the code of conduct that binds him as a psychiatrist is the closest he can come to understanding friendship. In Dr. Lecter's attempt to befriend Will Graham, the professional code of conduct he abides by serves as a model for how friends behave.

My claim is that Dr. Lecter's use of the ethics of his profession in his attempt to become friends with Will reveals the core of professional ethics: the attempt to artificially create and ensure the kind of trust that defines friendships. At the same time, Dr. Lecter's evolving relationship with Will reveals the limitations of professional ethics, which can never emulate the mutual trust of friendship because of the power imbalances inherent in the professional-client relationship. As their relationship evolves, the levels of trust and relative positions of power between Dr. Lecter and Will shift. They never quite achieve either a professional-client relationship or a friendship, but their relationship is always modeled on one or the other.

Being a Professional

Not all jobs are professions. Cashiers, cooks, and clerks are bound only by the moral and legal codes that bind everyone, regardless of their particular circumstances. Most often, when speaking of professions, we are referring to doctors and lawyers. There are other careers that we might think of as professions, and that likewise have unique codes of conduct—a case could be made, for instance, for considering members of the clergy, teachers, engineers, and accountants, among others, as professionals in the relevant sense. In considering the foundations of professional ethics, we must ask what is it about a profession that requires a separate code of conduct? And we should bear in mind that codes of ethics for professionals are in no way a new thing: the Hippocratic Oath, after all, has probably been around in one form or another since Hippocrates in ancient Greece, which makes it roughly as old as Western civilization.

The question of what constitutes a profession is complex, in part because a definitive list of professions seems impossible to come by. For a long time, to be a professional meant simply to be a doctor or a lawyer. However, with increasing specialization and the necessity of accessing ever more esoteric kinds of knowledge and skills, professions have proliferated—or, rather, jobs and careers that used to be non-professions have been professionalized. Joining the clergy, for instance, was once considered not a profession, but a vocation, a calling. There's some element of that remaining in how people think of the clergy, but it has been increasingly professionalized in the course of the last couple of centuries. So, rather than attempt to define a profession precisely, I will simply set forward some common traits that many professions have.

First, each profession involves some sort of expertise. A professional, typically, has some knowledge or skill that non-professionals lack. We hire lawyers because they know about the law and doctors because they know about medicine. But that is true of almost everyone. I know things you don't, and you know things I don't. Dr. Lecter is an expert at preparing human flesh for consumption, but that isn't his profession. So it is not just any expertise that makes one a professional. The expertise of a professional must be useful and important to others.

But it takes more than just expertise to make a professional. Someone may, for instance, be very knowledgeable about the law or medicine without being a lawyer or a doctor. To be a professional generally also means to be licensed or recognized as such by either a government or other members of the same profession. Such recognition is generally based on proof of expertise and adherence to the ethical code of the profession.

Now, revoking a license does not deprive a professional of her expertise—nothing can do that. It deprives her of recognition and the right to practice. This last aspect is, I think, a further condition for what makes a person a professional. One may be a professional even if one does not practice, but one must at least have the ability, the right to practice if given the opportunity. That opportunity often but not always comes in the form of having clients or patients. The clients make the professional a professional by placing their concerns in her hands.

This exemplifies an extraordinary amount of trust, especially in situations in which the professional in question is a virtual stranger. To protect the client, we say that there is a contract between the two parties. The client gives the professional her trust, and in exchange the professional uses that trust to help the client achieve her goals.

The Private Exit

Right up to the point when he snapped his neck, Dr. Lecter was actually a good and ethical therapist for Franklyn Froideveaux. Admittedly, intentionally killing one's patient is a serious violation of the Hippocratic Oath, but until that moment every action we see Dr. Lecter take regarding Franklyn is that of an ethical psychiatrist. So, we begin our discussion of psychiatric (and professional) ethics not with Will Graham, but with Franklyn.

We first met Franklyn leaving Dr. Lecter's office after a session. Franklyn left the office via the private exit for patients, which is significant in itself. At the core of most professional codes of ethics—and most especially the psychiatric code—is a concern for the client's privacy. The client must trust the professional. In the case of the psychiatrist and her patient, the client must trust the professional with the most intimate details of her life. Anything less than complete trust would undermine the attempts at therapy. One of the ways of ensuring that trust is through rules of confidentiality. Whatever Franklyn tells Dr. Lecter, indeed the very fact of their relationship, must remain between them. The secrets are Franklyn's, not Dr. Lecter's.

This is why Dr. Lecter tells Franklyn when they meet at the opera that "It would be unethical to approach a patient" (*Hannibal*, Season 1, "Sorbet"). It is unethical for a doctor to approach a patient in public, particularly if by doing so he would identify the patient as a patient. Dr. Lecter, attempting to be an ethical psychiatrist, fumbles a bit when Franklyn approaches him at the event—he doesn't know how to introduce Franklyn to his friend. He can't possibly admit that Franklyn is a patient, because it would violate confidentiality. At the same time, to introduce him as an acquaintance or a friend would send the wrong message to Franklyn, and possibly hinder the progress of his therapy. Thankfully (perhaps), Franklyn relieves Dr. Lecter of the burden by identifying himself as a patient—something he has every right to do.

Contrast this interaction with Dr. Lecter's interactions with Will. In the first season, Dr. Lecter is reluctant to identify himself as Will's therapist, but this reluctance extends beyond the public realm and into the privacy of his office and his home. "Office hours," he tells Will, "are for patients. My kitchen is always open to friends" (*Hannibal*, Season 1, "Coquilles"). While Franklyn desperately wants to be Dr. Lecter's friend rather than his patient, Dr. Lecter wants Will to be his friend rather than his patient. In a telling exchange, Dr. Lecter asks Will, "Am I your psychiatrist, or are we simply having conversations?" to which Will responds, "Yes, I think, is the answer to that" (*Hannibal*, Season 1, "Sorbet").

It is the less formal relationship with Will, the "friendship" (if we can call it that), that allows Dr. Lecter to discuss Will with Jack Crawford, not only acknowledging that he and Will know each other and interact (which of course Crawford knows, having introduced them), but the content of their conversations and his own reflections on them. Will, presumably, knows that Dr. Lecter shares this information. He nonetheless feels the need to extract a promise, of sorts, from Dr. Lecter that he will not publish anything that he learns from his relationship with Will. Will Graham is, after all, quite the topic of conversation among psychiatrists. It is one thing for Dr. Lecter to share with Jack Crawford, and another entirely for him to share with the psychiatric community at large.

On the other hand, when Will explicitly engages Dr. Lecter as his psychiatrist, he is just as scrupulous about protecting confidentiality as he was with Franklyn. When Jack Crawford asks Dr. Lecter his opinions about Will after this point, Lecter is blunt about telling Crawford that since Will is now officially his patient, he cannot share any information regarding him.

What, then, should we say about Dr. Lecter's willingness to share the contents of his conversations with both Franklyn and Will with Dr. Du Maurier? If Dr. Lecter and Dr. Du Maurier were simply friends or even colleagues, he would be in ethical hot water for discussing the details of Franklyn's therapy without first receiving Franklyn's permission. The confidentiality surrounding their sessions is entirely Franklyn's and so cannot be breached without his explicit permission. However, because his relationship with Will is less formal, more of a friendship than a professional-client relationship, the secrets they share belong to both of them. As it is, Dr. Lecter is ethically in the clear in sharing details with Dr. Du Maurier because of her status as his therapist. The same confidentiality that protects Franklyn's sessions with Dr. Lecter protects Dr. Lecter's sessions with Dr. Du Maurier.

In fact, of the various psychiatrists in *Hannibal*, Dr. Du Maurier has the murkiest track record when it comes to confidentiality. (Dr. Chilton's utter disregard for confidentiality rules is a problem unto itself, given his status as administrator at a publically-funded state hospital with intimate ties to the penal system.) Dr. Du Maurier acknowledges that she is on the very edge of the precipice, ethically speaking, in discussing Dr. Lecter with Jack Crawford. Even after Dr. Lecter signs a waiver freeing her to speak with Crawford (a questionable waiver, given the disclosures in his sessions about some of his patients), there is still a line that must be drawn.

If we could, perhaps, argue that Du Maurier was ethically covered by that waiver in her brief discussions with Jack, there is still no way to justify her interaction with Will. Simply acknowledging that she's heard of Will through her interactions with Dr. Lecter constitutes a breach of her patient's confidentiality—a trust that is in no way renounced when she stops being Dr. Lecter's psychiatrist. Again, the contents of the sessions still belong to Dr. Lecter, not to Dr. Du Maurier.

It should not, perhaps, surprise us that Dr. Lecter is so scrupulous about confidentiality. If there is anything that his sideline requires, it is an ability to keep secrets. But also, divulging others' secrets is rude. Hence Dr. Lecter's distaste for Freddie Lounds—as an investigative reporter, violating privacy and revealing secrets is basically her job description. Further, protecting his patient's confidentiality is one of the ways that Dr. Lecter protects himself. In his sessions with Will and Margot Verger, as well as his interactions with Randall Tier, it becomes clear that Dr. Lecter's therapeutic techniques are not always the most ethical, after all.

The confidentiality rules that govern many professional relationships are there to ensure the kind of trust that we have with friends. In the case of friends, explicit confidentiality rules are rarely necessary, because the organic nature of the relationship means that in coming to trust a friend, one also comes to trust their discretion. Because the professional-client relationship is artificial, explicit confidentiality rules are a necessary part of the groundwork for the trust that has to exist between them—specifically, the trust the client must place in the professional.

First, Do No Harm

It is one thing for a professional to keep a client's secrets; it is quite another for a professional to keep secrets from a client. Again, this is sometimes ethically required—Dr. Lecter can no more tell one patient about another than he can anyone else. But it is sometimes entirely unethical: as, for instance, when Dr. Lecter and Dr. Sutcliffe decide not to tell Will about his encephalitis.

I will present the case for the unethical nature of this conduct in a moment, but first I will attempt to show why it is not as black-and-white as it may appear. It is a topic of much interest in professional ethics how much information the professional is required to divulge to the client. The client, after all, has gone to the professional in part because the professional has information and expertise that the client lacks. The professional knows the goal that the client has in engaging her and, presumably, the best way to achieve that goal. As it turns out, there are some cases where the best way for the professional to help the client achieve her goal is to conceal information from her—sometimes even to the point of lying to her.

For instance, imagine a patient goes to a doctor complaining of a number of symptoms. The doctor runs a battery of tests and can find nothing wrong with the patient. After more rounds of tests and consultations with other doctors (with the patient's permission, of course), the doctor concludes that there is nothing physically wrong with the patient at all. Medically speaking, she is in perfect health. So, the doctor concludes that the symptoms are psychosomatic—they are a manifestation of the patient's belief that she is sick. Rather than confront her with the diagnosis, which will in all likelihood only lead to her going to another doctor and wasting even more time and resources, the doctor tells the patient that she is in fact ill with some fictional disease. The doctor then prescribes a placebo, and refers her to a psychiatrist under false pretenses—the particular illness, says the doctor, can also manifest in psychic disturbances, so the patient needs to be monitored by a psychiatrist.

Contemporary codes of professional ethics, including contemporary versions of the Hippocratic Oath, have largely been written with a view toward preserving and defending client autonomy. So, contemporary codes of medical ethics discourage the use of such placebo treatments and deceptions to help a patient. The professional is expected to adequately inform her client, even if having all of the relevant information may hinder the client's ability to pursue her goal.

But such emphasis is not without controversy. In the case above and cases like it there is a conflict between the professional's duty to treat the client with respect and the professional's duty to help the client achieve her goals. It is a basic question in professional ethics whether a professional has a right—or perhaps even a duty—to mislead a client in order to help the client achieve her goals. There is an inherent danger of abuse in any asymmetric relationship, like the professional-client relationship. If we grant that the professional has a right to deceive a client, then the client is robbed of the ability to ensure that the professional is actually acting in the client's best interests.

This brings us back, once again, to Dr. Lecter. Late in the first season, Dr. Lecter consults with Dr. Sutcliffe, a neurologist, about Will's condition. An MRI reveals that Will has encephalitis, which is causing his hallucinations and lost time. Dr. Lecter then convinces Dr. Sutcliffe to keep the results of the MRI from Will so that they can observe the effects of the disease. They will, he assures Sutcliffe, treat it before it's too late, but in the meantime they may gain some valuable insight into this rare condition and its effects.

Between them, and without consulting their patient, Dr. Lecter and Dr. Sutcliffe come to two decisions, only one of which is a clear violation of professional ethics. First, they decide not to inform Will of the diagnosis. Under the right conditions, this can be a justifiable decision by a professional—if such knowledge would hinder the client in the pursuit of her goals, then we can even make the case that a professional may be required to withhold it. Their second decision, however, is not only unjustified, it violates the oath they both took as doctors: the decision not to treat Will. Leaving a condition like Will's untreated doubtless does him some harm.

Again, these rules are in place to foster the kind of trust that grows organically in friendships. We generally do not lie to our friends and expect our friends not to lie to us. But few people would get upset at a friend who, for example, kept a surprise party secret from them. Our trust in our friends includes a trust that they will tell us the truth, or, at the very least, that when they conceal the truth from us, it is for a good reason. We have grown to trust our friends' discretion and judgment. With professionals, however, we expect their judgment to be bound by the rules of professional conduct.

This Is Your Hour

One of the reasons the professional/client relationship does not parallel a friendship, indeed one of the core reasons, is because the relationship of a professional to a client is always asymmetrical. Friendships may be more or less symmetrical, but at their core they are relationships between equals. Many, if not most, of the guidelines set out in professional codes of ethics are designed to protect the client, because in trusting the professional with whatever she has, she has made herself vulnerable. In a very real sense, patients are at the mercy of their doctors, clients of their lawyers, etc.

One of the common safeguards in professional codes of ethics is the requirement of informed consent. This is the requirement that Dr. Lecter and Dr. Sutcliffe violated by keeping Will's diagnosis from him and their refusal to treat him. Had Will been informed of his condition, it is reasonable to conjecture that he would have insisted on being treated for it. However, it was also his right to insist on not being treated. What matters is that he knows his options.

Informed consent is not, however, as cut-and-dried as it may at first seem. Arguably, for instance, the doctor who prescribes a placebo has not violated the requirement. The patient wishes to be treated for whatever malady she has, and the doctor prescribes the best treatment she knows of for that illness. It happens to be the case that in order for that treatment to work effectively, certain things have to be kept from the patient. The patient does not have all of the relevant information, but she does know that the doctor knows more than she does and that the doctor thinks this treatment will make her better. She consents to the treatment in light of the information she has, which the doctor deems to be all the information that is relevant to the decision.

The interesting problem for us, though, is not the question of how much and what kind of information a client needs to have to give informed consent to a course of action. What is interesting, because of Dr. Lecter's particular profession, is what exactly constitutes consent. Why this is interesting is because among the responsibilities that psychiatrists and psychologists are tasked with is the burden of determining whether a particular client is capable of making decisions for herself. Where lawyers may declare a person incompetent to practice law, and other doctors may declare a person incompetent to practice medicine, psychiatrists and psychologists have the authority to declare a person incompetent to exercise autonomy at all. In effect, psychiatrists can declare their clients non-persons.

So, how can professional ethics deal with a situation that seems to undermine one of the foundations of ethics as such—namely, individual autonomy? If Will's encephalitis was having a negative impact on his judgment and rationality (and it seems to have been, though not quite so severely as Dr. Lecter led him to believe), that shifts the power even more in the psychiatrist's favor. Now we have a situation of paternalism (or parentalism): a case where the professional takes it upon herself to make decisions about what is in the client's best interests without consulting the client, or even necessarily informing her. For one person to do this to another is at least rude, at worst downright evil; but in the case of the psychiatrist, it is not only allowable but in some cases positively condoned. If, for example, Dr. Lecter diagnosed that Will posed a danger to himself or others, it would be not just his right, but his professional duty to prevent that danger from manifesting itself—even to the point of effectively incarcerating Will against his will.

This authority may seem extreme, and it is, but in a way it parallels the kinds of duties and responsibilities that non-professionals have in their everyday lives. Think, for example, of Franklyn's dilemma regarding Tobias Budge. Tobias made some rather dark comments, and subsequently a man was murdered in a way very similar to what Tobias proposed. Should Franklyn go to the police with this information? There was no reason for him to report Tobias before the murder—he just made a rather off-color comment, which is not sufficient evidence to believe that Tobias posed any danger to anyone. However, after a murder is discovered that closely matches Tobias's comment, Franklyn has a reason to think Tobias may be dangerous.

Of course, rather than go to anyone in law enforcement with that information, Franklyn goes to Dr. Lecter—a questionable move, particularly given the confidentiality that is supposed to exist between them. Dr. Lecter, of course, fails to respect that confidentiality in this case, but there are two considerations that might clear him of any ethical wrongdoing. First, Dr. Lecter is ethically bound to do what he can to prevent future harms—including those that might be committed by associates of his patients. As Margot Verger notes, if she were to tell him that she was planning a murder, Dr. Lecter would be ethically bound to inform the police. Dr. Lecter is protected, secondly, because although he passes on information about Tobias to his associates in the FBI, he refrains from identifying Franklyn as the source of the information. This is an ethical tightrope to walk, but Dr. Lecter seems to stay on the right side of it. In fact, by the time he informs the FBI, Dr. Lecter has already met and dined with Tobias himself, and gotten a confession of their shared interests from him. Going and meeting with Tobias is about the most questionable act Dr. Lecter committed in this series of events—at least until he killed Franklyn.

The point is simply that the psychiatrist's authority to make decisions on behalf of her patients is essentially an extension of the non-professional's duty to prevent anyone from harming others or themselves. The added authority of the psychiatrist is based on her expertise and the trust that has been placed in her by other professionals, by the client, and by society more generally.

Am I Your Psychiatrist?

The story of *Hannibal* is the story of a friendship, of sorts. The relationship between Will Graham and Dr. Lecter has passed through roughly four stages. In the first stage, they were simply trying to get a feel for one another, attempting to establish in their own minds who the other person was and what relationship they had with each other. This early stage is bound solely by those ethical rules which govern all of our interactions with strangers. In the second stage, Will acts as Dr. Lecter's patient and believes himself to be such, more or less, while Dr. Lecter views Will more as a friend or potential friend. Here we have moved past the ethics of strangers, but have yet to establish what will take its place. Because Will is not an official patient, Dr. Lecter is not bound by professional ethics regarding him. At the same time, they have yet to establish anything like a real friendship, so their obligations to one another are not bound by that sort of code. If anything, their code consists of the explicit promises asked for by one and given by the other—such as Dr. Lecter's promise that anything he published based on his interactions with Will would be published posthumously. In the third stage, Will officially becomes Dr. Lecter's patient. Now their interactions are ruled explicitly by the psychiatric code of ethics. That stage is brief, however. It soon evolves into (something like) a friendship. Each of these shifts between stages is defined by a shift in the relative power of the two men—first, establishing that Dr. Lecter is the more powerful of the two, to Will subverting that stance by actually becoming Dr. Lecter's patient (thus binding him to the psychiatric ethic), to what ultimately becomes a relationship between equals on the same path—though with the acknowledgment that Dr. Lecter is further down the path than Will.

Although it has many of the trappings of friendship, their relationship never quite manages to be one, largely because the two men never actually trust one another. Each display of something like trust is a further manipulation, a baiting of the hook, intended to lure one of them where the other wants him to go. The closest they come, and can probably ever come, to friendship is their doctor-patient relationship.

6

The Psychiatrist as Sociopathic God

DERRICK L. HASSERT

HANNIBAL LECTER, M.D. After so many years, we continue to seek out the good doctor. In the persona of Dr. Hannibal Lecter there is much to admire and much that attracts: gourmet, skilled artist, cultural connoisseur, learned psychiatrist. And prolific serial killer, of course. Perhaps that last characteristic strikes you as the least admirable . . . perhaps not (I'm not here to judge). In his various incarnations, Dr. Lecter also enjoys chatting with his "protégés"—or victims, depending on mood, circumstance, or perspective—about the Big Questions concerning the nature of God, the nature of humanity, and the nature of evil. When probing Clarice Starling's understanding of the essence of her criminal prey in Jonathan Demme's *The Silence of the Lambs*, Dr. Lecter suggests a specific perspective on how to address such topics: "Of each particular thing ask: What is it in itself? What is its nature? What does he do, this man you seek?"

According to Lecter and the philosophy that serves as the foundation for his question, intrinsic nature is revealed through outward action. Going back as far as Aristotle, it has been argued that we know who or what someone is by their capacities: watch what they do over time and we'll see their nature open up before us. Watching Clarice Starling, we come to know her honesty and her devotion to principle as an agent of the Federal Bureau of Investigation. When considering Hannibal Lecter, we could ponder Starling's pointed question to the doctor: "Are you strong enough to point that high-powered perception at yourself? What about it? Why don't you . . .

look at yourself and write down what you see?" (Demme, *Silence*). Using the lens that the psychiatrist himself recommends, perhaps we can gain a better understanding of the nature of Dr. Hannibal Lecter.

Typhoid and Swans

In the novel *Red Dragon,* Dr. Lecter writes to Will Graham concerning Graham's taking of a criminal's life and the emotional turmoil resulting from that deed, noting that "it wasn't the act that got you down, was it? Really, didn't you feel so bad because killing him felt so good? Think about it, but don't worry about it. Why shouldn't it feel good? It must feel good to God—He does it all the time, and are we not made in His image?" (Harris, *Dragon*, p. 259). The novel *Hannibal* provides a broader context for Dr. Lecter's theological speculations, specifically the cannibalistic murder of his beloved sister Mischa by Nazi collaborators. Our moral compass quickly points to "Evil" when thinking about such an act. But why? According to Augustine of Hippo, evil is simply the destruction, corruption, or removal of a preexisting good. Based on this understanding, the wanton murder of a child is arguably the epitome of an evil act: what makes the death of a child so disturbing to the human mind is the destruction of all the potential and possibility inherent in that life, the countless futures brought to a conclusive and premature end, like a thousand deaths occurring all at once. Lecter prayed fervently that he would see his little sister again, but the only answer to his request was seeing his sister's baby teeth in the pit of a latrine. "Since this partial answer to his prayer, Hannibal Lecter had not been bothered by any considerations of deity, other than to recognize how his own predations paled beside those of God, who is in irony matchless, and in wanton malice beyond measure" (Harris, *Hannibal*, p. 256).

Since God arguably could have stopped this evil but did not, Lecter considers Him complicit in the act. Lecter deduces his understanding of God's character by witnessing what he understands to be His works. How Dr. Lecter views God is also reflected in his relationships with others; how he relates to others tells us a bit more about his character. Lecter sees God as a Being who allows capricious and unmerited suffering, most importantly, the death of an innocent child at the hands of those who embodied evil. Young Hannibal's initial acts of cannibalism were focused on consuming those deemed unworthy of the lives given them, rooted in vengeance and aimed quite clearly at those guilty of a heinous crime. Thereafter, by extension and whenever possible, Lecter preferred to "eat the rude . . . 'Free-range rude' " (Harris, *Hannibal*, p. 87). In his television embodiment, Dr. Lecter keeps a rolodex of the names of those who've slighted him next to his recipe box. In the film *Red Dragon*, he serves a subpar flutist to the symphony board. And there is the infamous demise of the diligent census taker, of course. Clarice observes that Lecter may see himself as doing a societal service by removing such objectionable elements from the midst of humanity. Where God failed in rooting out the weeds, Hannibal would not.

However, the "eat the rude" principle doesn't prevent Lecter from murdering those that happen to impede his freedom or tourists and curators whose identities he may find useful. Lecter may view these actions not as murder, but as necessitated killing, actions indispensable to his survival. Lecter places his own impulses and concerns above the rights and freedom of others, just as God placed His own inscrutable desires above the life of Lecter's sister. Lecter's actions can be viewed as imitations of his own nuanced concept of God, a Being possessing the properties of both good and evil. Unlike the philosopher Friedrich Nietzsche, Hannibal Lecter doesn't pronounce God dead—just incorrectly conceptualized. For those that Lecter views as having a potentially discerning nature such as his own or having traits he admires, he provides guidance and counsel. For those who stand in his way or transgress his tenets, he provides ruthless dispatch. Lecter seeks to emulate God as he understands Him. As Lecter remarks to Starling in the novel *The Silence of the Lambs*, "Typhoid and swans—it all comes from the same place" (Harris, *Silence*, p. 19). Lecter is both angry at God for allowing evil and yet seemingly eager to emulate His work, much like the traditional characterization of Lucifer. As we all know, this literary Lucifer of ours becomes a psychiatrist. Now imagine your mental health in the hands of a psychiatrist with a God-complex, where God's perceived character is not centered on forgiveness, benevolence, or love, but instead embraces good (and perhaps the beautiful over the good), evil, and capricious whim.

You Know What You Look Like to Me . . . ?

Like other branches of medicine, psychiatry is directive. A diagnosis is made and a treatment is prescribed with the goal of restoring psychological health. For those unsuitable for psychotherapy (such as people suffering from psychosis), various medications are often employed in order to restore the functioning of the rational mind. However, it has been argued that psychotherapy has the ethical advantage over drugs because the process respects and attempts to increase the independence of the patient. Nevertheless, even psychotherapy when improperly applied can result in psychological harm. Like other physicians, psychiatrists generally follow the old adage of *primum non nocere*: First, do no harm. As we've seen through his professional practice, Hannibal Lecter, M.D., may have a unique interpretation of that classic admonition and may view "psychological health" a bit differently than most of his colleagues.

In surprisingly brief interactions, Dr. Lecter sizes up an individual and determines the essence of what is before him. What can be observed speaks to nature, nature speaks to inherent potential, and potential informs what can ultimately be achieved in the progress of a patient. From this perspective, Lecter—like most psychotherapists—decides upon a *telos* or goal to which the therapy should point given the potential of the patient. When we look at an acorn and consider planting it in the ground we know we won't be getting pumpkins, because it isn't in the nature of the acorn to have the potential to make pumpkins. Likewise, regardless of how it's treated, a kitten will never grow up to be a Great Dane. Through his transitory yet careful observations, Hannibal Lecter can tell whether he's dealing with a common insect or with a caterpillar possessing the potential for becoming a butterfly (or a Death's-head moth). From a few pieces of behavioral evidence Lecter can deduce Clarice Starling's history and her character. Depending on the nature of the individual, Lecter's interventions can take rather unique paths based on what he sees as the possible ends. In the television series, Dr. Lecter has a pattern of encouraging patients with unstable minds to engage in homicidal behavior, seemingly as long as the murders are creative and aesthetically pleasing. Rather than navigating patients away from these endeavors, Lecter sees such behaviors as an unfolding or evolution of their natures and a realization of the inherent potential he sees within them. With some individuals even more radical therapeutic approaches are deemed necessary.

Show Me How You Smile . . .

Mason Verger is an exceptionally despicable character—even when compared with the exploits of a cannibalistic psychiatrist—a pedophile who uses the tears of children to flavor his beverages. When Dr. Lecter visits Mason's home as his court-ordered therapist, Mr. Verger seeks to entangle his psychiatrist in unprofessional behavior with the hopes of blackmail. While Mason shows Lecter the techniques of autoerotic asphyxiation and implements of torture, Lecter shares some apparently agreeable pharmaceuticals with his patient. While in a highly suggestible state, Verger is handed a shard of broken mirror and Dr. Lecter's prescription is that Mason peel off his face.

Why the disfigurement? The film *Hannibal* provides some clarifying dialogue: "Show me how you smile," he instructs Verger, "to gain the confidence of a child." From a very early age, children know that changing the outside of a living thing does not alter its nature: put a convincing cat suit on a dog and children know it still remains a dog. Slowly alter the outside of an imaginary creature and children know it remains the same in essence as it was before the alterations. However, children—and the rest of us—make initial classifications and judgments about character or nature based on physical first impressions. If I were to put on a police officer's uniform people would naturally deduce that I was a police officer—until someone asked me to do the job that goes with the uniform. A picture of the small canine in the convincing cat suit would probably be enough to lead people to believe they were looking at a cat. We are habitually drawn in by appearances and frequently learn too late that people and situations are not what they first seem. Lecter understands these facts about human psychology: sticking around to see Mason Verger's nature revealed through action would not be pleasant.

Per Lecter's request, Mason smiles for the doctor. "Ah, I see how you do it," Hannibal comments, and then recommends Mason peel off his face. As the patient is removing his own flesh, Lecter notes that the smile is still evident and advises Mason to "try again." More flesh is removed. "No, I'm afraid not" (Scott, *Hannibal*). Still more is sliced away. Once Mason's disfigurement is complete, Lecter breaks Mason's neck with the asphyxiation noose, leaving him paralyzed. With these actions, Lecter takes from Mason both his ability to draw children close through smiles and deception as well as his ability to physically dominate his victims. Dr. Lecter doesn't attempt to alter Mason's character through therapy. Instead, Lecter helps to create an appearance that matches essence, making it easier for children to discern the monster in their midst. In a tale such as *The Hunchback of Notre Dame*, assuming Quasimodo to be a monster because of his superficial form is an element of tragedy, whereas in this instance it is—from Dr. Lecter's perspective—the most appropriate and ironic form of therapy.

I'm Your Psychiatrist . . . I Am a Source of Stability and Clarity, Franklyn. I'm Not Your Friend.

Suffering from the general "neurotic" symptoms of anxiety and depression and apparently not possessing a mind that could be molded to murder, the television patient Franklyn Froideveaux appears rather average (*Hannibal*, Season 1, "Sorbet"). The name Franklyn Froideveaux pays homage to the Benjamin Raspail character from *The Silence of the Lambs*, a combination of Benjamin Franklin and Froideveaux, a street parallel to Raspail in Paris. Given their similar fates, Lecter's film epitaph for Raspail might be appropriate here as well: "Best thing for him actually, his therapy was going nowhere" (Demme, *Silence*).

As his treatment with Dr. Lecter progresses, Franklyn appears happier, improved from the despondent individual initially encountered. He also appears to be copying what he knows of the lifestyle and interests of his psychiatrist, popping up at the opera when the doctor is in attendance, professing a love for fine cheeses during session, and wearing outfits that could have been pulled from Hannibal's closet. By asserting that they share many of the same interests, Franklyn hopes to raise his standing with Lecter in expectation that his psychiatrist will also become his friend. In his longing for friendship,

Franklyn is no different from the majority of the human race. Without friends, Aristotle notes, no one would want to live. Indeed, Franklyn is not unlike Hannibal, who also longs for such closeness and understanding. While Dr. Lecter may seem transcendent and godlike in so many respects, Hannibal cannot find complete satisfaction in solitude. (Perhaps we should keep in mind that in Christian theology even God the Father has the eternal company of the Son and the Holy Ghost.) By nature, humans are both rational and social animals, with an instinctual desire for intellectual and emotional relatedness. We desire not just physical proximity to another, but mental nearness as well. For Aristotle, the highest form of friendship, a perfect or ideal friendship, flows from two individuals finding the same things—the same character—in one another.[1] While Franklyn wants Dr. Lecter to see him as an equal, it is perhaps too clear to Hannibal that Franklyn's imitation is superficial flattery.

Given that Franklyn desperately wants an intimacy for which Hannibal has no desire, the doctor decides to terminate Franklyn (as a patient—although circumstances later require Lecter to terminate him literally) and refer him to another therapist. As we know from the television series, Dr. Lecter is already quite busy therapeutically "helping" Will Graham blossom into something more like himself, viewing Will as his potential partner in a true kinship of equals. Here we see reflections of the relationship between Clarice and Lecter in the last act of the novel *Hannibal*. However, in his relationship with Will Graham, Dr. Lecter's behavior indicates that he doesn't necessarily believe Graham to be his equal at the onset: Hannibal is not content to accept Will as he is. Instead, Lecter must first embark on a systematic psychological and pharmacological program to transform Will, *raising* him to Hannibal's level. Dr. Lecter's unorthodox therapy includes framing Will for his own crimes and attempting to convince Will that murder is within his nature, as it is in Hannibal's. If Will truly embraced this belief, perhaps Lecter could reveal his true character to Will. Perhaps then Graham would indeed be Lecter's equal, with perfect friendship a possibility.

---

[1] For a more extended discussion of Hannibal Lecter's capacity for friendship, including in relation to Aristotle, see Chapter 10 of this volume.—Ed.

Like Clarice in the novel *Hannibal*, Dr. Lecter sees Will as a proper canvas on which to paint his own portrait. Given that Hannibal's motives are primarily to satisfy his own needs, any resulting kinship would not actually be the Aristotelian ideal of friendship. The other in the relationship with Lecter—Will or Clarice—is simply a means to an end; people are mere tools. As Hannibal turns people to food, he is also willing to devour them psychologically to attain his own ends. Hannibal does not love the other in his friendships as an equal, he loves the idea of being loved and therefore must attempt a fundamental transformation of the other. Keeping in mind that a perfect friendship is one between those of shared virtue or goodness, we should also keep in mind that Dr. Lecter seemingly embraces the label of evil, seeing in God both the qualities of good and evil. In the novel *The Silence of the Lambs*, Lecter berates Clarice when she attempts to dissect him "with this blunt little tool" that reminds him of the census taker, accusing her of having given up the essentialist categories of good and evil for behaviorism. "You've got everybody in moral dignity pants—nothing is ever anybody's fault. Look at me, Officer Starling. Can you stand to say I'm evil?" (Harris, *Silence*, p. 19). The other in a relationship with Hannibal Lecter must acknowledge and embrace their own evil in order to be his equal. The terms of friendship are dictated by Dr. Lecter for his own ends, with any friendship remaining a variation of base self-love and consequently imperfect.

A Tale of Two Clarices (and Two Lecters)

In the film *The Silence of the Lambs*, Lecter's artwork depicts an idealized Clarice in flowing robes standing serenely upon the path to the crucifixion and cradling a lamb—the symbol of Christ as a pure offering. Through this sketch we see Lecter's view of Clarice: Pure, noble, protective, sacrificial. In this idealization of Starling, derived from her heroic yet futile actions in trying to rescue just one innocent creature from slaughter (similar to Hannibal's sister), we glimpse the nature and potential that Lecter sees and admires. It is interesting that in the final act of the film *Hannibal* this symbolism is explicitly evoked, with Dr. Lecter restrained by Mason Verger with arms outstretched as in crucifixion—Lecter is now in the place of Christ, the Lamb—his death clearly anticipated. It is Clarice who intercedes to bring him down from the cross, again attempting justice and thwarting vengeance. In this act, for Dr. Lecter, Clarice realizes the potential he envisioned for her—the salvation of a God-like man from imminent death. In the process Starling is wounded and the doctor in turn plays the role of savior and physician, cradling Clarice in his arms as she cradled the lamb, bringing her to safety, and tending to her injuries.

From this point on there is a stark divergence between the actions of the literary and cinematic characters. The Dr. Lecter of the silver screen longs to see Clarice acknowledge and embrace her own principled and righteous nature, no longer dependent upon accolades from her government superiors: "Would they give you a medal, Clarice, do you think? Would you have it professionally framed and hang it on your wall to look at and remind you of your courage and incorruptibility? All you would need for that, Clarice, is a mirror" (Scott, *Hannibal*). In contrast, the literary Lecter seeks to manipulate and transform Clarice into something more in his likeness and fitting his desires. The cinematic Lecter would mutilate himself rather than harm Clarice, leaving her psychologically and physically much as he found her a decade before: First, do no harm. The literary *Hannibal*—who appreciates Starling's prowess as a warrior—takes hold of those things which are admirable and noble in order to twist and transform them into something that matches his own character. In the television show and in the novel *Hannibal*, Dr. Lecter provokes transformation as he sees fit. Hannibal's success in creating an equal worthy of his companionship is achieved only by the corruption of both the beautiful and the good in Clarice Starling. In this process there are echoes of Dr. Frankenstein's ability to create a mate for his creature, using material that had previously served a substantially different life. The ideal kinship longed for in human nature is subverted by Dr. Lecter's attempt to recreate his own quasi-divine image in another. Although the television Will and the literary Clarice come close to fulfilling Lecter's desire for perfect friendship, it will forever elude him, for his equal must be created through corruption, through the deprivation of what was good.[2]

---

[2] For an account of the relationship at the end of the novel, *Hannibal*, as *liberating* for Clarice (and Lecter) rather than corrupting, see Chapter 18 of this volume.—Ed.

We are left to wonder if the Clarice of the film and the Clarice of the novel are—before and after their respective interactions with Dr. Lecter—the same character. In one version of events Agent Starling is saddened and repulsed by Lecter's unorthodox culinary lobotomizing of Paul Krendler, whereas in the novel she gleefully asks for more of what is being served and sits casually at the table as Krendler is killed. True, she is under the influence of powerful hypnotic drugs, but even after their administration has ceased she stays by Lecter's side and becomes his companion. Was it always within Starling's character, an unrealized potential within her nature, to succumb to Dr. Lecter's corrupting influence? Studies in human obedience have revealed that we are capable of questionable and even cruel actions given the right circumstances, but afterwards we generally regret and then rationalize our actions. Is Clarice really just like any of us, or worse? Perhaps we would rather see Starling as the film presents her, ever courageous and incorruptible with Hannibal Lecter as her savage yet noble advocate. Based upon what we know of first principles, we are left to contemplate whether these two depictions really represent the same characters with the same natures. Perhaps the disparate behaviors of Dr. Lecter and Agent Starling between novel and film speak to distinct essences, or perhaps these really are the same characters, just on different journeys. Perhaps each had within them the potential for substantial change, good and evil. Something to ponder.

I Do Wish We Could Chat Longer . . .

Setting aside the idea that it is generally preferable to eat the rude, what can we learn from Dr. Hannibal Lecter? Even though Hannibal speaks of the great mass of humanity as "all those other poor dullards," in his longing for companionship we see an essential part of human existence. Hannibal's experience illustrates that although we can indeed choose our friends it is probably a mistake to mold our potential friends in ways that subvert their choices and their values, using them simply as means to an end. Doing so only creates a rather one-sided friendship based on utility rather than mutual respect. Also, plying people with mind-altering drugs may get you into trouble . . . but if you're a cannibalistic genius with a God complex, it may be difficult to resist the temptation to remake someone in your own image.

More helpfully, from Lecter's emphasis upon first principles we should be careful never to trust mere appearances, not with others and not with ourselves. Observe carefully, over extended periods of time, and we'll see character revealed. As rational beings we have the ability to reflect not only on the behavior of others, but on our own thoughts and behavior as well (what cognitive scientists would call "metacognition"). We can ask ourselves if our actions align with our values and who we wish to be and become. As the German poet, Goethe, once observed (and I translate loosely), "Behavior is the mirror in which everyone reveals their nature." This applies to everyone and everything, not just to Dr. Lecter and Clarice. While much of our cognitive processing goes on without our awareness, we still possess the ability to be mindfully aware of our choices and behaviors, guiding the actions that will shape our amazingly flexible brains. These choices therefore shape our habits and what will later be known as our character. Dr. Hannibal Lecter was careful to conceal his actions and consequently his true nature, showing others little more than what his own psychiatrist described as a "well-tailored 'person suit' " or a "human veil" (*Hannibal*, Season 1, "Sorbet"). What choices will we make, what behavior will we exhibit, and what nature will we reveal to ourselves and to the world?

III.

They Say He's a Psychopath

7
Psychopaths, Outlaws, and Us

RICHARD MCCLELLAND

Humans constantly seek to know "what kind of thing is it?" This is largely because we are biologically hard-wired to make such judgments. Thus, we can tell whether that blob we see in the distance is a human face. We can tell if the motion of that thing over there is caused by a biological agent or mechanical. We can distinguish natural sounds (the tree creaking in the wind) from artificial sounds (the axe falling on the wood). We can tell from a human's gait what its gender is and often its individual identity. The neural systems that support these automatic judgments are largely reliable and accurate under normal conditions. Such categorical judgments undergird a great deal of natural science and philosophy both. Indeed, it is arguable that neither would be possible for an animal that did not make such judgments reliably. Faced with the startling character of Hannibal Lecter, it is not surprising, then, that other characters in Thomas Harris's novels would ask, "what kind of thing is this?" Lecter appears in four of Thomas Harris's novels, and most fully in *Hannibal* and *Hannibal Rising*. In these stories, a lot of people want to categorize Lecter. Some think he is a psychopath, some that he is "a pure sociopath," some that he is "a monster." Getting the category right is important, for categories, when accurate, often tell us what the basic causal powers of a thing are and thus what to expect from it under various conditions and in various circumstances. I will argue that Lecter is best understood to be a certain kind of outlaw. But first we must clear some ground.

He Is Not a Psychopath

Humans are remarkable for their capacity for empathy. We now know that empathy comes in two varieties or has two main aspects (and two independent neural networks to support them). One is the capacity to understand another person's point of view, to "get" how the world looks to them. This is the thinking side, sometimes called cognitive empathy. The other is to have an appropriate emotional response to the condition of another person. This is emotional empathy, and it is often accompanied by the physical reactions that go with those emotions.

We know that psychopathic personalities typically display normal or near-normal cognitive empathy: they understand us and our points of view, often very well. However, they show relatively little capacity for emotional empathy: they understand us but they don't care about us.

It is now customary also to divide psychopathic personalities into two types, primary and secondary. Primary psychopathy is largely inherited and thus tends to run in families. If one member of a pair of identical twins turns out to be a psychopath, the odds are high that the other member of the same pair will also be psychopathic. Secondary psychopathy (sometimes called sociopathy) is learned behavior (though it may very well otherwise resemble that of the other kind of psychopath). It is learned at the hands of other members of a subculture that cultivates such behavior. Both types tend to be unempathic, given to impulsive behavior, poor control of behavior, poor forward planning, and spontaneous aggressive reactions to others.

The main reason for thinking that Lecter is not a psychopath, of either type, is that he shows a rich capacity for normal working of both kinds of empathy in concert. We can see this both in Lecter as a child and as an adult.

His Empathic Childhood

Hannibal is an extraordinarily intelligent and gifted child. In response to this, his father appoints Mr. Jakov to be his tutor. Jakov and Hannibal often go walking to discuss their lessons. Jakov often turns to speak into the air next to him, forgetting that he is walking with a child much shorter than himself. One day, Hannibal wonders to himself whether Mr. Jakov misses being able to talk with someone his own age. That kind of wonderment requires empathy to reach it.

Hiding from German and Russian soldiers in the family hunting lodge in the forest, in 1944, Hannibal goes to great lengths to protect his younger sister, Mischa. Once, given a crust of bread by his captors, Hannibal puts the crust in his own mouth until it is soft, and then gives it to Mischa. That, too, is the mark of an empathic response, realizing she would be unable easily to chew the dried bread. Hannibal and Mischa have been taken captive by a group of six men, themselves formerly collaborators with the Nazis and now on the run from both retreating Germans and advancing Russians. Grutas and his gang are entirely ruthless (here's your real psychopath). They have two other children captive when they come upon the hunting lodge, where all the adults have already been killed. They use these children for food. Eventually they come for Mischa. Hannibal tries in vain to prevent them from taking her, suffers a violent attack on himself, and loss of his beloved sister. Those efforts to protect Mischa also give evidence of empathy (of both kinds) in the young Hannibal (he is eleven years old).

Two years later, Hannibal has been rescued from a Soviet orphanage by his uncle, who takes Hannibal back to his estate in France. Hannibal is entirely mute at this time (we will come back to this later). The uncle dies suddenly of a heart attack. At his funeral the beautiful aunt, Lady Murasaki, is weary and Hannibal senses her fatigue. To help relieve it, he talks to the other mourners, so that Lady Murasaki does not have to. This sensing of his aunt's fatigue and his immediate use of his rusty voice to relieve her fatigue, is an empathic response: he consciously feels her fatigue and he deliberately and compassionately acts on that feeling.

Years earlier, when Hannibal's family has just recently retreated to the hunting lodge, Hannibal one day cuts loose from its vine a mature eggplant, polishes it up with his handkerchief and puts it where Mischa will see it. For Mischa loved the color purple. Here, too, we see the eight-year old Hannibal very directly tying his actions to his empathic awareness of someone else's desires. Psychopathic characteristics, and especially those that plague the human relationships of psychopaths, we now think, begin to appear in childhood. They can be reliably measured in children as young as three years of age. If Hannibal were a primary psychopath, he would by age eight already give evidence of this. And he does not. Indeed, quite the contrary: his empathic abilities are as advanced as his other intellectual and artistic abilities. What about Hannibal as an adult?

His Empathic Adulthood

Lecter becomes a successful psychiatrist and psychotherapist in Baltimore. It is, of course, possible for a psychopath to become a psychiatrist. But it is extremely rare. Successful practice of psychiatry, and virtually any form of psychotherapy, requires empathic ability, both cognitive and emotional, working together. We may infer, then, that the adult Dr. Lecter is not a psychopath, whether primary or secondary. Moreover, we sometimes actually see him practice his profession.

He treated Margot Verger therapeutically following her brutal rape by her brother Mason. In *Hannibal* we meet the older Margot, twenty years on. She reminds Lecter of their earlier encounters and especially the first one. She had stitches in her and was afraid of having to sit down. Lecter knew this and instead invited her to walk with him in the garden and to talk there, while they walked. For Margot to accept this treatment it would have been necessary for it to be a genuinely compassionate offer, one that took into account her possible suffering (without mentioning it) and did so honestly. False compassion would not serve the therapeutic alliance. And compassion is the handmaiden of empathy.

Twice in his novels, Harris mentions Hannibal's practice of going to public performances or public exhibitions and standing to one side to "read" the faces of the audiences. This reading is not literal: he is picking up the expression of human emotions from those faces. This is something that most adult humans can do very well, automatically and without thinking about it. The brain mechanisms of such emotional interpretation of facial expressions are well known and understood. Lecter is exercising his empathy.

For the most part empathy tends to cause us to act prosocially and cooperatively towards others. But there is no necessity about this and empathy can also be a weapon. Lecter is normal in this regard also. Senator Ruth Martin's daughter has been kidnapped by the serial killer Jame Gumb and imprisoned in a dry well in the cellar of his house. Lecter is interviewed by Martin, who thinks that he has special information that can identify Gumb (as indeed he does). Lecter taunts Martin with having breast-fed her daughter as an infant. "Thirsty work, isn't it?" Lecter says to her. Harris continues: "When her pupils darkened, Dr. Lecter took a single sip of her pain and found it exquisite" (Harris, *Silence*, p. 184). The whole exchange puts Senator Martin at a sharp disadvantage in her power struggle with Lecter.

Eventually, Lecter becomes the lover of Clarice Starling, a woman thirty-two years younger and a special agent with the FBI who is hunting Lecter. They become lovers as a direct outcome of Lecter's psychotherapeutic interventions with Starling following their joint escape from the certain death that Mason Verger conspires to bring them. That treatment succeeds in freeing both Starling and Lecter from neurotic fixations that have prevented both from forming intimate relationships with others in the past.[1] Indeed, Lady Murasaki once offered to become Lecter's lover (some time after the death of her husband). But Hannibal cannot respond to her offer positively, for he has already promised loyalty to Mischa. He has promised Mischa revenge for her own murder (for food). And until he achieves that revenge he is frozen in his virginal state. Starling suffers from a blockage tied to her memories of her dead father. Both find freedom eventually, and each other (as improbable as that may otherwise seem). This would not happen without an empathic ability in Lecter (at age sixty-five).

We should also note that Lecter cannot be a sociopath (or secondary psychopath). For he is not the product of some identifiable sub-culture that teaches its members psychopathic patterns of behavior. There is no sub-culture for Lecter.

Moreover, Lecter is a consummate planner and forecaster, both of the consequences of his own actions and those of other persons. He is like a chess master, planning many steps ahead of his opponents. Such planning, and the cool detachment that goes with it, are not the marks of a psychopath or a sociopath.

---

[1] For a fuller account of the nature and therapeutic quality of the Lecter-Starling relationship, see Chapter 18 of this volume.—Ed.

For all these reasons, then, we have to admit that Hannibal Lecter is not properly described as a psychopath or a sociopath. The term "monster" is no better, for it classifies him as Other, that is, as utterly alien to the rest of us. But, as we will see, he is anything but alien to the rest of us. To see this clearly we must first back up and consider his history.

His Traumatic History

When *Hannibal Rising* opens, Lecter's family is preparing to evacuate their ancestral home in Lithuania to escape oncoming German forces, part of Hitler's invasion of Russia in June 1941. They retreat to their hunting lodge in the forest and remain there until December 1944. Hannibal thus loses his home and spends three and a half years in hiding, fearing discovery by the Germans and, later, the Russians. This already has to be very stressful for a child, no matter how gifted that child may be. One winter's day, in the space of a few minutes and almost due to accident, the household servants, his tutor, both of his parents, and six soldiers are killed violently in the presence of Hannibal and his sister; only the children survive. A few days later, Grutas and his men show up and take them captive. There follows their brutalization, partial starvation, and the eventual killing (by axe) and eating of Mischa. Hannibal witnesses that killing and eating also. The loss of those we love by violent means is among the most traumatic events that a human can witness. Hannibal loses all the people he loves by violent means and within a very short period of time. What we see later on is a young boy, and still later an adult, who is suffering from post-traumatic stress disorder.

There is no uniform agreement among scientists as to exactly what constitutes PTSD, and it may well not have a single coherent biological manifestation. But three elements are very common: re-experiencing the traumatic events (especially by means of "intrusive" memories); behavior designed to avoid memory of the traumatic events (including suppression of conscious memories and other forms of dissociation); and unusual physiological responses to stimuli that resemble the traumatic events, either too much arousal or too little. All of these are found in Hannibal.

His dissociation begins with suppression of his memory of the actual killing of Mischa. He can remember events leading up to it, but not the actual killing itself. Neither can he remember consciously what happened after that until he is found wandering in the forest by a Russian tank crew, who shelter him and deliver him to a nearby village for safe-keeping. Indeed, Hannibal's amnesia lasts for some time after the events.

He is also mute when he comes out of the forest and remains so, as we have noted, for two years. Mutism is another form of dissociation, one that silences Hannibal's most powerful gift: his high verbal intelligence. His physiological response to highly stressful events in later life is to dampen arousal: his heart rate, respiration rate, metabolic rate, and emotions. He is calm when he attacks Paul Momund in the village market. He is calm much later when he attacks the nurse in the asylum. He is calm when the Sardinian kidnappers attempt to take him in Florence. And he is calm during the shoot-out at Mason Verger's farm, where Hannibal was threatened with being eaten alive by Mason's ferocious pigs. This preternatural calmness is the mark of Lecter throughout his childhood, adolescence and adulthood when under severe stress. It is a further manifestation of his PTSD. For the major symptoms of PTSD to continue in a trauma victim even for decades is not unusual. Holocaust survivors show the same pattern up to seventy years after the horrific events that engulfed them. Survival is bought at a very high price.

It is a further feature of Holocaust survivors that they also exhibit psychological resilience in the face of their otherwise traumatic history. Resilience is itself a complex, multi-level phenomenon. But basically it is the capacity to cope with those traumatic events and to make a good life afterwards. Survivors often are able to build new families, sustain professional careers, integrate themselves well into new cultural settings, and so on. Somewhat paradoxically, their dissociative abilities help with this. So also do their capacities for self-control, for planning, and for reflecting on their experience.

Hannibal shows the same pattern. He is a master planner, as we see even in his early deadly encounter with the butcher Momund. He out-plans and out-reflects all of his enemies, often preparing years in advance for hard times. Moreover, once he decides that it is necessary, he takes effective steps to recover his lost memories of the death of Mischa. He uses a combination of hypnotic and anesthetic drugs to help him do this, and also a quasi-self-hypnotic setting. These details (including the sodium thiopental he uses, which is known for its power to dampen anxiety) are scientifically accurate and of proven effectiveness in just what Hannibal is attempting. The recovery of those memories is enough to give him vital clues towards discovering the identity of Mischa's killers, one of them dead at the hunting lodge, the others free and flourishing in the world after the war. He hunts them down, every one. The combination of resilience and continued PTSD is common among severely traumatized persons.

A further aspect of Lecter's resilience is how he copes with his intrusive memories. Such events tend to be brief, emotionally disturbing, unconnected to other memories, and coming "out of the blue." Notable among these is the recurrent image of a young deer, wounded by an arrow, that Grutas and his men found in the forest, killed and ate a few days before they killed and ate Mischa. This is among the last of Hannibal's conscious memories before Mischa's death and when it suddenly intrudes upon his thinking (once while playing the harpsichord in his Baltimore house, once on the aircraft taking him back to America) he cannot stand it and screams like a child. But he finds a way to counter the emotional force of this memory. He kills the brutish deer hunter Donnie Barber with a crossbow bolt. And the sound of the string of the crossbow counters the flashback. His dominance and competence in killing Barber is enough to cancel out the helplessness and incompetence associated with his failure to protect his sister. This use of other autobiographical memories to counter the emotional impact of flashbacks is also accurate according to recent scientific studies. He will use the same technique later to aid Clarice Starling. In all of these respects, then, the resilient Hannibal manages to find his way to resources that can help him (or others) and to make use of those resources to aid in his later recovery and flourishing. He both *"navigates"* well to these resources and *"negotiates"* well with them (see Ungar 2012).

By giving us this history, Harris builds a biologically realistic bridge between us and Lecter. Harris thus succeeds in arousing our own empathic response to Lecter, especially as a boy and adolescent. That empathic response is a basis for understanding Lecter and not merely writing him off as Other than us. We may not identify with all of his purposes, all of his motives or all of his values, but we can identify with his plight. Just as Clarice Starling cannot resist the plight of the screaming lambs about to be slaughtered (in her memory), neither can Hannibal Lecter resist the plight of innocent sufferers like Mischa, or the plight of the bullied children whom he defends and avenges in the Soviet orphanage. He goes so far as to release the captive birds at Kolnas's restaurant, birds that will otherwise end up on customers' plates. Neither can we resist the plight of Hannibal himself. Our empathic response to him is both cognitive and emotional. But what about those motives, those values, and those purposes? There is more to be said about them.

His Motivations

So, Lecter is moved to aid "those in peril." He is also resilient in his pursuit of pleasure. Lecter has expensive and even exotic tastes, in food, wine, music, art, furnishings, musical instruments, artistic performances, automobiles, clothing. Harris gives enough details to show just how expensive his tastes are. He leases or buys cars, for example, that cost today hundreds of thousands of dollars. He drinks wines that cost thousands of dollars a case and hundreds of dollars a bottle. And so it goes. He will not deny himself, as Starling observes, even though the pattern of his exotic purchases is almost enough for her to track him down once he returns to the United States from Italy.

Hannibal has exotic intellectual tastes and interests as well. His education has been second to none. He subscribes to a number of advanced scientific journals ranging from physics and solar system studies to neurophysiology. He edits and reviews for scientific journals. He writes and publishes in them also, even while in the asylum. When free he pays premium prices for tickets to concerts, plays, and other public performances.

In all of these ways, Lecter is seeking one fundamental objective: his autonomy. The term itself means "self-governing" or "self-ruling." It is a form of mastery or competence that enables a person to make real in the external world the purposes and values that are most central to his or her identity. Here, indeed, is another facet of his resilience. For competent persons can broaden and build their repertoire of patterns of action. They can also marshal the necessary resources, including personal relationships, goods of the body, situations or circumstances that they need to achieve their purposes. Lecter is a master at these tasks.

A further part of his autonomy is his attitude towards institutions, including the institution of medicine to which he has otherwise devoted himself. More particularly, he has one attitude towards institutions that have failed of their promises or are in the process of declining in their quality and value. And that attitude is one of contempt. In his book *Exit, Voice, and Loyalty*, the sociologist Albert Hirschman argues that when our institutions or organizations start to fail or to decline we have basically three possible responses. We can exercise continued loyalty to the institution and its values, despite their decline. We can try to exercise a voice for reform inside the institution. Or we can exit the institution. Lecter plumps for exiting as his basic strategy. He goes even further, however, in seeking to undermine the faith others have in those same institutions. This is especially so for Clarice Starling. Her loyalty to the FBI, an institution that finally turns on her and destroys her reputation, is attacked by Lecter. And eventually she, too, exits. Indeed, it is arguable that her exiting is the essential move that saves both her and Lecter himself from destruction. It is also a powerful bond between them. The destruction of faith is one of Lecter's favorite amusements, but by no means the only one.

Early in his stay with his uncle and aunt in France, Hannibal is seen by a psychiatrist, Dr. Rufin. Rufin observes that Hannibal is constantly pursuing several independent trains of thought, always one of which is for his own amusement. Many years later, Clarice Starling describes Lecter's amusing of himself as "whimsy." We know a good deal about amusement. It is a very positive and durable emotion. Given his powerful memory for events and scenes, Lecter is in a position to retain his amusements and to use those memories as a resource during harder times. Amusement, then, can also serve to broaden and build an individual's emotional resources and action repertoire. Its positive emotions can become a positive spiral to counter the negative spiral that external events may otherwise cause. As such, amusement is also part of Lecter's resilience and serves his drive for autonomy.

But Lecter is also a killer, you protest. And surely this separates us decisively from him, placing him "beyond the pale."

His homicides have nothing to do with us, after all. They are inexcusable and are what makes him a monster.

Oh, really? Let's look more closely.

His Killing

It is true that Lecter kills. However, his killing is always instrumental and rational; his killings serve clearly identifiable purposes. They are not merely random nor compulsive nor ritualistic. He kills to achieve revenge, for example, and revenge is a common motive found in all humans and in all human cultures known to us. Its pleasures can be intense and durable. It is even codified in many cultures, both ancient and modern. Lecter also kills to punish, and so do we. Although capital punishment is not uniform any longer in human societies, not long ago it was such. For the longest part of human history, reaching back as far as our resources can take us, we find killing as an ultimate form of punishment (likewise in our closest primate relatives). It is often justifiable especially when those who are killed are otherwise likely to escape any form of justice for their crimes. But we can go further than this.

There are excellent reasons for thinking that homicide is a human adaptation. It can, in particular circumstances, effectively solve problems that bear on an individual's or group's biological fitness, their capacity for successful reproduction. Humans kill in predictable circumstances. They kill, for example, to prevent the loss of a valuable mate. They kill to protect other valuable resources. They kill to enhance or to defend social status and reputation. We are among the most cooperative species on the planet. But we are also among the most aggressive species on the planet. And our aggression often takes the form of killing, for perfectly clear and compelling reasons (see *The Murderer Next Door* by Buss).

Lecter is thus doing what humans and other primates have done for millions of years. He also does his killing in just the ways that evolutionary theory predicts. Of course, sometimes what Hannibal Lecter thinks is a valuable resource to be protected or enhanced by killing is something we would not find so. Thus, he kills the curator of the Capponi Library in Florence so that he himself can take that man's place. He kills the incompetent violist in the Florence orchestra so that a better musician can take his place, thereby improving Hannibal's own experience of the orchestra. We are not likely to find these deaths defensible. But just as you are not likely to blame Jason Bourne for his killings, neither are you likely to blame Hannibal Lecter for most of his. Why would you? He's just like you. When he tells Will Graham that Graham was able to track him down because Graham is just like him, he is talking also to us. And now we can say something positive about his kind.

Hannibal as Outlaw

In the ancient and medieval worlds some persons were declared to be outlaws. This was sometimes punishment for homicide or treason, sometimes for much lesser offenses. But the effect was the same: to place that person beyond the protections of the law. They could thus be killed by anyone else without fear of further punishment. The Romans did this, the Greeks did this, medieval Britons, Scandinavians, Germans, Slavs, all did this. And we in turn are fascinated and even mesmerized by the figure of the outlaw. Think of our many films, television series, and novels that celebrate the outlaw. But the situation is more complicated than simply being shoved out the door of civil life and its institutions.

Some outlaws live both inside and outside of the law. Lecter is such a one. For he rents houses, leases cars, engages in commerce, manages his wealth, carries on professional tasks, goes grocery shopping, and attends the theater. In all of these ways he is fully integrated into civil society and follows its norms and conventions in order to achieve his purposes. How else would one do it? What else would be the point of one's outlawry? He also defends the weak against the predatory strong. He punishes the guilty; promotes the autonomy of others, exercises empathy and compassion, does not lie and does not steal.

But he also lives outside of the law. He hides from the authorities. He alters his facial appearance. He uses false passports. He avoids being fingerprinted. He kidnaps people. And he kills whom he determines to kill, he himself and all by himself. He is jury, judge, and executioner in his own cause. He lives as independently as he can, never yielding final loyalty to any institution. His being outside of the law is also what makes him vulnerable to the deadly schemes of those who hunt him:

Inspector Pazzi in Florence, the Sardinian kidnappers, Mason Verger, Inspector Popil in France, and so on. No one is as vulnerable to the aggression of others as the outlaw.

There is no good critical study of the concept of the outlaw, much less of our fascination with outlaws. But we can see some of what is going on. For we too are killers, at least potentially (and many of us actually). We too seek our pleasures. We too thirst and hunger for autonomy at the same time seeking the valuable spouse or partner. But it is the killing that is perhaps the hardest for us to face. For here our aggressive human nature is most clearly revealed to us. In Hannibal Lecter, then, we are given a mirror within which to discern the outline of that nature. Perhaps only in the context of a fiction could we do so in a sustained way. For in such a context we are safe (just as we are safe in the movie theater). And in such safety we can look and see what Lecter shows us: there is an outlaw in all of us.

8
Consuming Homicidal Art

JOHN MCATEER

Hannibal Lecter once killed a flutist from the Baltimore Philharmonic Orchestra. He then fed some of the victim's internal organs to the Philharmonic's board of directors at a dinner party he was hosting. The flutist, Benjamin Raspail, had been one of Dr. Lecter's psychiatric patients. In the novel *The Silence of the Lambs*, Hannibal tells Clarice Starling that he killed Raspail for "whining" too much during therapy (Harris, *Silence*, p. 54). In the 2002 film version of *Red Dragon* it is implied that Hannibal killed Raspail for being a bad musician.

The interpretation of Hannibal's motive has evolved as the story has been told and re-told. Every version of the story agrees that Hannibal is a gourmet cook, well known for his culinary connoisseurship. He made an *amuse-bouche* from Raspail's thymus and pancreas—what chefs call the "sweetbreads." But is Hannibal a psychopath who kills people simply for being annoying? Or an extreme aesthete so committed to high culture and good manners that he kills those who fail to live up to his exacting standards? And which would be worse?

Homicidal Art

When novelist Thomas Harris invented Hannibal Lecter, he based his character on real-life serial killers he had become aware of during his career as a crime journalist. But criminologists like to point out that real-life serial killers do not act like Hannibal. For example, one recent academic article concluded that real-life serial killers tend to have lower verbal IQ scores, in contrast to the highly intelligent and hyper-verbal Dr. Lecter (DeLisi et al.).

One of the most obvious ways fictional serial killers differ from real ones is their method of killing and disposing of bodies. In the world of Thomas Harris's novels, serial killers treat their murders like art. For example, the Tooth Fairy calls his murders "My Work. My Becoming. My Art." (Harris, *Dragon*, p. 165). He opens the eyes of his dead victims so they can "watch" him like an "audience" at a "performance" (Harris, *Dragon*, p. 17). In the TV series *Hannibal*, the idea of homicidal art is pushed even further. One killer cuts his victim's throat and plays his vocal chords like a cello (*Hannibal*, Season 1, "Fromage"). Another builds a totem pole from human bodies (*Hannibal*, Season 1, "Trou Normand"). And, in perhaps the most striking "artwork," one killer creates an enormous three-dimensional "mural" using dead bodies of varying skin colors (*Hannibal*, Season 2, "Kaiseki").

In real life there have been cases of cannibalism and killers who kept body parts as "trophies." Perhaps the most famous case was Ed Gein, the inspiration for several of Hollywood's most memorable murderers, including Norman Bates in *Psycho*, Leatherface in *The Texas Chainsaw Massacre*, and Buffalo Bill in *The Silence of the Lambs*. According to one especially vivid account of Gein, "On moonlit evenings, he would prance around his farm wearing a real female mask, a vest of skin complete with female breasts, and women's panties filled with vaginas in an attempt to recreate the form and presence of his dead mother" (Fox and Levin, *Extreme Killing*, p. 4). There is an element of performance here, but this is a long way from homicidal art. Gein was motivated by psychological drives, not artistic ones.

Thomas Harris's original homicidal artist on the other hand, is interested in the aesthetic dimension of his murders. The Tooth Fairy films his murders and watches them again and again at home, partly for sexual gratification but also in order to critique his performance. Watching the film, he judges his performance harshly: "Even at the height of his pleasure he was sorry to see that in the film's ensuing scene he lost all his grace and elegance of motion, rooting piglike with his bottom turned carelessly to the camera. There were no dramatic pauses, no sense of pace or climax, just brutish frenzy" (Harris, *Dragon*, p. 74). The Tooth Fairy aspires to the kind of cultivation attained by Hannibal Lecter whose "pulse never got over eighty-five" while murdering a nurse, "even when he tore out her tongue" (Harris, *Dragon*, p. 56). Although there are many homicidal artists in the world Thomas Harris imagines, Hannibal remains unique. He is more intelligent, more cultured, than others. While the Tooth Fairy or Buffalo Bill might have some sort of twisted aesthetic predilection, Hannibal Lecter actually seems to have good taste. He has a genuine appreciation for Bach and Italian architecture and fine wine. He is a classic "aesthete."

Like his aesthetically refined hero, the Toothy Fairy loves fine art—he listens to Handel and finds inspiration in the paintings of William Blake—but the act of murder reduces him to the frenzy of an uncultured brute. He aspired to more: "with experience, he hoped he could maintain some aesthetic distance even in the most intimate moments" (Harris, *Dragon*, p. 74).

Going the Distance

Aesthetic distance is a concept first introduced by psychologist Edward Bullough in the early twentieth century. Bullough points out that the same object can be experienced differently, depending on the psychological attitude we bring to it. For example, in ordinary circumstances—say, while traveling—foggy weather produces annoyance, anxiety, or even fear. If you just want to get on with the business of practical affairs, fog can get in your way. But if you are able to set aside any practical goals you have and just look at the fog itself, it can be seen as beautiful. He uses the metaphor of taking up a critical "distance" from the object.

> Thus, in the fog, the transformation by Distance is produced in the first instance by putting the phenomenon, so to speak, out of gear with our practical, actual self; by allowing it to stand outside the context of our personal needs and ends—in short, by looking at it "objectively," as it has often been called, by permitting only such reactions on our part as emphasize the "objective" features of the experience. (Bullough, p. 89)

Bullough argues that to properly experience an artwork we must find the right balance between the objective and subjective experience of the artwork. We must be neither over-distanced nor under-distanced.

Horror films like *Hannibal* provide a good example of how this works. If we are unable to distance ourselves from the image of Hannibal cutting open a still-living person's skull and then feeding the victim his own brain (sautéed with shallots, minced caper berries, and grated black truffles, of course), then we will be so horrified and disgusted that we will be unable to continue watching the film. If, on the other hand, we over-distance ourselves from the scene, we may be too objective, too cold, and not experience the horror at all. We might be thinking about whether it is physiologically possible to feed someone his own brain, or about how the filmmakers were able to achieve the special effect. The key to the appropriate aesthetic experience is to get caught up enough in the film to feel the horror without being sent running from the theater.

Empathy Disorders

Arguably, one element of aesthetic distance is empathy. If a viewer or reader is to appreciate the horror of Hannibal's murders, he or she must empathize with the victims. Someone who doesn't have feelings of concern for the suffering of the victims won't be able to have the appropriate aesthetic response. For this reason, it is tempting to think that psychopaths are incapable of aesthetic experience insofar as they lack empathy for others.

Indeed, there is some evidence that real life psychopaths tend to have an underdeveloped aesthetic sensitivity. For example, in one of the first clinical studies of psychopathy, psychiatrist Hervey Cleckley discussed a patient who was unmoved by art: "It is impossible for him to take even a slight interest in the tragedy or joy of the striving of humanity as presented in serious literature or art. He is also indifferent to all these matters in life itself. Beauty and ugliness, except in a very superficial sense, goodness, evil, love, horror, and humor have no actual meaning, no power to move him" (Cleckley, p. 40). Cleckley's patient fits the clinical definition of a psychopath. The terms "psychopath" and "sociopath" are used somewhat interchangeably in the mass media. The technical psychiatric term for this condition is Antisocial Personality Disorder. According to the DSM-5 (a standard classification system used by mental health professionals), the diagnostic criteria for Antisocial Personality Disorder include a lack of empathy which manifests as callousness: "Lack of concern for feelings or problems of others; lack of guilt or remorse about the negative or harmful effects of one's actions on others" (Meloy and Yakeley).

It is important to notice here that lack of empathy only means the psychopath lacks *concern* for others, not that they can't *understand* their feelings. This fits with Thomas Harris's portrayal of Hannibal Lecter. In *Red Dragon*, Frederick Chilton says Hannibal is a "pure sociopath" (Harris, *Dragon*, p. 56). Will Graham disagrees. Will says psychologists only call Hannibal a sociopath "because they don't know what else to call him." Will does point out that Hannibal "has no remorse or guilt at all," but adds that "he's not insensitive" (Harris, *Dragon*, p. 49). In other words, Hannibal has empathy but not a conscience.

Far from lacking empathy, Hannibal is quite sensitive to the feelings and perspectives of others. This is one reason he is attracted to Will Graham. "The reason you caught me is that we're *just alike*," he tells Will (Harris, *Dragon*, p. 62). In the 2001 movie version he specifies: Will and Hannibal are alike because they both have a talent for "imagination," an uncanny ability to get inside other people's heads (Ratner, *Red Dragon*). Hannibal understands what others are thinking and feeling— he simply doesn't care. Likewise a survey of real life psychological case studies reveals that, instead of an empathy deficit, the true mark of a psychopath seems to be their "inability to take an interest in anything that does not serve, directly or indirectly, to satisfy some desire" (Maibom and Harold).

Can Psychopaths Have Aesthetic Experiences?

Philosophers Heidi Maibom and James Harold hypothesize that the psychopath's pathological egocentrism would yield an inability to achieve aesthetic distance. Remember Bullough's theory that we must set aside our "personal needs and ends" and attend to the "objective features" of the artwork. In other words, aesthetic distance means engaging with the art object as an end in itself, not as a means to satisfy your own subjective desires. If you only value an artwork because it is worth a lot of money or depicts a sexually arousing figure, then you are not appreciating the work aesthetically. You are treating the object as a means to achieving an external good (money or sexual gratification).

Maibom and Harold assume that psychopaths treat *everything* as a means to external goods, and so can engage neither persons nor artworks as ends in themselves. Remember the clinical definition of a psychopath involves a lack of empathetic concern for others. The DSM-5 links this to "egocentrism" and "self-esteem derived from personal gain, power, or pleasure" as well as "manipulativeness" and the desire to "control others" (Meloy and Yakeley). This is certainly true of Hannibal Lecter who is fond of discussing the "power" that God feels when he "kills" people through natural disasters. Hannibal clearly takes great pleasure not only in killing but in toying with people. In the TV series, *Hannibal*, Will Graham says Hannibal wound him up like a top and set him spinning "to see what I would do" (*Hannibal*, Season 1, "Savoureux"). In Maibom and Harold's terms, Hannibal treats Will as a mere means to Hannibal's egocentric pleasure.

There is something right about this interpretation. Perhaps it explains why most psychopaths can't achieve aesthetic distance. For example, the Tooth Fairy is too caught up in his own egocentric sexual and homicidal desires to create objective beauty. But Hannibal doesn't seem to fit this explanation. If it is impossible for a psychopath to appreciate art, then Hannibal shouldn't be able to appreciate Bach and Italian architecture.

What this hypothesis fails to take into account is that it is compatible with aesthetic distance for a viewer to engage with an artwork instrumentally as a means to her *own* aesthetic pleasure. Sure, for it to be genuinely *aesthetic* pleasure, such instrumental aesthetic engagement would require a certain kind of psychic distancing (setting aside such practical interests as desire for money, sex, or other goods external to the art object), but aesthetic distancing does *not* require setting aside the desire for the pleasure that can result from the contemplation of art *itself*. The whole point of aesthetic distance is to enable us to achieve just that sort of pleasure!

Therefore, since the psychopath doesn't necessarily lack any cognitive skill, and since aesthetic distancing doesn't necessarily require abstracting from egoistic desire, then the psychopath should, in principle, be capable of aesthetic appreciation. There is no reason Hannibal Lecter could not exist in real life.

From Consuming Art to Consuming People

On the other hand, this account does entail that psychopaths are incapable of experiencing the value of an object for its own sake. While they can be sensitive to the object's aesthetic properties, they cannot judge that it is good for the object to exist apart from their *own* experience of it. They wouldn't care if anyone else ever got to experience the object—unless, of course, the psychopath somehow got pleasure from other people's aesthetic experience, as for example if sharing an artwork with someone led them to praise the psychopath's good aesthetic taste. But in that case the psychopath is still treating the artwork—indeed, the other person, too—as a means to his own pleasure.

This explains why psychopaths would lack ethical sensitivity, since ethics does require non-instrumental valuing of persons. Furthermore, this account means that psychopaths treat art like food—something to be consumed for pleasure—which in turn suggests that if a psychopath took an aesthetic interest in people, he would treat them, too, as objects to be consumed for pleasure. "Hannibal the Cannibal" is simply the logical extreme of this line of thought.

The Death of Aestheticism

Our discussion has revealed something interesting about the relationship between art and ethics. The philosopher Ludwig Wittgenstein famously said that "Aesthetics and ethics are one" (Wittgenstein, p. 77). But this chapter has shown that to be false. Someone could be good at one but not the other. But it also implies that they are not entirely unrelated, either. The tradition of aestheticism argued that morality was entirely irrelevant to art. For example arch-aestheticist Oscar Wilde once wrote, "There is no such thing as a moral or an immoral book. Books are well written or badly written. That is all" (Wilde, p. vii). According to this view, all that matters to art appreciation is beauty of form. The logical extreme of aestheticism turns out to be homicidal art.

For example, the Muralist from the *Hannibal* TV series arranges his victims' bodies into an artwork, using their skin color to create an abstract pattern almost resembling the rose window of a Gothic cathedral. With enough aesthetic distance, an objective viewer could see a kind of true beauty in this macabre mural. And if aestheticism is true, then this would be an entirely appropriate way of engaging with this scene. There could be no objection to homicidal art *as art*. One could certainly object that an artwork made out of dead bodies is immoral, but, from a purely aesthetic point of view, it could still be a rewarding aesthetic experience and hence a great work of art.

Our discussion of aesthetic distance shows that things are not as simple as aestheticism believes. The aesthetic point of view does not in fact silence all the demands of morality. Sometimes our attempts both to respect an artwork and humanity as ends in themselves genuinely conflict. In those cases, morality trumps pure aestheticism. We *ought not* take up a purely aesthetic point of view toward dead bodies.[1]

In terms of aesthetic distance, we might say that anyone who is able to experience dead bodies as beautiful is necessarily over-distanced. To see why, consider that the Muralist's artwork is essentially a sculpture made from human bodies, just as other sculptures are made from marble or bronze. From this point of view, we see that the material is not irrelevant to the artwork. Materials are commonly listed on museum and gallery walls, precisely because they are relevant to the interpretation of the work. Thus it would in fact be a mistake to disregard the bodies and appreciate only the form of the work. The materials matter. Anyone whose aesthetic attitude fails to take into account the materials at all is over-distanced from the work.

Ironically, I think Hannibal would agree. For him, the fact that the works (or meals) are made from human bodies is the *whole point*. And knowing them to be human flesh actually adds to the pleasure of consuming them. But he's a psychopath. A normal person would be incapable of taking aesthetic pleasure in the death of another human being. So we can say that Hannibal's moral deficit actually does turn out to be an aesthetic deficit in cases of homicidal art. He finds some art beau-

---

[1] This tension is further explored in Chapter 15 of this volume.—Ed.

tiful that he ought not to enjoy—art that is bad from both a moral *and* aesthetic point of view.

It might seem perverse to learn how to consume art from a psychotic aesthete. But anyone who advises us to "eat the rude" is bound to have something interesting to say about the relationship between ethics, aesthetics, and gastronomy.

9
Not Knowing Serial Killers with Hannibal Lecktor

JASON DAVIS

Best Hannibal Lecter? Your time starts now. If you said "Sir Chianti Hopkins, who else," that's a Fannibal fail. If you said Mads Mikkelsen and recited the Hannibal-Joker comparison by Sean aka The Freak, half of the horror blog *Girl Meets Freak* ("Mikkelsen's Hannibal is to Hopkins' Hannibal as Heath Ledger's Joker is to Jack Nicholson's Joker," Bottai and Peaschock), you get some brownie points. But if you answered, "Isn't it spelt L-e-c-k-t-o-r?" then you win the Skype date with Tom Noonan.

Picking Brian Cox's eight minutes as the killer with the nursery rhyming nickname means you're probably one of two types of fans of Michael Mann's *Manhunter*. You're either in Column A, which is: You've got pre-Internet memories of VHS nights and TV movie repeats of *Manhunter* and *Silence of the Lambs*, and you loved more what a Scottish actor did with the character of Hannibal than what a Welsh actor won an Academy Award for. Plus, you're still getting more clueless looks of "Who's Brian Cox?" than agreed-upon props for preferring a 1980s Hannibal (played as a coldly restrained, gum-chewing, phone-hacking killer) over a 1990s Hannibal (played as an unblinking, campy dungeon dweller with a shop front window for a cell). Or you're in Column B: You know *Manhunter* from downloads or YouTube, so you're probably born digital enough to know where Brian Cox fits into the Hannibal-verse from the Interwebs. You get your eighties Hannibal fill from podcasts like *The Projection Booth*, where unrepentant Mann-ophiles bromance the Cox, or *Sordid*

Cinema, who ran their own Hannibal-listics test and called out *Manhunter* as the best film in the franchise (Conceição et al.). You probably know the origins of Michael Mann's idea for using Iron Butterfly's "In-A-Gadda-Da-Vida," from his correspondence with the deluded and Wikipedia page-less killer Dennis Wayne Wallace. Wallace said the 1968 Top 30 hit was a love song he shared with a woman he obsessed over, and ended up killing people for (Feeney, p. 65). But you'd also Tweet as DVD commentary-worthy what Kristine, aka the girl half of *Girl Meets Freak*, floats as the reason for Mann's mix tape pick of "In-A-Gadda-Da-Vida" for the film's shotgun shootout: "to signal Dolarhyde's transformation to the Dragon because, you know, dragons are like iron butterflies?" (Bottai and Peashock). When hit up for the best version of *Manhunter* to check out— theatrical, director's cut, or restored director's cut—you'd say go with every flavor and watch the *Manhunter* extended fan edit of all the releases. And as for the fan edit version of *Red Dragon* that's got Hopkins *Manhunter*-ed out of the picture enough to keep it paced as the Graham and Dolarhyde show— "It's just you and me now, sport" (Mann, *Manhunter*)—you know it won't have any tracks by Shriekback to save it from also deserving mister X's hilarious *Film Threat* take down of Danny Elfman's score for *Red Dragon*: "when Graham enters a bloody crime scene, Elfman lets loose with a cue that seems more at home in a William Castle or Hammer Horror film" (Robinson).

So with everything the Interwebs have on 1980s Hannibal, that'd be enough to force a recount from the Nostalgia Critic's beat out of *Red Dragon* over *Manhunter* (Walker). How is it that people who know *Hannibal* are, well, still ignorant of *Manhunter*?

Do You Know How You Caught Me, Will?

But there's another sense of "best Hannibal," and that's to best or beat Hannibal by outthinking him at his own "knowing game." The knowing game is Lecktor taking advantage of what he wants Will Graham to know and not to know about the Pilgrim and his lunar cycles. To anticipate the knife twist of getting Lecktor wrong, you'll need to do more than second guess what a psychiatrist, murderer, profiler, and prisoner freely gives up as expert advice. What don't I know about what

Lecktor is feeding me? After all, Graham's controlled recreation of the fantasy world of the Tooth Fairy makes known aspects of what was unknown about the physical world, things that were in the blind spots of police procedure, like the latent finger-prints on Mrs. Leeds or how Graham's been watching the same home movies that Dolarhyde has all along. But there's a constant unknown for Graham. And that's how much he can possibly know that will help with keeping himself psychologically separate from, and so in control of, what he mentally recreates when he's profiling the Tooth Fairy.

Lecktor knows this. He's alert to why Graham wants to see him in prison; how the Tooth Fairy is picking his blooms. That's Graham's excuse to get his mindhunting mojo back by comparing notes with Lecktor. But Lecktor's onto Graham getting him to do the predatory thinking for him without Graham having to immerse himself too deeply, or for too long, in a set of behaviors, desires, and patterns of thinking he doesn't yet know enough about. So Lecktor cuts him off from giving up that knowledge as pre-digested. Making Graham do his own "field work" is Lecktor's opportunity to get Graham messed up enough either to risk his own life chasing Dolarhyde or to be permanently switched on as a homicidal killer.

Then there's Lecktor's fan mail from the Tooth Fairy. Did Lecktor allow it to be discovered knowing it would lead Graham to risk himself as bait? Or did he know that FBI dis-information about the Tooth Fairy in the *Tattler* would end up with Freddy Lounds as collateral damage in Graham's gamble? When Lecktor congratulates Graham for setting Lounds up for his fiery Hot Wheels death, that's Lecktor the psychiatrist coaching Graham to accept how alike they are as explorers of the joy of killing. Lecktor left Graham and the FBI ignorant about what Dolarhyde would most likely do. Sure, that's a probability Lecktor bet on. But he had a purpose in keeping Graham ignorant. And that was a strategic deprivation of knowledge on Lecktor's part: to get at Graham, one way or another.

Outthinking Lecktor is going to take more than just getting inside the mind of a serial killer. It requires thinking not only about what you don't know about a situation, a course of action, or why something that wasn't known was left so unexamined. Overcoming unknowability, what you're routinely ignorant of and why, involves thinking differently in ways that get at what's not letting something become known even when in plain sight. Ignorance isn't always just a lack of knowledge. And sometimes the best question to ask is *why* you don't know what you don't know, rather than *how* you might know it.

If all this mentioning of knowns and known unknowns is making you think you're hearing Donald Rumsfeld's "There are known knowns" phrase, that's a good association to make. The former Secretary of Defense's famous expression is an example of how ignorance can be related to knowledge. And weirdly enough, Hopkins's Lecter in *Red Dragon* does resemble Rumsfeld. Re-watch the scene in *Red Dragon* where Lecter, chained to the ceiling of an indoor exercise yard with an armed guard watching overhead, is talking to Graham (Ed Norton). From side on, Hopkins's Lecter looks uncannily like Rumsfeld, so much so, that it's hard not to hear morsels of Rumsfeld's soundbites coming from Lecter's mouth in that sing-song voice combo of Truman Capote and Katharine Hepburn. "You know the pilgrim's killing on a lunar cycle, Will. That's a known known. And you know he's giving special attention to the women of the families he's killing, but you don't know how he's selecting them. That's a known unknown. What you don't know that you don't know about the Tooth Fairy, well, that's the unknown unknown. And I think that's why you're here to see me, Will, isn't it?" Best Hannibal. Your time before the next full moon starts now.

Lecktor-ology Meets Agnotology

The study of ignorance, especially how ignorance can still exist even when we know better or know otherwise, does have a name. It's called *agnotology*. The high-cultured Lecter of *Silence of the Lambs* or *Hannibal* would know what the Greek words mean that the term "agnotology" is derived from. But I bet 1980s Lecktor would know it from the Greek terms used in clinical psychology. *Agnōsis* is the Greek word for *not knowing*, making agnotology the study of why something remains or is kept unknown. Putting it another way, agnotology is concerned with knowledge like that other philosophical term, "epistemology," which is about how we know what we know. But agnotology asks questions about what we don't know and why. For

Robert Proctor, the historian of science who has developed much of the questioning that aims at understanding why ignorance persists in the face of scientific understanding, such as the tobacco industry's efforts to generate doubt about the health hazards of smoking ("doubt is our product"), the study of ignorance-making involves more than just understanding ignorance as the "not yet known" or non-knowledge on the other side of a steadily retreating frontier that knowledge is pushing against. The focus, Proctor reminds us in the introduction to *Agnotology: The Making and Unmaking of Ignorance*, "is on knowledge that could have been but wasn't, or should be but isn't" (Proctor and Schiebinger, vii).

Both Graham and Lecktor reflect different aspects of ignorance in relation to knowledge about serial killers. That Graham knows why and where to dust for prints on the corpses of the Leeds family goes beyond what the Atlanta PD detectives can know about finding more trace evidence from forensic facts and routine investigation. But it's the psychological processes of identifying too much with a killer's fantasies and re-imaginings of the staging of the dead families as the Tooth Fairy's audience, with the mother as the centerpiece in a post-mortem mystery theater of becoming, that makes it dangerous knowledge. And Graham wants to stay ignorant enough about how and why he can know these things. John Douglas, the FBI profiler who was the inspiration for the characters of Jack Crawford as well as Graham, shares his fictional counterpart's desire to keep the public ignorant about his own profiling techniques. In *Mindhunter: Inside the FBI Elite Serial Crime Unit*, he argues for continuing ignorance about most of his own profiling techniques at the risk of "giving away any closely guarded investigative secrets that could provide a 'how-to' to would-be offenders" (Douglas and Olshaker, p. 31).

With Lecktor, it's obvious how the serial killer specimen craftily keeps his clinical captors ignorant of what can be known about him. Lecktor knows about the Leeds and Jacobi cases from the newspapers, but doesn't keep copies of the articles lest he's thought morbid. Or that's what he wants his captors to think. And as for Lecktor's offer to help with profiling the killer of the families, it keeps everyone ignorant of his contact with the Tooth Fairy; and it lets him access crime scenes and the autopsy details of fresh kills that he can luxuriate over in memorized playback behind his eyes. And this gets to what we, as viewers, are ignorant of with regard to Lecktor.

Graham's panic-induced exit from the cell accompanied by Lecktor's "Smell you later" is obviously how we know Lecktor's gotten through Graham's mental defenses. And there's much in that scene of Graham's one and only face-to-face encounter with Lecktor. Matt Zoller Seitz and Aaron Aradillas show in their amazing video essay on *Manhunter* how the shot composition and editing make it look like Lecktor is a distorted mirror-image of Graham as Graham puts questions to the killer for whom he almost ended up as a meal (Seitz and Aradillas). And seeing Graham behind the cell bars reminds us where he'll end up if he becomes a killer like the one he's identifying with. But it's the very beginning of their encounter in the cell that gets us closer to how creepily that scene really plays out. Uttering that memorable line with his back to Graham says so much about how Lecktor, with his powers of smell and memory, would already have the advantage over his victims, detecting them even without seeing them. If you stay at the aftershave joke, however, you're not thinking about how other aromas discernible to Lecktor's acute power of olfaction would've added to his enjoyment: the sweet cooking smell of his victims as stewed or baked cuts of meat infused with ingredients. And as for the chemical breakdown of his victims, after the savored taste of people pieces cooked at fifteen-to-twenty minutes per pound, there's the metabolizing of their flesh as nutrients within Lecktor's body. If you haven't thought about where the smelling joke that Lecktor tells (probing for details about Graham having kids) finishes up, through Lecktor's gut and out the other end, you're staying just with the Lecktor you think you know from what you can see and hear, rather than thinking with your nose. *Smell thyself.*

But how does ignorance relate to what we know about or don't know about real serial killers? Think about what would happen in the law enforcement world after Graham kills Dolarhyde. You're an FBI Internal Affairs Division special agent. There are multiple shooting deaths of local law enforcement officers that resulted from responding to calls by FBI agents investigating a suspect strongly connected to the homicides of two families. The lead FBI agent elected not to wait for a backup SWAT unit. There's the wrongful death of a tabloid journalist connected to the same FBI agent who used said tabloid to bait the same homicide suspect. Then there's the supplying of homicide case files on two murdered families to an imprisoned serial killer who was later found to be in correspondence with the suspect connected to those very same murders. Why wouldn't you investigate what wasn't known but could've been? What could've been done about the risks of such uncertainty?

It's not so much "who knew what and when?" but more a case of "why were decisions made without questioning more of what wasn't known?" Was there an overreliance on profiling that led Graham to identify too much with the Tooth Fairy? And was there an overreliance on Lecktor as a source of knowledge that he would exploit? What this questioning points to is how ignorance is at work in what we think we know about serial killers. As Robert Proctor says of agnotology as a knowing game (and you'll soon see how applicable this is to what the FBI said they knew about serial killers), the focus is on the need "to think about the unconscious, and structural production of ignorance, its diverse causes and conformations, whether brought about by neglect, forgetfulness, myopia, extinction, secrecy or suppression. The point is to question the *naturalness* of ignorance, its causes and its distributions" (Proctor and Schiebinger, p. 3).

And this gets us back to where we started out, with "best Hannibal Lecter." In a curious way, that people are more familiar with Anthony Hopkins as Hannibal than they are with Brian Cox is connected to why the American public in the 1990s got a very different account of the phenomenon of real world serial killer activity from the FBI: they didn't know what they didn't know because of the phenomenal success of *The Silence of the Lambs*.

And the Academy Awards for Best Picture, Best Actor, Best Actress, Best Director, and Best Adapted Screenplay Go To . . .

How much did the success of *Silence of the Lambs* affect what the American public knew from the media about the FBI's Behavorial Science Unit, the BSU? More than you might've guessed. By the mid-1980s, the FBI was politically and socially accepted as best placed both to understand and to deal with the major social problem of serial murder. After all, it was the FBI's behavioral science experts at Quantico that alerted the American public to the rising problem of roaming serial killers, responsible for up to a quarter of all homicides every year, with some of them operating across state lines. Why wouldn't the best solution to the country's growing serial murder problem include beefing up the FBI's profiling and crime analysis resources as well as creating new powers for the FBI that increased its jurisdiction over serial murder, and ultimately justification for the BSU at Quantico? But in 1990, the biggest challenge to the profiling system developed by the BSU wasn't from rising rates of serial murder, but from a deeply flawed psychological assessment that wrongly identified suicide/murder, rather than an accident, as the cause of the deaths of forty-seven naval personnel in an explosion aboard the *USS Iowa* in 1989. The BSU's psychological analysis was found invalid by an American Psychological Association review panel, and the dramatic display of the professional fallibility of the FBI's profiling prowess was targeted by the news media for skepticism and even outright dismissal. All of that was soon overshadowed, however, by the Oscar accolades heaped on *Silence of the Lambs*, and the media's favorable depiction of the BSU led to increased media access to the FBI's serial murder experts and profilers.

As Philip Jenkins investigates and documents in his groundbreaking study, *Using Murder*, and his follow-up research published almost a decade later, "Catch Me Before I Kill More," much of the FBI's knowledge about the scale of serial homicide, and therefore both the necessity of the scope of their powers and the public perception of serial murder, was based on falsehoods. Jenkins argues that serial murder in the 1970s and '80s was "neither new nor distinctively American" (Jenkins, p. 4). It's a highly infrequent phenomenon accounting for at most one or two percent of homicides, not a quarter of them. And the majority of serial killers are "homebodies," not interstate rogues. Their victims are mostly in the same locale or region as themselves. Jenkins's research shows that the FBI's support and promotion of a serial killer panic is a perfect case study in ignorance-making about serial murder. The public perception of serial murder was a false one. The FBI's justification for bigger budgets, more powers, the behavioral wizards and access to their authority and knowledge by the media and Hollywood filmmakers, was all based on ignorance of what was already known, ignorance that prevented investigation of the BSU's fallibility and statistical falsehoods. Ignore the FBI experts behind the curtains of the serial murder panic. Where to now, Special Agent Dorothy, when the mindhunting wizards are exposed?

Riffing in the Known Hannibal-verse

Best Hannibal dream sequel? Mike White, co-host of the film podcast *The Projection Booth*, once pitched a friend's take on how one possible Hannibal Lecter sequel (one, thanks to character licensing restrictions, we'll never get) would play out: Clarice Starling needs a recovering Will Graham to help track down Lecter, sans ponytail. But can Starling trust Graham's "mindhunting" to keep her safe from Graham himself, let alone Lecter? *Let the knowing games begin.* Would Starling work out what she doesn't know about strategies Lecter might use to try to trigger Graham's homicidal urges? Do Graham and Starling know how Lecter is shortlisting his more deserving victims to feed his own needs? And which world of 24/7 news cycles should the sequel have for media coverage of the known knowns and known unknowns about Lecter? The one filled with talking heads, soundbites of FBI press conferences and 911 calls of coast-to-coast Lecter sightings, syndicated hosts interviewing profilers and true crime writers (think Freddy Lounds meets Glenn Beck), all replaying in between thirty-second fillers on murderabilia hunters, Lecter cult collectors, and arrested copycat killers? Or the one where, as Slate.com and CNN remind us, our fascination with serial killers is dwindling? We're not in serial killer country anymore, Dorothy. (See Beam, "Blood Loss: The Decline of the Serial Killer"; Fox and Levin, "A Surprising Truth about Serial Killings.")

Was that last "What If" another trick question about Lecktor? Kind of. Riffing on "What Ifs" for an imaginary sequel is another knowing game that expands the known Hannibal-verse of pop-cult knowledge about serial killing. If the *Silence of the Lambs* film echoes a Grimm fairy tale, which fairy tale would Starling's teaming up with Graham be a retelling of? Or what if this team-up sequel was *Scream*-ified and went meta with Lecter on serial killer culture? This riffing on what can be known, even to rearrange the storytelling pieces into ways that make it unfamiliar, doesn't stop at established franchise material that has purely coincidental resemblances to anyone, living or dead. We know enough about the serial killer lore behind Thomas Harris's creation of Jame Gumb. That character was a composite of Ted Bundy, Ed Gein, and Gary Heidnik. So flipping through the flipbook of real-life serial killers, which murderer or three could be the inspiration for the non-Lecter killer or killers in the imaginary sequel? Or would a real killer with neither a Wikipedia page nor a serial killer trading card be a better unknown source for a character that Lecter targets? And how do you find out about an unknown predatory killer anyway? This is where Lecter gets to be both the cause of ignorance about serial murder and, in the imaginary sequel we deserve, something of a guide into the land of the unknown unknowns about serial killers.

Lecktor at Large among the Less-Dead

Cut to the chase. In my imaginary sequel, Lecter makes telephone contact with Graham and Starling. He tells them that he's keeping a low profile, casing out a murderer whose sex worker victims don't make it into the local papers. The serial murderer, Lecter informs Graham and Starling, "was doing his killing in Poughkeepsie, New York, a town on the Hudson River halfway between Albany and New York City—too far south to enter the Albany television market and too far north to be covered by the New York City TV footprint. *That's like saying it never happened*" (Vronsky, p. 40). If that geographical location sounds a little too exact to be made up as film dialogue, you're right. Those lines by my imaginary Lecter are from Peter Vronsky's book *Serial Killers: The Method and Madness of Monsters*. And the serial killer is, or was, real.

Kendall "Stinky" Francois murdered eight sex workers between 1996 and 1998. He kept their corpses in the attic of his parents' place. But his victims were never eaten or kept alive in a prison pit. And they weren't skinned or made into sculptures, just strangled lifeless and stored in garbage bags. Add to the low publicity this not-made-for-TV, "typical," single-digit serial killer career would've made, and Vronsky's point about a killer and his victims staying invisible outside of a metropolitan television footprint is another example of how media-fed public knowledge about serial killers is adding to our ignorance of them. Who in the media would care enough to want their audience to know about missing sex workers outside of the world of their own metro area? "No one wanted to know how this killer was picking them," the imaginary sequel Lecter tells Starling and Graham. "Because nobody knows they are gone. Some of them never became active missing person cases. They're the missing missing. They're the unknown unknowns, Will. When they are found dead, if they ever are, their deaths don't matter as much. They are the 'less-dead'."

To put the "less-dead" into Lecter's mouth is to cue up another real-world reference that's used to think about the known unknowns and unknown unknowns influencing what we know about serial killers. And, intriguingly enough, the term "less-dead" originated with a criminologist, Steven Egger, who first linked wider public ignorance about serial murder generated by pop-cultural serial killers in a paper he gave at the 1992 annual meeting of the Academy of Criminal Justice Science, just two weeks before *Silence of the Lambs* won five Oscars at the Academy Awards. The "less-dead," as Egger explains in his own entry for the term in the *Encyclopedia of Murder and Violent Crime*, "refers to the majority of serial murder victims, who belong to marginalized groups of society." He continues:

> They lack prestige or power and generally come from lower socio-economic groups. They are considered less-dead before their deaths, they virtually "never-were," according to prevailing social attitudes. In other words, they are essentially ignored and devalued by their own communities or members of their neighborhoods and generally not missed when they are gone. Examples are prostitutes, the homeless, vagrants, migrant farm workers, homosexuals, the poor, elderly women, and runaways. They are vulnerable in locations they frequent, and easy to lure and dominate. (Egger, p. 279)

Would Lecter ever target the "less-alive"? That'd spoil the appeal of snuffing out the deserving, especially after his ret-conned origins as an aristocratic killer of Nazi-collaborators, substituting evermore his eaten sister with the flesh of his victims. But those preying on the "less-alive" would be on Lecter's menu as convenient take-away if he was the at-large focus of an FBI manhunt. That's what Egger is getting at with the idea of the "less-dead." The media and police can and do contribute to public ignorance about the victims of serial killers. So, as much as our continuing fascination with the mythical individuality of serial killers means we'd recognize their names more than those of Nobel Prize winners, very few people would be able to name even one victim of a serial murderer.

Good Will Hunting and the Dark Matter of the Hannibal-verse

If what the characters in *Manhunter* know about Lecktor makes up the known Hannibal-verse, then what they don't know *and* don't know that they don't know isn't just ignorance that gets pushed back by knowing more than they did before. The stuff that's not known about Lecktor is more like the "dark matter" of the Hannibal-verse. And Lecktor relies on ignorance as much as he's an ignorance-making demon in the world of Will Graham. Mindhunting with Lecktor means you're not going to bump into what you don't know. It's going to roll out at you like a fiery wheelchair. The pull of these Lecktor effects— the invisible, cognitive influence he has on what can be known or what he keeps unknown—extends from the fictional world into the real world of what people think they know about serial killers. The mythological and fairy tale elements of the Hannibal-verse overtake our thinking about serial killing, creating ignorance where there could have been knowledge. And Hannibal, the "never-has-been," as in *there-never-was-nor-ever-will-be* a real killer like Hannibal, is one real answer to the question of why we're ignorant of the "never-were" victims of real, no-name, no-brand, serial killers.

IV.

I Gave You a Rare Gift, but You Didn't Want It

10
The Light from Friendship

Andrew Pavelich

Thomas Harris introduced the characters of Will Graham and Hannibal Lecter in the novel *Red Dragon*, and in that version of the story, we're told that Will met Hannibal while investigating a murder, and almost immediately saw that Hannibal was the killer. It was meant to show how well Will understands the minds of killers, and how he makes intuitive leaps even before he fully understands them. Will then visits Hannibal in the mental hospital to "catch the scent" of the killer he is currently chasing, and Hannibal taunts him by claiming that they are more alike than not. It's a powerful scene that sets Will up as a super-investigator who alone can bring down the kinds of psychopaths that populate Harris's novels.

When Bryan Fuller created his series, he kept Hannibal and his psychosis, and kept Will and his powerful intuition, but changed the relationship between the two characters. When the show began, the audience assumed (or at least I did) that it would be about how Will catches killers-of-the-week while missing the big one that's right under his nose. And while the show definitely had that theme, it also became a show about how Will and Hannibal, who share a kind of disconnect from the people around them, become friends. In the series, Hannibal often points to Will as either his friend or his potential friend, and Will spends most of Season 1 confiding in Hannibal as something between a therapist and a friend. Will then spends Season 2 seemingly masquerading as Hannibal's friend in order to catch Hannibal in an act of murder, but at some points in this masquerade, the two seem closer than ever before. In the end, Hannibal stabs Will, and feels the tragedy of being betrayed by the one person who has ever been his friend. But was he right? What does it mean to be a friend? And, given the kind of person that Hannibal Lecter is, could he ever have been friends with Will Graham?

Aristotle on Friendship

To get a handle on whether the characters of Will Graham and Hannibal Lecter really are friends, we need to take a step back and look at friendship in general. There have been some classic descriptions of friendship in the history of philosophy, but probably the most important is one of the first: that of the ancient Greek philosopher Aristotle.

Aristotle had a lot to say about friendship, but it starts with the basic idea that friendship is more important than we usually give it credit for. He thought that having friends is a necessary part of living well—both emotionally, morally, and practically. As human beings, he says, we naturally have affinity for others. If we are living rightly, then we will love our own lives, and we will want to share these lives with others. Friendships allow this.

> For without friends no one would choose to live, though he had all other goods; even rich men and those in possession of office and of dominating power are thought to need friends most of all; for what is the use of such prosperity without the opportunity of beneficence, which is exercised chiefly and in its most laudable form towards friends? (Aristotle, *Nicomachean Ethics* 1155a)

What's the point of power, or wealth, or even of goodness, if we cannot share this with someone we care about? Without friends, none of our achievements matter.

Aristotle also says that friendship must be recognized, and reciprocated. In part, he says, this is because we all wish for the best for ourselves, and our friends reflect our own concerns. We must know our friends, and they must know us. Friendship ultimately is aiming at equality between two people; it's about two people being joined in all things. For this reason, Aristotle says that ordinary people cannot be friends with a king; there is simply no room to meet as equals, even if each party is wishing the best for the other. As Aristotle writes, "To be friends, then, they must be mutually recognized as bearing goodwill and wishing well to each other" (Aristotle, *Nicomachean Ethics* 1156a).

To put it all together, then, for Aristotle, the highest form of friendship is between people who are good, and good to each other:

> Perfect friendship is the friendship of men who are good, and alike in virtue; for these wish well alike to each other qua good, and they are good themselves. Now those who wish well to their friends for their sake are most truly friends; for they do this by reason of own nature and not incidentally; therefore their friendship lasts as long as they are good—and goodness is an enduring thing. (Aristotle, *Nicomachean Ethics* 1156b)

In the world of *Hannibal*, there are a few candidates for this kind of friendship. One is the relationship between the members of the FBI forensics team. They have an easy time with each other, and seem to accept each other for who they really are. However, we rarely get a chance to see them outside of work, and so they may just have a kind of "work friendship." Not that such a relationship isn't real, but it's not as deep as the perfect friendship that Aristotle talks about. For this, I think we should look to the relationship between Jack Crawford and his wife "Bella," at least after she is honest with him about her cancer. They want the best for each other, and they want each other to be equals. They may not always agree about what's best (an example being her attempted suicide), but they care about each other and place each other at the center of their lives.[1]

Aristotle's philosophy of friendship is a very influential one that tends to line up with a lot of our everyday ideas: we want friends so that we have someone to share our lives and share our fortunes with, and we want our friends to reciprocate our friendship. Our friends must, as Aristotle says elsewhere, share our souls. But if we are going to discuss friendship and Hannibal, we also have to look elsewhere in the history of

---

[1] For more on the role of Aristotle's notion of friendship in discussing Hannibal Lecter's relationships with others, see Chapter 6 of this volume.—Ed.

philosophy. Hannibal, after all, is hardly a conventional character, and his friendships will not be conventional either. We must
turn to one of philosophy's great outsiders: Friedrich Nietzsche.

Nietzsche on Friendship

Nietzsche is a notoriously difficult philosopher to understand.
He is probably most famous for writing that "God is dead," but
this doesn't exactly mean that he thinks that there is no God.
What he means instead is that God does not matter—or more
precisely, that God *should* not matter. If we understood the
world in the right way, then we wouldn't bother wondering
what God wants, or what God says. God, Nietzsche says, is
irrelevant to our lives.

Part of what makes Nietzsche hard to grasp is that he
doesn't think that everyone is capable of really believing the
things that he says are true. One of the core concepts in
Nietzsche's philosophy is that there are two kinds of people in
the world: most of us, the ordinary masses of humanity,
unquestionably worship a higher being, and tell ourselves that
this being has given us absolute moral truths. We do this,
Nietzsche says, to shield ourselves from actually having to
make decisions in life, and as such, we hide ourselves from the
truth. Opposed to this group are those very few who know the
truth, who know that there is no higher authority—that even
if there is a God, there is no reason to take him as the arbiter
of morality. Nietzsche calls these people *"Übermenschen"* in
German, sometimes translated as "supermen," but probably
more aptly (and literally) translated as "overmen." They are
people who stand over the rest of us, due to their willingness
to embrace the truth about the universe. They even stand as
equals to God—obviously not equals in power, but equal in creativity and desire. This, Nietzsche says, is actually what God
wants in us: "Companions the creator seeks, not corpses, not
herds and believers. Fellow creators, the creator seeks—those
who write new values on new tablets" (Nietzsche, *Thus Spoke
Zarathustra* I: "Prologue"). The overmen do not wait for God to
approve their actions—they act as they wish, without regard
for what the masses call "morality."

It should come as no surprise that this is how Hannibal sees
himself. Consider two of the times that Hannibal actually talks

about God. When he is helping Will examine his feelings about having killed Garret Jacob Hobbs, he says: "Killing must feel good to God, too. He does it all the time. And are we not created in his image?" (*Hannibal*, Season 1, "Amuse-Bouche"). Much later in the series, when Hannibal serves Will roasted ortolans, he explains that it is traditional when eating them to cover one's head before God, but he doesn't do this himself, saying, "I don't hide from God" (*Hannibal*, Season 2, "Kō No Mono"). This all lines up with what Nietzsche said about the overmen—they are not subservient to God, but equals. Autonomy and freedom from ordinary morality are the hallmarks of Nietzsche's overman, not subservience.

Hannibal actually mentions Nietzsche once, when serving a trout that Will caught. He says: "More flavorful and firm than farmed specimens. I find the trout to be a very Nietzschean fish. Trials of his wild existence find their way into the flavor of the flesh" (*Hannibal*, Season 2, "Su-zakana"). For the overman, life is all about struggle and growth. When we realize that this is the only life that matters, Nietzsche thought, we can truly live, and accumulate the real experiences of life— much like the trout. And in this process of creativity, conflict, and struggle, life (ours and the trout's) acquires its taste. The overman does not want comfort. He wants life.

An entire book could be written about Hannibal and Nietzsche, but here we're interested only in friendship. For Nietzsche, friendship is about cultivating the *Übermensch*; it's a striving of two people to each become more than just ordinary humans. Friendship in this sense does not preclude conflict, or even open combat; it may even encourage it. One can imagine enemies in war thinking of each other in this sense of friendship—as equals who are equally set apart from the rest of humanity and are striving to grow. Their fight does them both good. This may not make sense in a modern version of war, where death is quick and impersonal, but it makes more sense in a classical view of war, with the combat of champions, each becoming greater through the struggle.

> If one wants to have a friend one must also want to wage war for him: and to wage war, one must be *capable* of being an enemy.
> In a friend one should still honor the enemy. Can you go close to your friend without going over to him?

> In a friend one should have one's best enemy. You should be clos-
> est to him with your heart when you resist him. (Nietzsche, *Thus
> Spoke Zarathustra* I: "On the Friend")

This is the kind of friendship that Gilgamesh and Enkidu, or Achilles and Hector, could have had (even though they didn't become friends in life, Achilles certainly respected Hector in death). Friendship is about striving, and becoming better—which makes friendship, for Nietzsche, largely a matter of self-interest.

Nietzsche and Aristotle actually share a great deal in their thoughts on friendship—they both view it as an essential part of the best life, and they both view the relationship between friends as one of shared interests. The difference, or at least one big difference, is that for Aristotle, friendship was ulti-mately about honesty and reciprocation. For Nietzsche, friend-ship is about growth, which can take place through conflict, and can include dishonesty. This difference is going to be important when looking at Hannibal and Will.

Hannibal's View of Will

Hannibal Lecter has a hard time making friends. Over the course of the series, as he becomes close to Will, he seems to get excited about the possibility of friendship. Up until then, as his therapist Dr. Du Maurier says, Hannibal is "disconnected from the concept of friendship" (*Hannibal*, Season 1, "Relevés"). There are many people in his life who seem like friends (Jack Crawford being one), but their relationships are only really on the surface. Again, Dr. Du Maurier puts it well, saying that Hannibal wears a "person suit" to navigate the world (*Hannibal*, Season 1, "Sorbet"). Acting like friends with Jack is a part of that suit, but he sees in Will the possibility of more. We get the sense as an audience that this would be the first real friendship that Hannibal has ever had.

Why is it so hard for him to make friends in the first place? It's not, I think, just the fact that he has murdered people and eats their corpses. I think that there is something about Hannibal that lies behind the murders, and this is what sepa-rates Hannibal from the rest of the human world. It's all very Nietzschean, but to see how, exactly, we have to look at his rela-tionship to animals.

Will often says that the Chesapeake Ripper looks on his victims as pigs, to be slaughtered. There's some truth to this, but he's not quite right, as it turns out. Hannibal causes the slaughter of lots of actual pigs (as most of us do), but as he tells his dinner guests, he uses an ethical butcher. For actual pigs, Hannibal is perfectly willing to kill them and use them for his dinner, but he is not willing to cause them unnecessary suffering. But this is not how he treats his Chesapeake Ripper victims. He causes them tremendous unnecessary suffering—removing their organs while they are still alive. Why? Because he thinks that they are, in fact, less than pigs. They don't deserve even the respect owed to pigs. (It's worth noting that this is a major departure from the original description of Hannibal Lecter in the novels, as someone who tortured animals before moving on to killing people. This is how actual psychopaths often progress, but it was changed, even in the later novels, presumably in part to make Hannibal more relatable. We can tolerate our characters killing people, but they cannot kill animals—except for food on a daily basis.)

Hannibal treats the animals that he cooks and eats as instruments for his ultimate pleasure, but he also recognizes that they have feelings, and that they don't deserve to suffer more than necessary. Hannibal seems to treat most of the people in his life the same way. He has some fondness for them, like pets, but will kill them in an instant if it is a matter of his own interests. We can imagine that if he had found Dr. Du Maurier in her home at the end of Season 1, he would have killed her in a relatively pain-free way. She had to die, but she had never been rude, and so she didn't deserve to suffer. Dr. Du Maurier, Jack Crawford, Alana Bloom: Hannibal sees them all like pigs. His Chesapeake Ripper victims are less.

It's extremely interesting that the show does not let us see Hannibal performing one of his Chesapeake Ripper killings. We see him kill many times, but in his guise as the Chesapeake Ripper, we see only the results. Why? I suspect because the show-runners know that this would be too much for us to maintain anything like sympathy for the character. Probably rightly—we can live with our main character as a murderer, but watching him torturing his victims would be harder for audiences to swallow.

One can imagine a similar hesitancy in the character of Hannibal. He can share with others that he has taken lives (he has several public killings in the show, and admits to killing someone as an ER doctor). But he cannot share that he has hurt people, on purpose. One gets the sense that Hannibal wants to share this part of this life, but not with just anyone. Obviously he can't share it with anyone who would turn him in, but he also can't share it with the other killers on the show. For example, Matthew Brown, the orderly from the mental hospital from Season 2: that killer didn't savor the moment, didn't remove trophies while the victim was still alive, didn't understand why his victims cling to life. Hannibal also didn't try to befriend Tobias Budge, the killer cellist from Season 1. The reason for this is a little less clear, but I like to think that it's because he was rude to Franklyn, who did not deserve it. Hannibal was fine with killing Franklyn, but didn't want to leave him in the hands of someone who would hurt him.

Think of how the world is ordered for Hannibal. There seem to be the following categories:

- Rude people, whom he will happily kill in the most painful of ways;
- Animals, and the vast majority of people, whom he will kill for the slightest need, but not with unnecessary pain;
- People he finds interesting, like the rest of us relate to pets—whom he may have to hurt, but whom he would prefer to have in the world rather than not (including Alana Bloom);
- Will Graham, who goes beyond this last category into something else; and
- Himself.

Hannibal wants a friend, and he sees in Will Graham the potential to become the kind of person that could be his friend. Hannibal sees himself as helping Will to take the next step. Obviously he lies, manipulates, and vicariously tries to kill Will, but I don't think he sees any of this as acting contrary to a friendship with Will. Nietzsche would probably agree.

So we can see what Hannibal sees in Will—the possibility of a real friend. Why does Hannibal want to become friends? Probably to do something new. He has never had an equal in his life, and it might open new doors. Thus Hannibal's manipulation of Will into becoming more serves Will, but also serves

Hannibal. According to Nietzsche, at least, Hannibal is acting like Will's friend.

Will's View of Hannibal

What does Will think of Hannibal? To answer this, we really have to look at the various time points in the series. When they first meet, Hannibal tells Will that he hopes that they can become friendly. Will sees it differently at first, but quickly comes to think that Hannibal is someone who is at least not taxing in the way that other people are.

Their relationship becomes something more than psychiatrist and patient after Will kills Garret Jacob Hobbs. From Hannibal's perspective, I think that this marks the beginning of his idea that Will can possibly become more like him. Will was entirely justified in shooting Hobbs—in fact, he regrets not shooting him more accurately—but he still suffers tremendously from the killing. Why? Encephalitis was a factor, but not the only one. Part of what the show does so well is take seriously the immensity of taking another life, where other TV shows would sweep such killings under the rug. This, I think, is a part of what Hannibal sees in Will: the valuing of all life, even those lives that deserve to be taken. And for Will, Hannibal as a therapist is just about perfect, since Hannibal does not treat Will's discomfort as psychosis.

Hannibal is a good therapist, but he's also more.[2] We can see how by looking at what Hannibal says to his other patient, Franklyn, who makes overtures of friendship—Hannibal tells him that his therapy is a "source of stability and clarity," but not friendship (*Hannibal*, Season 1, "Sorbet"). Hannibal is all this to Will, but more too, and Will knows it.

The next part of the story starts when Will is hospitalized. Will now knows the truth about Hannibal. At first, his reactions are to turn to the law. Then, he tries to have Hannibal killed. When Hannibal visits him in the mental hospital, Will says, "You're not my friend. The light from friendship won't reach us for a million years. That's how far away from friend-

---

[2] For a more elaborate consideration of Hannibal Lecter as therapist, see Chapter 5 of this volume.—Ed.

ship we are" (*Hannibal*, Season 2, "Kaiseki"). From Will's perspective, it's all over, and in a sense, Hannibal would agree. Whatever they had earlier is gone. The difference is that while Hannibal wants to develop something new and truer with Will, Will fixes his attention on punishing Hannibal for his crimes.

The third part of their relationship is Will pretending to be Hannibal's friend, trying to get him to expose his true, murderous self. Did Will ever actually consider joining Hannibal? The show tries hard to make us wonder, but in the end, I don't think he did. He was setting Hannibal up from the beginning. As soon as Hannibal kills Beverly Katz, and as soon as (for all Will knows at the time) he kills Abigail Hobbs, there's no question of Will joining him. If Hannibal had admitted that he had not killed Abigail, Will might have been more inclined to commit to his lifestyle, but even so, I don't think he would have committed all the way.

The only real question for Will is what kind of person he wants to be. He is, for a time at least, willing to become a killer—for all moral purposes, he is one by the end of Season 2, killing one man whom he didn't have to kill (Randall Tier), and attempting to kill—and regretting not killing—another (Clark Ingram). I think that Will might have been happy to become the kind of killer that television has given us before, the best example being Dexter Morgan (of the series, *Dexter*): the serial killer who only kills those who deserve it. Hannibal is more: he doesn't kill for justice or morality, he kills because he can. His purpose in killing is often just to make artistic points. This is a kind of person that Will Graham just cannot become, and as such, he can only see Hannibal as evil.

In the novel *Hannibal*, Thomas Harris makes Hannibal Lecter into this kind of "moral" killer, only going after the kind of person whom the reader would think deserves it. Hannibal in that novel is not the kind of person who would kill an innocent girl to goad the FBI. Hannibal in the television series sometimes kills people who deserve it (even a few times killing a fellow serial killer, à la Dexter), but more often he kills people who are rude, or who get in his way.

Will never really could have been the kind of killer Hannibal is. Will wants to catch Hannibal, not help him, and although he understands him, he does not want the best for him. Will was looking for a soulmate—a friend in the classical Aristotelian sense—and Hannibal was not it.

The Tragedy of *Hannibal*

Bryan Fuller has said in an interview that the show is really about heterosexual male friendship, in a way that few other television shows are (*A.V. Club*, "The Walkthrough: Suzakana").[3] He has also said that the tragedy of Season 2 is the ultimate betrayal of this friendship (*A.V. Club*, "The Walkthrough: Mizumono"). But I think that ultimately it wasn't, since Hannibal and Will were never mutually friends. When each one thought the other was closest was when they were being lied to the most, and neither conception of friendship—neither Will's Aristotelian view, nor Hannibal's Nietzschean one—can withstand such lies.

It should be clear that Aristotle leaves little room for lying between friends. For him, friends are true soulmates, who share everything about each other, and share everything with each other. Such a friendship could withstand what we might call "white lies" ("your new haircut looks nice," "you didn't embarrass yourself too much at the party," etc.), but not lies about things of central importance. There would be no question, from Aristotle's perspective, that a big lie, even if it were intended ultimately to help, can have no place in true friendship.

For Nietzsche, big lies might actually be required in friendships, since for him, friends are about growth, not comfort. Hannibal lies to Will about his encephalitis to help him grow, and he sees no problem thinking of himself as Will's friend while doing so. But from Hannibal's perspective, even as he lies to Will systematically, Will's lies to him are far worse. Will is lying not to help Hannibal or to challenge him, but to capture him and take his freedom. Will's lies are not about growth or striving, as Hannibal thinks his are.

So, in neither Aristotle's sense nor Nietzsche's are Hannibal and Will friends—there are times when each thinks they are, but they are mistaken, and for each, the exposure of that

---

[3] For more on the idea of Hannibal as a series devoted to exploring heterosexual male bonds (sometimes called "homosociality"), see Chapter 11 of this volume.—Ed.

mistake is tragic. But even more tragic, and part of what makes the show so great, is that there is just the smallest hint of something like true friendship, right before the bloodbath that ends Season 2. We actually get a glimpse of this from both sides: first, when Hannibal, at dinner before the climactic murders, asks Will to leave right there, and abandon their plans to trap Jack. Hannibal has smelled Freddie Lounds's perfume on Will, and knows that Will has been lying to him, but is willing to let it all go. Of course, Will cannot. Later, amidst the bloodshed, Will tells Hannibal that he could have just left town, implying that had he done so, Will would not have chased him. Both of these are moments where one of the characters shows real concern for the other, and while neither really makes sense in light of their respective ideas of friendship, they show something of the deep connection between the two. In these moments where Will and Hannibal are closest to truly being friends, any friendship between them is already impossible. As much as they may want to, they cannot escape the knowledge of their betrayals of each other, already in progress.

11
A Rare Gift

SELENA K.L. BREIKSS

> *Time did reverse. The teacup that I shattered did come together. The place was made for Abigail and your world. Do you understand? The place was made for all of us, together. I wanted to surprise you. And you . . . You wanted to surprise me. I have let you know me. See me. I gave you a rare gift, but you didn't want it.*
>
> —HANNIBAL LECTER (*Hannibal*, Season 2, "Mizumono")

Bryan Fuller's television series *Hannibal* is a macabre crime thriller based on the characters in Thomas Harris's *Red Dragon*—the novel which precedes *The Silence of the Lambs*. The complex relationship between Dr. Hannibal Lecter and Special Agent Will Graham is a dynamic bond of masculine emotional intimacy, competition and exclusion, and an unspoken fraternal order. Lecter and Graham navigate the multiple boundaries of their relationship as colleagues and friends, doctor and patient, victim and assailant, sexual rivals and emotional allies. Hannibal and Will's relationship is further complicated by their interactions with the series' secondary characters—namely, with Alana Bloom, a romantic interest of both men; Abigail Hobbs, the daughter of a serial killer for whom both men briefly share a parenting role; and Jack Crawford, the director of the Behavioral Science Unit within the FBI and their direct contact for the Bureau.

Hannibal and Will have a ridiculously complicated relationship. As mentioned above, they are not only colleagues, but their bond maintains an intricate balance of doctor-patient, friend-enemy, and victim-assailant affinities—only to be complicated further as surrogate fathers and sexual rivals. The men are consistently in a state of competition and collusion, in a nearly simultaneous fashion, in their personal and professional lives. This relationship is at times positive for both men, as they are able to deeply understand each other and offer reciprocal emotional feedback and understanding (regardless of their revolving position as friends and enemies). "Homosociality" is a specific term for this type of bonding, coined by Eve Kosofsky Sedgwick in her book, *Between Men*. The use of "homosocial" refers to the non-sexual, platonic bond between two men and encompasses the intimacy of their relationship (what we might sometimes call a "bromance"), and is especially visible when examining Hannibal and Will's friendship, mentorship, and rivalry. Their bond is only between them, leaving those around them—namely Jack, Alana, and Abigail—as mere bystanders, and later victims, of their entanglement. This homosocial bond with Will is Hannibal's "rare gift": the opportunity and promise of a friendship, which will be expressed through the production and consumption of haute cuisine made from their collective gathering of meat, and will result in a bond that extends deeper than mere curiosity. Hannibal manipulates and molds Will, excited about the potential friendship. As we learn in the final scenes of the second season, as Will lies gasping in a pool of his own blood, this was Hannibal's design.

We're Both Alone without Each Other

Throughout the series, Hannibal and Will exist in a continuum of lopsided give and take. In his book, *The Accursed Share*, French philosopher Georges Bataille offers a glimpse into this sort of relationship. He conceives of it as not limited specifically to literal gifts and economic gains and losses, but rather more symbolic shifts in reciprocal bonds. Every moment of pleasure—for example, shopping sprees, sexual contact, and indulgent feasts—can also be included with the idea of "the Share" being tied directly to the display of economic *and* social surplus. We can see this in *Hannibal* with the grand meals prepared by Hannibal and the social elements tied to these events. Hannibal is demonstrating his power within his relationships with Will, Alana, and Jack as he is not offering strictly food, but an elegant, multi-course meal which conveys his superior position. This position is not only his wealth and social status, but his constant ability to maintain dominance and control as they all seek to capture the Chesapeake Ripper. These actions are what Bataille calls the shifting of bonds in relationships; as Hannibal becomes more confident in his ability to mask his killings, the more meals he shares with his colleagues. He is so self-assured in his ability to hide his crimes that he not only invites his potential captors into his home, he serves them the evidence that they hope to find as an epicurean, cannibalistic feast.

Bataille's "accursed share" is a unique take on Marcel Mauss's book, *The Gift*, insofar as Bataille's description of the competitive relationship between the giver and the receiver is a response to Mauss. Mauss, yet another prominent French philosopher, explains that gifting is not specifically done for economic purposes, adding that it also includes an element of social bonding, but to an even greater extent can contribute to rivalry. Giving a gift, according to Mauss, can be as much about establishing social dominance as it is about anything else. Mauss's theories are especially useful in coming to understand the homosocial relationship between Hannibal and Will: they are first positioned as colleagues—which adds an immediate professional rivalry—then, as doctor and patient, giving Hannibal the edge as Will's support as he sinks into delirium. Will, dealing with the swelling in his brain, cannot fully reciprocate the emotional generosity, lending Hannibal the upper hand in the relationship. Hannibal has overcome Will to the extent that Will's internal monologue is replaced with Hannibal's voice. Will makes this quite apparent at the beginning of Season Two, when he tells Alana, "I hear Hannibal's voice in the well of my mind. I hear him saying words that he's never said to me. It isn't my imagination. It's something else" (*Hannibal*, Season 2, "Kaiseki"). Hannibal's influence has become excessive to Will, despite the doctor's (superficially) good intentions. Hannibal's idea of the gift of friendship, companionship, and mentorship had become a burden on Will's self-identity, and is a perfect example of Mauss's idea of gifting to overpower or overwhelm the rival. The idea of their platonic relationship being a "gift" to Will is deeply ironic, given the toxicity and mayhem that Hannibal has introduced into Will's life.

I Don't Know if I've Got Any "Self" Left Over

The homosocial bond between Will and Hannibal manifests in three forms throughout the series—the Stag, the Wendigo, and the "Willdigo." The Stag, which has been present since the first episode, is a hallucination but also serves as a source of comfort for Will. It is ultimately symbolic of his mental stability and wellbeing. The Stag appears in his dreams and nightmares as a sort of beacon of normalcy. Will is not frightened or suspicious of the Stag, but rather curious and trusting of the beast. On many occasions, the Stag is attempting to lead him away from Hannibal. It's as though Will knows deep down that this isn't the healthiest relationship, and yet is still drawn to Hannibal out of a sort of morbid curiosity, a need to know and experience a bond with a person like the enigmatic doctor. The dynamic state of the Stag throughout the show—from a dreamland companion to the victim of the Wendigo—reveals the slow dissolution of Will's hesitations surrounding Hannibal, the entrapment and framing of Will for the Chesapeake Ripper's murders, and his ultimate surrender to the seduction of the duplicitous and charismatic Dr. Hannibal Lecter.

The Wendigo is a beast of legendary proportions. The origins of the folkloric animal stem from Algonquin myths surrounding the taboo of cannibalism. The Wendigo can either possess a person or the person can become the beast, most commonly when human flesh is eaten as a means of survival. In most narratives, the Wendigo is a grotesque being, a large, gaunt figure. It is half-human, half-animal with large multi-pointed horns, an emaciated body and sunken eyes, with a stench of decay and decomposition. As Will sinks deeper into the delirium, the Stag is nearly replaced by a Wendigo figure, complete with withered body and horns, except the mangled face which has been replaced with Hannibal's blackened visage. This beast is not only symbolic of Hannibal's eventual push of Will into madness, but also a marker of both Will and Hannibal's transgressions.

The "Willdigo" isn't a term designated by Bryan Fuller or offered anywhere in the script, but it is a fantastic nickname created by the Fannibals (the cheeky nickname for the community of avid fans of *Hannibal*). The Willdigo is the salt to the Wendigo's pepper. Near the end of Season 2, the Wendigo eviscerates the Stag and the Willdigo emerges out of its carcass.

The newborn beast is identical to the Wendigo, with the blackened, emaciated body, but with one difference: Will's face replaces Hannibal's on this creature.

Eating Her Is Honoring Her; Otherwise It's Just Murder

Hannibal reminds Will (and the audience) that, "cruelty is a gift humanity has given itself" (*Hannibal*, Season 1, "Coquilles"), a natural transgression embedded in the human essence. The homosocial bond between Will and Hannibal becomes dependent on their shared transgressions. Hannibal and Will both embody perceptions of good and evil simultaneously. During the Chesapeake Ripper trial, Will is positioned as evil but is mostly good, while Hannibal is positioned as good while being mostly evil. However, the mark of evil is not lifted from Will entirely after the declaration of a mistrial. In his book, *Erotism: Death & Sensuality*, Bataille discusses transgression as the ability to move beyond a taboo without disrupting its social and cultural rationale. Offering murder as a specific example, Bataille notes that the act of killing another human is not universally banned, because if it were, war and military assassinations would not exist whatsoever. Through this, we have to bear in mind—especially with Hannibal—that naming something as taboo does not deny that it is a possibility. When watching the preparation and display of Hannibal's gorgeous feasts, we separate these images from the reality that the meat he's butchered in his cellar is human flesh. We know that this is taboo, the violation of a corpse, yet we gawk at the frivolity and splendor of his gourmet meals. Hannibal's transgression is buried in this beauty. His cannibalism has transcended the taboo.[1]

It's Nice to Have an Old Friend for Dinner

Hannibal's epicurean cannibalism removes the grotesque—and for some, the immorality—of eating human flesh. The off-screen production of Hannibal's feasts includes a culinary

---

[1] For more on the nature of Hannibal Lecter's cannibalism, see Chapter 2 of this volume.—Ed.

designer, Janice Poon, who also runs a blog aimed at helping fans recreate their favorite dishes from Hannibal's dinner table. This only reiterates the idea that food and shared meals are a site of bonding, nourishment, security, and ritual as the Fannibals can experience the meals while watching the series. Hannibal's corrupted—and yet celebrated—ethics surrounding the gathering of his meats are nearly justified as he says to Will, "Whenever feasible, one should always try to eat the rude" (*Hannibal*, Season 2, "Tome-Wan"). His victims often include corrupt politicians, other serial killers, copycats, and people who threaten to expose the more private moments of his life. His morally bankrupt attitude is cemented in his statement, "I don't hide from God," while he chews and swallows the entire body of an ortolan, an endangered songbird which he's prepared as a debauched delicacy (*Hannibal*, Season 2, "Kō No Mono").

Our ritual of eating goes beyond the needs of eating three daily meals. The process of food production begins with the source from which it is then harvested, prepared, trussed, and served. Once the food makes it to the table, it is then offered as a plated meal or served in a family style manner. Each of these steps adds meaning to the meal itself—everything from the source, to the preparation, to the passage of the serving dishes—and reinforces the rituals that make up what we'd consider a traditional meal. The practice of eating food with another person or a group impacts our identities. The preparer of our meal becomes a literal and symbolic source of the basic need of nourishment. Hannibal performs all of the stages of meal preparation from harvester to server, enriching his dining companions. He carefully selects his sources, ensuring that the meat is not bitter with fear, nor—at least as he sees it—undeserving of becoming the entrée for his elaborate meals. Hannibal does not "eat the rude" only for the sake of his cannibalistic urges. He prepares these meals in his ritualistic fashion for himself and his colleagues as a way to display their superior virtue, literally consuming rudeness as the means of its physical and symbolic disposal.

Fear Makes You Rude, Will

Hannibal almost requires our suspension of disbelief in order to cope not only with the gruesomely elaborate crime scenes, but also with watching Hannibal destroy Will by triggering a mental collapse. Mental illness is confined, studied, medicated, and—at best—treated. Confinement shames the person and exerts a social power over those deemed "mad," contributing to the invisibility and suppression of the mentally ill. Think of the conversations surrounding Will—by Jack, Alana, Dr. Chilton, and Hannibal—while he is confined at the Baltimore State Hospital for the Criminally Insane. Even more so, think of the use of the cage in which Will is often held, positioning him as a spectacle, subordinate to those who have their freedom (ironically, even the real Chesapeake Ripper, Hannibal Lecter). Will's encephalitic infection is compounded by his unique empathy disorder—which he describes to Jack in the first episode, saying, "My horse is hitched to a post that is closer to Asperger's and autistics than narcissists and sociopaths . . . I can empathize with anybody" (*Hannibal*, Season 1, "Apéritif"). Will's conditions—the infection and the empathy disorder—draw strange reactions from his colleagues, especially Hannibal. While his empathy disorder fascinates them, the delirium caused by the infection leads them to discuss him as though he is dead. Hannibal is guiding Jack and Alana to accept Will's symbolic death, positioning them as unknowing accomplices in his experiment with Will's mental state, eclipsing his own mental instabilities by framing Will for the Chesapeake Ripper's crimes.

We're All Pathological in Our Own Ways

In his book, *The History of Madness*, the French philosopher Michel Foucault offers a description of Hieronymus Bosch's painting, "Cutting the Stone" (alternatively titled "The Extraction of the Stone of Madness," or "The Cure of Folly"). This early Renaissance piece shows a patient, seated in a chair, with a doctor, a monk, and a nun surrounding him. The doctor is cutting into the patient's head, revealing a small flower. What's odd about this painting is the fact that the doctor is wearing a large funnel as a hat and the nun is balancing a textbook on her head. Since the life and works of Hieronymus Bosch were so poorly documented, there is no formal explanation for the event in this painting. Foucault suggests that the strange headwear calls into question the sanity of the doctor and the two witnesses when he says, "Bosch's famous doctor is far more insane than the patient he is attempting to cure, and his false knowledge does nothing more than reveal the worst excesses of a madness immediately apparent to all but himself" (Foucault, p. 25). Sound familiar? Look up the image: can you imagine Will as the patient and Hannibal as Bosch's doctor? Substitute Jack Crawford for the monk and Alana Bloom for the nun, too. Now reread that passage by Foucault. Hannibal's psychiatrist, Dr. Bedelia Du Maurier, is on point when describing Hannibal's concealed psychosis: "I've had to draw a conclusion based on what I glimpse through the stitching of the person suit that you wear. And the conclusion that I've drawn is that you are dangerous" (*Hannibal*, Season 2, "Sakizuke").

Jumping from Foucault's interpretation of Bosch's painting, with the four characters in the roles I've described above, we can look further into the discussion of madness in Foucault's text and throughout the first two seasons of the show. Bosch's doctor may be a charlatan in hindsight, but at the time, was likely a trusted professional. Mesmerized by his poise, his demeanor, and his status, Jack and Alana neglect Will's fears surrounding Hannibal, as Will is marked as sick and unreliable (as diagnosed by Hannibal). Despite the close and bonded relationship that Will and Hannibal have, Will's testament to Hannibal's instability goes unheeded and uninvestigated until it is far too late. Hannibal is far from a fraud as a doctor, but is definitely not as even keeled as he tends to project. Our monk, Jack, looks on eagerly while awaiting a positive outcome from Hannibal's treatment of Will. Alana, our nun, waits idly with her head resting on her hand and a finger at her temple, signaling intrigue and observation—the "professional curiosity" which Alana repeatedly reminds us is the source of her interest in Will. The book balanced on her head represents futility as Bosch's nun seems to hope that the knowledge held in the book will trickle down from its pages and into her head—a futility much like her "professional" interest in Will and her attempts to understand his peculiarities (as if being physically near him would lead to understanding the complexities of his condition). In front of the nun is a yellowed flower, the same variety of blossom coming from the head of the patient. The doctor, the monk, and the nun are all taking part in removing the universal symbol of life from the head of the patient, and Alana—having abandoned her more intimate relationship with Will for Hannibal—retains a small portion of his former self (the nun's yellowed flower). So, we might say, Jack and Alana are accomplices to Hannibal's stripping the life out of Will by taking advantage not only of the state of delirium induced by the swelling in his brain, but also of the dependence and trust established within their homosocial relationship.

They Love and Kill What They Love

Will's fragile and crumbling mental state deeply impacts his romantic involvement with Alana, causing her to see him more as a wounded dependent than as a viable love interest. Her focus shifts to Hannibal who is—at least on the surface—a more emotionally stable and balanced lover. This creates tensions between Hannibal and Will, as their tenuous bond is now further complicated by erotic rivalry. In *Deceit, Desire, and the Novel*, the French philosopher René Girard explains triangular relationships as "Mimetic Desire." This is when A has a desire for Y, and B—noticing A's desire—begins to desire Y as well. Out of their shared desire for Y, A and B become rivals. Applying this model to *Hannibal*, Will is A, Alana is Y, and Hannibal is B. Will and Alana were involved first, but it was cut short due to the Ripper investigation. Hannibal only showed any interest in Alana after her involvement with Will. After Will is released, Alana is upfront with him and says she is with Hannibal now, adding to the already existing rivalry between the two men. Easy enough, right?

Continuing with the path of Mimetic Desire, the rivalry between Hannibal and Will is "Mimetic Violence," or a reciprocal rivalry. This happens when the friction between A and B (Will and Hannibal) is no longer focused on Y (Alana), and they begin to imitate each other's hostilities. For Hannibal and Will, this appears in the response to Will's encephalitic infection. Hannibal could have chosen to seek medical treatment for Will, especially after he suspects an illness with the disfigured clock drawing and the confirmation by Dr. Sutcliffe, but instead ignores the spreading infection to push Will to the point of breaking. After the confirmation of his suspicions, Hannibal murders Dr. Sutcliffe in order to silence him and eliminate any risk of exposing his experiment with Will's damaged mental state. For Girard, this is the point where A and B no longer focus on their shared desire for Y, but rather focus on each other's demise and, for Hannibal and Will, the dissolution of their homosocial bond. Solidifying his attempt at defeat, Hannibal force feeds Will a severed ear while he's unconscious. Will regurgitates the ear and, after it's found to be from Abigail Hobbs, Will is arrested as the Chesapeake Ripper. Hannibal's rival is subdued, and he is fully free to act on his desires for Alana.

Having finally received treatment for his ailment, Will begins to catch onto Hannibal's deceptions, and while he is incarcerated at Baltimore State Hospital, his attempt to murder Hannibal by proxy with the assistance of the hospital orderly, Matthew Brown, signals what Girard calls the "Mimetic Attraction," or the escalation of the rivalry. Matthew abducts Hannibal and hangs him by a noose with a precariously balanced bucket barely reachable at his feet. Jack and Alana ultimately rescue Hannibal, and while he survives the attempted murder, he is deeply affected by Will's reciprocated violence. Recognizing that Will is better utilized as an ally and friend, he frames his colleague and hospital director, Dr. Frederick Chilton, as the Ripper, stripping any shadow of a doubt from Will, freeing him completely from the charges.

Just after Will's release from the asylum, Randall Tier, a former patient of Hannibal's, is enlisted by his former psychiatrist to murder Will using a reinforced bear suit, intended to mimic the impact of being mauled by an actual bear. As Randall attempts to kill Will, the Wendigo appears in place of Randall and his bear suit, and Will beats the Wendigo to death. Coming out of his rage, Will realizes he has actually killed Randall. Acknowledging that they are now even in their attempts to kill each other, Hannibal instructs Will to honor his kill and he creates an articulated bear skeleton, accented with the flesh and face of Randall Tier. As Will examines his work, the eyes come alive and he hears Randall's voice whisper, "This is my becoming. And it is yours" (*Hannibal*, Season 2, "Naka-Choko"). Continuing with Girard's pathway of Mimetic Desire, Will and Hannibal have reached a point where their reciprocated violent acts have become entirely parallel, and there is a "lack of differentiation" between the two men. The homosocial bond that binds them is reinvigorated through their newly shared desires and plans to escape together. This stage is reinforced by the birth of the Willdigo, nearly indistinguishable from the Wendigo, except for the replacement of Hannibal's face with Will's.

Generally, in the stages following the lack of differentiation, there are two outcomes described by Girard: a paroxysm—a sudden and violent attack—or the delegation of someone as a scapegoat to suffer all the consequences on behalf of the group. Mason Verger is Hannibal's scapegoat—a ritual sacrifice. Will believes that Hannibal is able to justify killing Mason as it purges him of his "lesser rudeness" (*Hannibal*, Season 2, "Tome-wan"). Mason has forcibly sterilized his sister (and Will's former lover), Margot, as a way to control her by removing the possibility of producing an heir. Hannibal, seeking retribution, offers Mason powerfully psychoactive and analgesic drugs. When Will comes home to find Mason, sitting in the dark, feeding strips of his face to Will's dogs, Hannibal's plans for Mason's death are interrupted.

Will Graham Is and Will Always Be My Friend

This is where we come full circle to the passage I've quoted at the start of this chapter. The teacup has shattered and it's just about to come together. Since Hannibal has not been able to successfully complete the scapegoating via Mason's death, and realizing he has been entirely betrayed by Will, he's left with the paroxysm as his only exit. With the final episode of the second season, we're left hopeless as nearly all of the starring cast lie bleeding out in Hannibal's home: Jack in the wine cellar, Alana on the front steps, and Will and Abigail in the kitchen, with Will attempting to stanch the flow of blood from the wound in her neck, just as he did when her father slit her throat, while simultaneously attempting to slow the bleeding from his own stomach. Hannibal offered Will the rarest gift he could offer—companionship, mentorship, and friendship—but Will didn't want it.

12

A Little Empathy for Hannibal Is a Dangerous Thing

TIM JONES

Empathy is basically the ability to inhabit, fully and non-judgmentally, the frame of reference and point of view of another person. It's all the rage these days—and not only for FBI profilers like Hannibal's nemesis, Will Graham. Social theorist Jeremy Rifkin argues in *The Empathic Civilization* that, far from the cynical picture we usually get of people growing more insular and selfish as the years go by (like your grandparents would probably moan at you), there's actually been a recent shift in the other direction. Thanks to the increasing number of stories about other people from all across the world that are now only a few clicks of the mouse or taps on the screen away, we're rapidly approaching what Rifkin calls "global peak empathy." Inhabiting the mindset of someone else and imagining what the world feels like from his or her own perspective has never been easier or come more naturally. Go us!

I say "Go us!" because empathy *sounds* awesome. The potential value of increased levels of empathic contact from person to person is made pretty clear by psychologist David Howe in his book, *Empathy: What It Is and Why It Matters*. Once we've established an empathic connection with someone else, this bond has the power to foster "cooperation" and "collaboration" in situations where there might otherwise only be competition or hostility. It also has the power to soothe and heal pain and distress. That pretty much every major approach in counseling and psychotherapy trains its practitioners in the use of empathy as one of its most basic foundations proves Howe's point. No matter whether you're a cognitive behavior therapist or more person-centered, one of the principal things you'd do with your clients as part of your efforts to help them through their distress is show an empathic understanding of their story and their problems.

So if we're reaching a state of "global peak empathy," this can only be a good thing, right? It's pretty timely for Bryan Fuller's reimagining of Thomas Harris's characters in *Hannibal* to show up and give us an answer to this question. But we mightn't like the fact that rather than singing empathy's praises like Howe does in his book, Fuller's show places at its front and center a whacking great big warning about empathy's dangers. When we see the impact that being a brilliant empath has on Will once he's met Hannibal, we might wish that empathy weren't on the rise, but on the decline instead. This is a show that tells us to be as *un*-empathic as possible, for the sake of our very sanity and perhaps even for the safety of society itself. All that this "global peak empathy" might give us is a world of remorseless serial killers like Hannibal!

Empathy: What It Is and Why It's Dangerous

If we take a longer look at what exactly empathy *is*, it should become more obvious why it's so dangerous to form an empathic connection with a guy like Hannibal—a wonderfully suave, charming (even sexy?) culinary genius, with whom you'd love to share a bottle of wine and a night at the opera, but who, underneath this dazzling surface, is a cannibalistic killer. Then we'll see why the show is sounding such a loud warning about a global trend that it'd seem more obvious to be pretty happy about.

What exactly are empaths doing when they form an empathic bond with the person in front of them? Empathy is defined by hugely influential psychotherapist Carl Rogers as the ability "to assume . . . the internal frame of reference of the client, to perceive the world as the client sees it, to perceive the client himself as he is seen by himself, [and] to lay aside all perceptions from the external frame of reference while doing so . . ." (Rogers, p. 29). To empathize with another person, then, is to cast your personal judgments on his or her philosophy and behavior aside, so that you can see these things exactly how he or she sees them him- or herself. And then you must successfully communicate this move to the client, so that he or she *feels* this willingness to achieve a total understanding of exactly where he or she is coming from, in terms not just of thoughts, but of feelings too, including those uncomfortable ones buried pretty far beneath the surface, which might never have seen the light of day outside the therapist's room.

A therapist like Rogers would reach out like this several times each day, demonstrating to every one of his clients a willingness to enter their worlds and join with them in a moment of pure, human contact. Imagine yourself in the shoes of someone like *Hannibal*'s FBI profiler Jack Crawford, whose wife Phyllis is in the final stages of terminal lung cancer. He'd experience the power of someone showing him that they understand exactly how he's feeling about the situation, that they see and appreciate all the thoughts and emotions spiraling through Jack's head, whatever they might be—whether they include guilt about being unable to do anything to protect his wife from the disease; or fear of the impending bereavement and a life spent without her; or, perhaps, a sense of being trapped by a situation beyond his control and wishing for *any* release possible, even if the only way this release can happen is the illness getting on with it and running its course. Not a nice thing to be thinking, but what he may well *be* thinking nonetheless.

In the first cases, just knowing that another person is taking the time to acknowledge what a guy like Jack is going through can kick-start a healing process all by itself. When we feel we're worth being encountered in this deeply meaningful way, all sorts of resources for coping that we didn't know existed start coming to the surface. In the latter, darker instance, this isn't exactly a feeling that someone like Jack would feel comfortable owning up to at all, or even safe to acknowledge fully to himself. He might have to keep it pretty deeply buried for the sake of his very sanity. But if the counselor can sense that this *is* what's happening within Jack, and communicate this to Jack himself from a neutral, non-judgmental perspective, then Jack might feel safer owning up to these feelings and putting them out in the open. He can then explore them for himself with the therapist's support and work through them in a healthy way, rather than bottling them up.

The crucial idea when empathizing with darker thoughts like the example given above is remaining non-judgmental. The empathizer steps out of any feelings he or she might hold about the client's situation, and inhabits, in as pure a sense as possible, the client's own outlook on the situation. The empathizer might be absolutely horrified that someone might secretly wish that a loved one's terminal illness be over and done with. He or she might regard this as the height of betrayal. But while empathizing, this becomes irrelevant. What matters is reconstructing, living and communicating a sense of what the client is going through, completely unfiltered through the empathizer's own judgments or moral position.

And this is where *Hannibal* sees the big fat danger signs. You might *need* to keep your own moral position intact if you don't want some particularly unpleasant mindsets, like Hannibal's, to completely erase your own.

Where There's a Will

While empathy is probably most commonly used in therapeutic encounters like the above, in the case of FBI profilers like Will, it's being put to a different purpose. A therapist would use empathic contact to help people right in front of him or her; *Will* uses it to help people from a distance by catching bad guys like Hannibal who'd seek to do them harm. If he can fully inhabit their frame of reference, and see the world exactly how they see it themselves, then he can second-guess their motivations, predict their next move, and stop them in their tracks.

The opening sequence of *Hannibal*'s pilot episode dramatizes pretty beautifully how this works. We first meet Will looking on at a house full of dead bodies, with blood splattered casually across the walls. He's staring at the camera, looking slightly lost, and we're left to think for a moment that this might be because he's traumatized by what he's seeing. But instead his vacant gaze is because his own perspective on the scene is literally slipping away from him. And then he seems to experience a moment of perfect calm as he gives himself up to this process and his own point-of-view disappears entirely. He's then Will Graham no longer, and is literally inhabiting the viewpoint of the killer looking on at his handiwork. When Will says of the male homeowner, "He will die watching me take what is his away from him" (*Hannibal*, Season 1, "Apéritif"), he's effectively stepped back in time to the moment of the act itself and reached a moment of perfect empathic contact with Garret Jacob Hobbs, the killer he's hunting. Will's living out the thought-processes and philosophy of Hobbs as Hobbs would experience them for himself, unmediated by any separate judgments that Will might make, were he to consider them from his own point of view.

Very useful to the FBI. But surely very scary for Will. At least he's not stuck in this horrible mindset permanently. When we see him later in the episode, he's Will again, speaking as Will speaks, and thinking how Will thinks. Like any empath should be, whether a counselor or a profiler, Will is able to leave the philosophy of the killer behind once the role is no longer necessary or appropriate. This ability to withdraw back to our own moral positions and emotions is an absolutely key ingredient to any empathic encounter.

There's something about Hannibal himself, though, that derails this process and leaves Will's own moral center slipping away beyond his reach. And this, the show suggests, is why empathy is pretty dangerous. You might be horrified at what empathizing with a cannibalistic serial killer like Hannibal makes you feel and accept as reasonable, only to retreat back towards your own frame of reference on Hannibal's activities and find that it's no longer there. Episode Three of *Hannibal*'s first season, "Potage," sees Will ask if you can "catch somebody's crazy." It might not be an answer that we want to hear, particularly in a world approaching "global peak empathy" like Rifkin thinks, but the show basically answers "yes, you can!" And forming an empathic bond with someone as charmingly dangerous as Hannibal is the primary means of infection.

There's Something about Hannibal

To empathize with Hannibal is to understand as an indisputable fact, just as he does, that weak or hypocritical people are ripe for hunting and ritualized degradation, and that human meat is no less deserving of being kept from our plates than the animal meat that many of us consume pretty regularly. And that following this philosophy and acting it out in the real world isn't wrong at all, and not just right either, but *beautiful*.[1]

Fuller's show works pretty hard to demonstrate to its viewers what Will's going through when he struggles to retrieve his own perspective from this philosophy of Hannibal's. We see for ourselves exactly how beautiful some pretty disgusting things can look, if only they're framed the right way. If you think about it for a moment, there's nothing at all pleasant about being buried alive in the woods and transformed into an incubation system for rare fungi, like the victims in the show's second episode, "Amuse-Bouche." But (and I hope this isn't just my own reaction to the episode!) look at how director Michael Rymer manages to make this fate look almost poetically beautiful. In the same episode where Will is first being encouraged by Hannibal to see the wonderful side of his desire to kill Hobbs in the pilot, we're placed directly alongside him by being shown how beautiful serial killing can look for ourselves.

What Hannibal is doing to Will, the show is doing to us. And if we're a bit creeped out by this because we keep a healthy sense of the horror that remains so close to the beauty, then we can well imagine how Will feels whenever his own perspective on murder flickers back into life against the mindset Hannibal is leading him towards. We at least get a bit of a respite every time there's an act break, or we can turn the show off once we've finished marathoning a few episodes, with the box sets or online. Unlike poor old Will.

The best illustration of exactly why Hannibal's perspective is so hard to escape from is probably the closing sequence of Episode 7 of the first season, "Sorbet." Again, note how beautiful it all looks: how proud Hannibal is of the meal he's putting together in the kitchen and then placing before his guests; how much care he takes over pouring and checking the wine and cutting up the . . . whatever it is he's cutting up; how sumptuously the long tracking shot over the dinner table showcases the final result of all this painstaking preparation. His world, and the steps he's taken to bring it into being, looks truly . . . delicious. It's quite the effort to remember what's actually underlying all the luxury spread before us.

---

[1] For a discussion of Hannibal Lecter as an aesthete that ranges beyond the bounds of the television series, see Chapter 13 of this volume.—Ed.

Watch, too, the knowing way in which Hannibal warns his guests that "nothing here is vegetarian." *They* then laugh because the very notion of him needing to give such a warning to a room full of rapacious carnivores, who wouldn't entertain the thought of giving up the luxury of meat-eating, not even for a moment, is indeed laughable. *He* takes on the slight hint of a smirk we see in the episode's closing shot, not because his joke is funny on the same level that his guests recognize, but because of the hypocrisy beneath their laughter, which they're unaware of. If they knew what they were really eating, all the trappings of high-society surrounding them would collapse into horror, and rather than laughing, they'd end up in quick need of the smelling salts. While to Hannibal, eating animal and eating human are basically the same thing.

And if we laugh ourselves, we're presumably not laughing for the reasons his guests are laughing, but because we're delighting in the hypocrisy that Hannibal is drawing out from beneath high-society's fragile veneer of civility. We're encouraged to appreciate the joke on Hannibal's level, not theirs. And it's a good one.[2] He's right to make the point. There's something savage in the guests' delight for meat, and if this savagery were put before them in a way that would make it recognizable for them, they'd be completely unable to stomach it. How pathetic of them! It's enough to make you relish the thought of finding the nearest carnivore, tricking them into eating an acquaintance and then laughing at them when they say how much they're enjoying the lovely meal you've prepared!

Oops. But look how easy it is to be drawn into Hannibal's worldview. His closing look towards the camera and his raising of his glass, not just to his guests but to us as well, is practically an invitation to share this position of judgment with him and against his guests. For just a moment, we're again in exactly the same place as Will. It's lucky for us that this is right where the episode ends and we can snap back to reality.

But until this cut to black, we've been seduced by the acting, the direction, and the dialogue into taking on Hannibal's point of view, just like an empath would do more willingly as part of his or her daily work. And the scene shows perfectly that

---

[2] For a deeper analysis of Hannibal Lecter's sense of humor—including this sort of joke, and others—see Chapter 14 of this volume.—Ed.

Hannibal's philosophy is so hard to disengage from because it's just so damn clever, so suave, so delightful. The most horrible things are framed so effortlessly as the very height of sophistication. Who wouldn't want to be as smooth as Hannibal is when he stands in triumph at the head of the dinner table, staring down at the stupid, uncomprehending guests whose utter ignorance means that they deserve everything that happens to them?

By the end of Season 2, Will appears to have pulled himself back from a permanent alignment with Hannibal, but this isn't without a huge amount of personal trauma on the way. Perhaps it's only possible because Will's someone who's recognized as a gifted empath and so has probably had lots of training on how to pull back from getting too close. Laypeople like us wouldn't have a chance if our encounters with Hannibal weren't confined to bite-sized forty-two minute tasters.

So Tell Me Hannibal, How Does That Make You Feel?

But like I said before, Will isn't trying to use empathy in order to help Hannibal, like a counselor or psychotherapist traditionally would, but to catch serial killers, without even realizing at first that his new friend is one of their number. A way of redeeming empathy from the show's scary portrayal of its dangers comes from imagining how it might work if a truly empathic encounter with Hannibal happened in a context more therapeutic than police-procedural, like in the example I gave using Jack earlier.

This isn't necessarily any safer for the empath. After all, Hannibal's psychotherapist, Dr. Du Maurier, is a bit crazy too. She might have had a screw loose to begin with, but it's more likely that she's just a little bit further along the same path Will was going down before the Season 2 finale, with an empathic connection with Hannibal (in this case during a therapy session) leaving her unable to retrieve her own perspective from his perverse, yet seductively beautiful, way of seeing the world.

But empathy still deserves an attempt to show what it could really do for a person like Hannibal, if used by a particularly skilled counselor who could avoid the fates of Will or Dr. Du Maurier. At its height, or what therapists Dave Mearns and

Brian Thorne call Level 3 Empathy, it has the ability to "show an understanding of the client beyond the level of the client's present expression" (Mearns and Thorne, p. 59). This level of work between therapist and client can even reveal underlying feelings and emotions "quite opposite" to the thoughts and behaviors manifesting "on the surface." And it's at this deepest level that empathy could become most therapeutically useful for Hannibal.

Imagine, for a moment, one such possible therapeutic encounter:

> **Therapist [*let's call him Tim, just because*]:** You've been talking a lot about the contempt you feel towards people weaker than yourself . . . About how they deserve what you do to them . . . I'm not sure if you're aware of this or not, Hannibal, but when you're bringing up these things, I'm getting the sense that there's something else there too . . . Like you're fidgeting in the chair a lot. And you don't seem to be able to make eye contact with me.
>
> **Hannibal:** [*Long awkward silence*]
>
> **Tim:** I wonder if *you've* ever felt weak or helpless, like the people you've been talking about?
>
> **Hannibal:** [*In a tone of spontaneous dramatic breakdown*] Yes! I was only eleven! My family was killed by the Nazis! I watched helplessly as they abused my sister! I couldn't do anything!
>
> **Tim:** I'm hearing a real sense of powerlessness here. You saw all these horrible things happen and there was absolutely nothing you could do to stop them.
>
> **Hannibal:** [*sobbing in an operatic fashion*]
>
> **Tim:** You don't just sound sad. You sound disgusted with yourself. With how weak you were back then.
>
> **Hannibal:** Too damn right! I was pathetic! Letting that happen to my own family!
>
> **Tim:** You were pathetic. Just like the people you've been killing recently.
>
> **Hannibal:** Yes. That's exactly it. I guess . . . I guess I'm actually striking out at that part of me that couldn't do anything to help.

Tim: That's really brave of you, Hannibal. All this time you've been attacking the helpless little boy who couldn't do anything to save his family . . . You're all sorted now. That'll be $150 please.

Hannibal: You're brilliant. If you have any cards, I'll hand them out to all my guests at my next dinner party. Where I shan't be serving person anymore, I promise.

Getting someone like Hannibal to this point would take even the most brilliant therapist way, way longer than a ten-minute section of an individual session. It could take years of exploration to even broach that sort of area—along with a really bold therapist who has the courage to stay with Hannibal's frame of reference this whole time, rather than breaking the empathic connection by chipping in with his or her own judgment on either the situation itself, or Hannibal's understanding of it.

But this is the kind of self-knowing that empathy can foster. If Hannibal felt the genuine empathic support of his therapist, he might feel safe enough to examine his actions to an extent he's never done before, and eventually discover deeply rooted causes of his present behavior that he wasn't even aware of himself. Causes that could stem from the events given in *Hannibal Rising*, where a totally helpless and weak young Hannibal had to watch impotently as his family was killed and their home destroyed. In the right therapeutic environment, Hannibal might discover that the wish to ritually degrade anyone he meets who appears weak or helpless is actually the wish to hurt the little boy whose powerlessness led to the deaths of his beloved family. He'd see that his anger towards people in the present day is actually his anger towards the young Hannibal that they remind him of.

The true value of empathy should now be a bit more obvious than NBC's show makes it appear. Imagine where an empathically-guided exploration of these discoveries could take Hannibal in future sessions. He could examine his past from an adult perspective and realize that what happened to his family was never his fault at all, but only ever that of the monsters who actually did all the bad stuff. His anger towards his own helplessness could then fade in favor of a kind sympathy. And he'd no longer need to displace his self-hatred onto people he meets in the present.

One less serial killer for us to worry about when we're heading home at night!

So there are two possible versions of Rifkin's world of "global peak empathy," one much more desirable than the other. Either we'll follow Will's path and go a bit mad when a philosophy as terrible as Hannibal's appears so irresistibly attractive that, once we've forged an empathic connection with him, our own sense of right and wrong is almost impossible to reclaim. *Or* people with pasts like Hannibal's can be helped to work through their baggage of thoughts and feelings in a way that stops them having to be channeled into unhelpful behaviors like becoming a serial killer.

Given what we see happen to Will in the show, it would be a particularly brave empath who risks guiding Hannibal on this journey of discovery! And given the wider risks for society as a whole, if we didn't manage to pull ourselves back, and Hannibal's philosophy spreads from one person to the next, it might be safer for all of us just to stay away instead, no matter how dangerous he'll continue to be for the hapless folk who end up with an invitation to dinner . . .

So it's best for both of us if I end this chapter by saying to you exactly what Jack says to Will in "Tome-wan," the penultimate episode of Season 2: "Don't let empathy confuse what you want with what Lecter wants." If you happen to see him the next time you're out and about, you should probably walk on by, however nice your intentions. *You* might want to help him out, but *he'd* want to carry on killing people and eating them. And I'm guessing you'd rather not become so enamored of his philosophy during your empathic contact with him that you end up going even further than Will and embracing the role of cannibalistic serial killer for yourself!

V.

It's Beautiful in Its Own Way, Giving Voice to the Unmentionable

13
An Aesthete *par Excellence*

Jason Holt

We see him from behind, his hair slicked back toward us, the simplicity of a white t-shirt that seems somehow elegant despite the setting. The left hand splays open a book of poetry for eyes that savor it at leisure. Not much later, the book lies on a table, in the same incongruous setting, with notes of piano in the air, Bach's "Goldberg Variations" coming from a tape recorder—the table a spread of drawings lovingly detailed from an eidetic memory and keen imagination by a surgically skilled hand. This is a pure aesthetic moment, yet also an overture, we know already, to a very different kind of scene.

This aesthetic moment belongs to Dr. Hannibal Lecter in *The Silence of the Lambs*, right before he butchers a pair of guards, cutting the face off one for an impromptu mask, stylizing the corpses in effecting his unlikely escape from the cell where the Memphis police have temporarily caged him. The soundtrack crescendos as Dr. Lecter, with a nightstick in tempo with the music, rains blow after blow on one of the guards—on us, in fact—seen from the guard's perspective in an inspired use of the subjective cam.

One may be tempted to interpret these scenes, the aesthetic moment and the butchery, as discontinuous, to think of the aesthetic moment as fake, a kind of camouflage used by Lecter to lull his captors into a false sense of only mild insecurity. Even the stylized guard's corpse strung up on the cage may seem but a diversion to draw attention from the literally face-masked Lecter posing supine as the other guard. But although these strategic benefits are undeniable, it makes more sense to interpret the scenes as continuous. Lecter's aesthetic appreciation is genuine, not disingenuous. The manner of stylization of the cage-pinned corpse clearly mattered to the one who posed it. Perhaps most importantly, it is apparently the same music, more fully orchestrated, that crescendos, a metronome for the nightstick blows, as if the nightstick is Lecter's gruesome conductor's baton. We also know from earlier that the butchery will have left Lecter's heartbeat unaccountably, inhumanly, chillingly calm and steady. Afterwards, the blood-spattered carnage everywhere, the piano reasserts itself as if under the light touch of Lecter's rhythmically gliding hand.

What gives this progression of scenes continuity is the simple fact that Hannibal Lecter, enigmatic monster that he is, is an *aesthete*, one who prizes the rewards, the pleasures, afforded by art and beauty: art, in its various styles, whatever it depicts—and whatever its raw materials; beauty, in its different forms, wherever it might be found, in however unlikely a place. For the aesthete, such pleasures don't just matter, they matter *a lot*, as they do for Lecter, who isn't just an aesthete but an aesthete *par excellence*. Such aestheticism is in fact the very key to unlocking the mystery of his character, elaborated as it is into such an alien, such a grotesque extreme that few if any could wish for the strength of stomach to follow.

This perspective makes an implicit assumption about the relative importance of various depictions of Dr. Lecter. Setting aside the seminal novels by Thomas Harris, I take Sir Anthony Hopkins's portrayal to be canonical, prominently though not exclusively in Jonathan Demme's 1991 masterpiece *The Silence of the Lambs*. This makes sense given the undisputed pop cultural preeminence of Hopkins's Lecter and Demme's *Silence*. Sir Anthony, alongside his significant body of film work, is notably also a composer and painter, a true artistic polymath; no wonder his portrayal of Lecter throws into sharp relief the doctor's aestheticism. That said, I'll always have a soft spot for Brian Cox's inaugural movie portrayal in *Manhunter*, which deemphasizes, at least by comparison, the doctor's aestheticism. The aesthetic is more evident in the Gaspard Ulliel effort in *Hannibal Rising*, its culinary and gastronomic side full-blown in *Hannibal*, both Hopkins's film and Mads Mikkelsen's TV incarnations.

Discriminating Taste

For aesthetes, art and beauty occupy a more prominent pl[ace] in their value system than for most other people. Aesthet[ic] value, the value of art and beauty, can be understood in con[-] trast to other sorts of value, in particular intellectual and moral values. Consider as the ultimate trio of values the *good*, the *true*, and the *beautiful*, respectively the realms of moral, intellectual, and aesthetic value. Forget the problematic equations of the poet Keats (truth = beauty) and philosopher Plato (the good = the true = the beautiful), and appreciate that, in their ordinary senses, these terms are representative of entirely distinct values. In simple terms, being a good person has nothing to do with being smart or attractive, just as being smart has nothing to do with being attractive (which philosophers have lamented since Socrates) or good, just as possessing beauty has nothing to do with being a good or intelligent person. As an intellectual aesthete, Dr. Lecter clearly prizes two of these values very highly, leaving the other, we know which, an irrelevant castoff. A thing will have aesthetic value because of its power to provoke aesthetic experience, and for aesthetes such experiences are among life's greatest pleasures.

What makes an experience an *aesthetic* experience? It's a particular pleasure associated with the appreciation of art and beauty. Whether you're enjoying a painting of the sunset or the actual sunset, both enjoyments may count as aesthetic. You like looking at them, how you feel in, and reflect on, the moment of looking. Think of how you feel when you're listening to your favorite song, or watching a beloved movie. The pleasures, the thoughts and feelings that come in actively appreciating these works of art, that's what gives the experience an aesthetic quality. This is partly a kind of detachment. Think of Lecter's steady pulse when butchering his victims, or the way you respond to a nude study differently than to porn. At the same time, there's a kind of intensity of response in appreciating art, a keenness of attention, more focused and significant than in most ordinary experiences. What makes such "detached engagement" so rewarding, not just to aesthetes, is that it resolves internal conflicts, with intellectual and emotional responses in harmonious balance, in sharp contrast to everyday life.

...reciation of art, or anything really, can be
... in different ways. Lecter, for instance,
...owledge of art history, not to mention a
...appreciation of human anatomy, which,
...is fine drawing abilities, perhaps surprisingly
...ardo da Vinci. Seriously, if you look at da Vinci's
...al drawings, I challenge you not to see just a little bit
...er there! But the doctor also has other types of knowl-
...e and know-how relevant to his aestheticism. These include
... surgeon-grade precision with a scalpel, which mirrors the
rendering precision of his sketch pencil, along with chef-worthy
culinary chops—where taste meets taste. Taste in either sense
also depends on the taster's level of perceptual sophistication,
on how well they discriminate the relevant properties of what
they're judging: connoisseurship, in essence. Think of Lecter's
olfactory prowess, and his particular penchant for an exotic
sort of acquaintance with mundane humanity. Here looms a
potential feedback loop: aesthetic pleasure motivates improving its underlying knowledge, skill, and discrimination, which
in turn enhances further pleasure.

One thing that hasn't been mentioned yet but must be is the
affinity between art and play. The psychopath's attitude toward
their victims is often very much cat to mouse, or player to play-
thing. Play in its purer forms involves the freedom, responsive-
ness, and creativity of art, with a similar type of enjoyment. We
know what fun Lecter has with anagrams and other wordplay,
the half hints of coded puzzles—"If one does what God does
enough times, one will become as God is"—with reluctant play-
mates Graham and Starling, who are unwilling, unlike Lecter, to
treat it as a game. In fact, Lecter doesn't exactly view Graham or
Starling as mice so much as potential cats, as far as the game is
concerned. He even handicaps himself, suggesting possible
moves to *Manhunter*'s Graham: "You haven't threatened to take
away my books yet"; to *Silence*'s Starling: "No, no, no, you were
doing fine. You'd been courteous and receptive to courtesy, you
had established trust with the embarrassing truth about Miggs,
and now this ham-handed segue into your questionnaire? Tut-
tut-tut, it won't do." This, of course, is just an entrée into what
Lecter really wants to play: a game of quid pro quo.

Lecter's attitude toward serial killing, half playful, half serious, reflects his aestheticism, which cuts a very wide swath in

being able to take aesthetic pleasure from things that most of us would find utterly repulsive. Many people prefer even their aesthetic encounters to be with rather lighter fare. Many moviegoers would opt for the lightness of a romantic comedy over the darkness of a Hannibal Lecter film. Such preferences are fine, of course, but art history is chock-full of aesthetically powerful works depicting not just dark but horrific things: Goya's disturbing painting of Saturn cannibalizing his son, for instance. As far as *depictions* go, of course, most of us understand aesthetic pleasure taken in a Goya painting or Demme film depicting cannibalism. We stop, however, at the divide between fiction and reality. *But Lecter doesn't stop.* He's able to derive aesthetic pleasure from, not just the depiction, but also the *reality* of such horror. Nor is it horror that matters to him, otherwise he wouldn't be so harsh a critic of other serial killers, or so technical in preparing a dish. Lecter is above all *discriminating*. He'd reject a Nazi aestheticism, cigarette cases and lampshades made from human skin, not as extreme evil—as we would—but as extreme bad taste. Such a hate-based aesthetic would strike him as utterly stupid. Lecter only really hates people who've been evil to him—or rude.

Blindness That Enhances

Being blind is something most people don't have much experience with, especially permanent blindness. We do, however, like Clarice Starling in Buffalo Bill's basement toward the end of *Silence*, have some sense of what it's like to have situational blindness, as nicely conveyed by Demme's use of the subjective cam giving us the killer's night-vision-goggled perspective on Starling's fumbling in the dark. Most of us think, however, and it is almost clichéd to say so, that blind people sometimes find that their condition has an upside, that the blindness is associated with, and the basis of, enhanced abilities in other areas. For instance, many blind people have improved spatial memory, and more sensitive nonvisual sensory perception: improved hearing, more sensitive touch. From a neuroscientific viewpoint, the explanation of this phenomenon is pretty straightforward, in that lacking visual input, some of the brain is essentially freed up and can contribute to other sorts of processing. Remember Reba McClane, Dolarhyde's coworker in

Manhunter, running her fingers through the sedated tiger's fur, feeling its breath on her forearm, listening to its heartbeat?

Consider an analogy I would like to suggest between literal blindness and the metaphor of a psychopath being *morally* blind. A psychopath fails to see the moral dimensions of what they do and the moral status of other people, or they understand morality but fail to see the point of it. Lecter's psychopathy is blended with an intelligence too brilliant to be lacking an understanding of moral issues. Rather, his personal code of values and integrity aside, he just doesn't care. I'm thinking it's still appropriate to call this a kind of moral blindness, even though it's less a matter of not detecting the morally relevant features of a situation—for instance, that a potential victim is a *person*—and more a matter of ignoring these features, of being unmoved by them where the rest of us, in different degrees, would be so moved.

One of the fascinating aspects of Lecter's character is that it shines a spotlight on values and abilities that he has but that are not intermixed, unlike most of us, with muddying shades of morality: the evil genius, the amoral aesthete. The psychopath's moral deficit in this way shows such qualities as they do possess—in Dr. Lecter's case, a brilliant intelligence and sophisticated aesthetic sensibility—in starker, purer outline, in a way allowing us to appreciate these qualities and the beauty and significance of such abilities for what they are in themselves. For this reason Lecter is a kind of abstraction, from morality, of intelligence and aestheticism. Without the pure psychopathy we would have a more complicated, more realistic representation of a sophisticated and aesthetically sensitive intelligence. By being what he is, Lecter helps us appreciate just how important, and often unnoticed, the aesthetic is in our lives, from enjoying popular artworks like Hannibal Lecter films to savoring everyday rituals like your morning cup of coffee. With more or less sensuality, more or less aestheticism, we may relish eating a well-prepared liver—though we'd be pickier than Lecter, and less picky too, about what kind of liver.

Unlike Dr. Lecter, most of us are comparatively blind to the importance of the aesthetic in life. But of course, Lecter is blind to our moral concerns. Perhaps, as with a literal blindness that enhances other senses, it is precisely Lecter's moral blindness that enhances his powers of aesthetic discrimination, along perhaps with his astonishing olfactory sensitivity and gustatory breadth. We know he can identify perfumes and colognes on habitual wearers—Graham's Old Spice, Starling's L'Air du Temps—and this surely informs his sensitive palate. Smell, of course, is a primitive sense, an evolutionarily old, beastly sense, and this is retained, regardless of how sophisticated, how intellectualized it is, in Lecter's aesthetic sensibility. He seems more able to appreciate art than most of us, even those with some claim to the title aesthete. Just consider his stint as an art scholar in *Hannibal*. It may be—though let's hope not!—that having a Lecter-like aesthetic sophistication depends on a Lecter-like psyche.

The ACME Question

Part of what makes Hannibal Lecter a compelling, even archetypal, character is that we can't quite figure him out. He can figure out what makes *us* tick—those in his various peer groups: serial killers, psychiatrists, profilers—but we can't, it seems, figure out what makes *him* tick, whatever we learn of his formative years in *Hannibal Rising*. He's an enigma. Or as Will(iam Petersen's) Graham puts it in *Manhunter*, when asked what was diagnosed as wrong with Lecter, "Psychologists call him a psychopath. They don't know what else to call him." But he's also, even among other psychopathic killers, a most unusual case, which we see with crystal clarity when we're introduced to him in *Silence*, last cell on the left. He's a completely different beast from the other criminally insane inmates: "They don't have a name for what he is." Nor is this just a matter of education, intelligence, or decorum. Lecter defies analysis. He's too smart, too unusual, for conventional understanding and techniques: "He's much too sophisticated for the standard tests" (Demme, *Silence*). As *Manhunter*'s Graham puts it, "We tried sodium amytal on him three years ago to find where he buried a Princeton student; he gave 'em a recipe for potato chip dip." As serial killers go, Lecter is clearly a cut above.

Now I'm not suggesting that we can necessarily fully plumb Dr. Lecter's psyche, not at all. Although we might, but perhaps never should, resolve the enigma he presents, it may prove insightful to seek at least a partial account of his character by considering what I'm calling here *the ACME question*.

Specifically, if there is some hypothesis we can make about Lecter that can help explain different, seemingly incongruous, but essential aspects of his personality, that fact will give us good reason to accept that hypothesis: a curve that best fits a set of data points will be justified for that reason. This principle of "inference to the best explanation" is familiar both in philosophy and in science, and applies even in the case of fictional entities like Hannibal Lecter. The ACME question concerns and comprises four of these essential and ill-fitting aspects of Dr. Lecter's personality: 'A' for art, 'C' for cannibalism, 'M' for murder, 'E' for etiquette—each of which is vitally important to Lecter, though the set seems ill-matched. Why would someone who values brutal murder care about fine art? How could a cannibal's decorum give Emily Post a run for her money? Is there anything about Lecter that integrates and explains this apparently ragtag collection of tendencies?

Of course: the aesthetic. It's Lecter's aesthetic sensibility that underlies and unifies these different aspects of his concern and personality, at once ultra-civilized and ultra-savage. Lecter's appreciation for art isn't at all motivated by financial investment or cocktail-party snobbery. His art-scholar expertise rather expresses and facilitates his appreciation of works of art *as* works of art: for what they represent, what they express, for the skill and style with which they're created, and for the aesthetic pleasure that comes from interpreting and creating them. His cannibalism is no less refined. He's a gourmet, after all, a cannibal gourmet—both as a chef, where he exhibits a subtle creativity adapting Cordon Bleu techniques to preparing human tissue, and as an epicure, where he demonstrates an appreciative and discerning palate. Though he sometimes, in the form of attack, tears into live unprepared flesh with his teeth, this is not the aesthetic Lecter aspires to and often achieves. He prefers a slow burn. Lecter's attitude toward serial murder is similar, as he's quite at home adopting the posture of both artist and critic. As an artist he creates difficult, often symbolically rich tableaux using his victims as raw material. As a critic he often demeans the imperfect efforts—as psychologically shallow, forensically clumsy, interpretively trite—of other serial killers.

But how does Dr. Lecter's odd obsession with etiquette fit in here? His first murder, we see in *Hannibal Rising*, is spurred by the victim's bad behavior toward Lecter's aunt: menacing but essentially disrespectful. In *Silence*, after his escape, Starling is convinced that Lecter won't come after her because "he would consider that rude." In general—that is, when he's not killing or eating anyone—except for occasional bouts of provocative rudeness, he's scrupulously polite and decorous. Those like Graham and Starling who respect him, in both senses, likewise refer to him, title intact, as "*Dr.* Lecter." To them, and up to a point, Lecter responds in kind. If we think of etiquette as a set of arbitrary conventions which are essential to culture, part of the order that civilization imposes on nature, then we can see how someone like Lecter who's fastidious about etiquette may be that way because in a world of chaos such politesse can provide deep aesthetic satisfaction. "Discourtesy," says Lecter, "is unspeakably ugly to me"—an aesthetic complaint (Demme, *Silence*).

In short, although this doesn't and isn't meant to dispel completely the enigma that is Dr. Hannibal Lecter, what unifies his value system, what integrates his personality, what makes him the archetype he is, is precisely the aesthetic. Yet what makes sense of Lecter makes sense of us, the audience, as well, and what we—through the horror—keep coming back for.

14
A Funny Thing Happened on the Way to the Dinner Party

Joseph Westfall

Two cannibals are eating a clown.
One says to the other, "Does this taste funny to you?"

Hannibal Lecter is a funny guy.

To be sure, generally speaking, his sense of humor is a tad bit more refined than average. Some of his jokes and witticisms might go over all those other poor dullards' heads. Sometimes, his humorous comments are only funny if you know certain things about Dr. Lecter, things that, at least until the time of his incarceration, he seemed quite interested in keeping private—or, at least, known only to a special few. But even if we do not always understand his humor, even if the jokes we do get seem to us sometimes more cruel than funny, we would be remiss in our accounting of the good doctor were we not to include "witty" among his essential characteristics: he is intelligent, yes, a genius, even; he is clever, and manipulative, persuasive in the extreme; he is gifted, a talented artist and composer and scholar and psychiatrist *and chef*. While there might be some reasonable debate about whether he's evil or a psychopath, we can all agree that he is both a serial killer and a cannibal. As Paul Lewis notes, "Dr. Lecter draws on his impressive intellect and vast store of knowledge in both committing crimes of great brutality and in coming up with witty accounts of them" (Lewis, pp. 34–35). In short, whatever else he might be, Hannibal Lecter is a funny guy.

First Principles

What makes something funny? Although there are many competing philosophies of humor, the most widespread explanation is actually one of the simplest: something is funny when it unites within itself a contradiction between two incommensurable elements—and when, generally speaking, we experience that contradiction as amusing (rather than, say, as terrifying or inappropriate or incomprehensible). Thus, the Keystone Cops unite the orderliness presumed of police work with the production of chaos to humorous effect; Charlie Chaplin's most famous character, the Little Tramp, unites the customs and mannerisms of bourgeois society with extreme poverty; and so on. In contemporary humor, Will Ferrell has virtually made a career of unifying the contradiction of self-importance and idiocy in his characters—the most recent incarnation of the classically comedic character, the buffoon—in a way that keeps us laughing, time and time again.

This general answer to the question, "What makes something funny?" is often called "the incongruity theory of humor," and one of its most striking features, as the philosopher Noël Carroll has pointed out, is that it shows us that humor has a structure very similar to that of horror. Although "at first glance, horror and humor seem like opposite mental states," Carroll points out that, just as with a funny joke which unites incongruous elements to form a self-contradictory whole, so we can see that horror—especially in its most common literary and cinematic form, the monster—similarly unites incongruous elements to form a self-contradictory whole (Carroll, "Enjoying Horror Fictions," p. 145). An undead monster like Dracula (or Frankenstein, or the mummy, or the zombies of *The Walking Dead*) is the self-contradictory unity of life and death; on the other hand, a more bestial monster—perhaps paradigmatically, the werewolf—is the incongruous unity of human and animal.

Carroll makes an effort to extend his analysis of the monster into discussions of humor—he uses, frighteningly enough, the example of the clown (especially as used by Stephen King in *It*)—but clowns seem to be *either* horrifying *or* amusing, maybe even alternating between the two, but never both at the same time. (Pennywise does not seem capable of eliciting laughter, nor Bozo genuine horror.) In any case, thinking about clowns doesn't seem terribly useful in coming to understand the wit of Hannibal Lecter: Dr. Lecter is no clown. In addition, Carroll tries to explain how he might include someone like Dr. Lecter in his definition of monsters (he spells it "Lector," and calls such characters—like Norman Bates from *Psycho*—"psychotics," although Thomas Harris seems to have made every effort to resist identifying Lecter straightforwardly or simply as a psychopath; Carroll, "Enjoying Horror and Humor," p. 148).[1] But again, insofar as we find Dr. Lecter frightening, Carroll's theory doesn't explain how we might also—*at the same time*—find him funny.

Carroll thinks that we cannot find the same things amusing and frightening, precisely because, on his understanding of horror, we must feel like the monster (or psychopath) is dangerous—and, on his understanding of humor, we must feel safe from such dangers in order to find them amusing. Hannibal Lecter, however, is simultaneously humorous and frightening, not only both dangerous and amusing, but amusingly dangerous (and dangerously amusing?). His humor *gains* from the horror he inspires, and he is *more* frightening given his capacity for disarming us (and his "friends" and victims) with his wit and charm. Thus, if we're going to understand what makes Dr. Lecter such a humorous fellow, we're going to have to go beyond the dominant view among philosophers—and delve a little more deeply into Hannibal Lecter's humor itself.

Sometimes, Lecter uses mild jokes and witty observations to gain the trust of his companions, or in the manner of a polite and engaging host. He is, as we Fannibals know, a most charming man. But I think it's safe to say that charm is not a central component of Dr. Lecter's sense of humor. Generally, he uses charm in more direct ways: the gift of the Scarlatti score (or the Dante sonnet, in the film version) to Signora Pazzi in *Hannibal*; the sympathetic ear he lends Alana Bloom in the television series; the exquisite food with which he makes friendly overtures to nearly every character in that series, as well. Even when he playfully teases Alana or engages Jack Crawford or Will Graham in witty repartee, Hannibal Lecter isn't especially funny. No, Dr. Lecter's humor comes from a darker place.

---

[1] For more on the suitability of Carroll's notion of the monster to considerations of Hannibal Lecter, see Chapter 17 of this volume.—Ed.

Much of the time, when Lecter is funny he is mocking somebody or something, and although we are amused by his mockery, we don't find it particularly witty or charming. This is the predominant type of humor Lecter uses in the novels of Thomas Harris, as well as their film adaptations. In addition to mockery, however, there are two others. When under duress—when captured by the Sardinians in Mason Verger's employ in *Hannibal* (in the novel, the film, and the television series), for example—Lecter often makes light of his tormentors and captors, or his situation. And then, on occasion, Lecter tells jokes or makes wry comments that are really only funny to the movie or TV audience—not the people around him—or (and there are obviously very few of these) other characters who are aware of the true nature of Dr. Lecter's culinary proclivities.

We have, thus, three basic types of Hannibal Lecter humor: (1) mockery, (2) expressions of power, and (3) inside jokes. Naturally, some specific instances of Dr. Lecter's humor will fall into more than one category, but it's useful to examine the categories separately, I think, in any case.

I Hope You're Not Too Ugly

The type of humor Hannibal Lecter uses most frequently in the novels is of the mocking sort. After having encouraged and enabled Francis Dolarhyde, the serial killer known to the public as "the Tooth Fairy," to travel to Florida to attack FBI investigator Will Graham and his family—and after Will suffers a grievous facial wound, courtesy of Dolarhyde—Dr. Lecter writes Will a letter from prison, in which he notes, "My dear Will, you must be healed by now . . . on the outside, at least. I hope you're not too ugly" (Ratner, *Red Dragon*).

In the novel upon which Brett Ratner's film is based, the letter never reaches Will Graham. It is intercepted and destroyed by Jack Crawford. In the novel, the joke forms the closing line of Dr. Lecter's note, and it reads, "I wish you a speedy convalescence and hope you won't be very ugly. I think of you often" (Harris, *Dragon*, p. 335). In this way, the novel version has a somewhat more menacing tone than in the film. Neither the joke nor the letter—nor the assault on Will Graham at his home—appear in the first film adaptation of *Red Dragon*, Michael Mann's *Manhunter*.

In the *Red Dragon* film, the line, read to us in the inimitably snide voice so much a part of Anthony Hopkins's interpretation of the character, is in fact rather funny—despite its lack of cleverness (as far as humor goes, it's more a jeer than a joke), and the violence of which it makes light. But these elements—the crass directness of the joke, as well as the cruelty of the barb—are characteristic of a large percentage of the humorous things Hannibal Lecter says or does in the novels, as well as in the films based upon them. In addition to killing and eating people, Dr. Lecter appears to be quite fond of cruelly mocking people; we might say he *skewers* them (*ba-dum-tss!*). This is especially true of people who have suffered violence, great tragedy, or loss, as Will Graham has at the end of *Red Dragon*; as Clarice Starling has in the opening chapters of Thomas Harris's *Hannibal*, when Paul Krendler has basically assured the end of her career at the FBI after the shootout at the Feliciana Fish Market; or as Senator Ruth Martin has in her meeting with Dr. Lecter in Memphis in *The Silence of the Lambs*, where he has promised to help in the search for her daughter, Catherine Martin, the last woman abducted by the serial killer Jame Gumb (also known as Buffalo Bill or, in the novel, Mr. Hide). Recall Lecter's obscene references to Senator Martin having breastfed her daughter—"Tell me, mum, when your little girl is on the slab, where will it tickle you?"—and then his parting shot: "Oh, and Senator, just one more thing: *love* your suit" (Demme, *Silence*). Generally speaking, Dr. Hannibal Lecter's primary response to weakness is a snide and cruel but humorous one: "mock the weak" is perhaps a milder correlate of his more infamous dictum, "eat the rude."

Mockery is not the highest form of humor, to be sure, and although it can be genuinely funny, the laughs are usually short-lived—and always at someone else's expense. Thus, despite his proclamations to the contrary ("Discourtesy is unspeakably ugly to me"—uttered by Lecter in both the book and film versions of *Silence*, as well as in the TV series), it would seem that Dr. Lecter is in some ways and at some times—again, almost exclusively in the novels and films—quite rude. This is true despite the narrator's musing in *The Silence of the Lambs* (and Will's in *Hannibal*), that "it was as if the murders had purged him of lesser rudeness" (Harris, *Silence*, p. 22; *Hannibal*, Season 2, "Tome-wan"). And this, also despite Clarice Starling's insight, in conversation with the ex-orderly, Barney, that "she recognized for the first time the compliment implied in the monster's ridicule" (Harris, *Hannibal*, p. 90). While Lecter does mock those whom he seems genuinely to respect—Will and Clarice chief among them—he also turns his biting mockery on lesser figures, perhaps most notably (and least respectfully) his former patient and victim, Mason Verger, and his "keeper" while he is incarcerated in the Baltimore State Hospital for the Criminally Insane, Dr. Frederick Chilton.

One of the most telling moments of mockery in the Hannibal Lecter series appears in the film version of *Hannibal*. Dr. Lecter has left Europe and returned to the United States, and he is in telephone conversation with Clarice Starling, goading her on but refusing to remand himself into FBI custody. Clarice notes that Mason Verger, a former patient whom Hannibal Lecter had drugged and then persuaded to cut off his own face (and feed it to his dogs) and, in the film, Lecter's only surviving victim, is intent on killing him. Lecter notes that, on the contrary, Verger wants to see him "suffer in some unimaginable way," and then asks, "Have you had the pleasure of meeting him . . . face-to-face, so to speak?" When she responds in the affirmative, Dr. Lecter adds, with what seems like more than a little relish, "Attractive, isn't he?" (Scott, *Hannibal*). His mockery—one of the funniest lines in the film—draws attention to Verger's disfigurement, while at the same time, by taking the form of a rhetorical question, makes Clarice complicit in the mocking observation. Just as he will attempt to persuade Clarice later in the film to join him in his eating of the rude Paul Krendler's brain (successfully, in the novel), here he attempts to implicate her in the mocking of the most obvious weakness of Mason Verger, his lack of a face.

Lecter is speaking of Frederick Chilton when he observes to Will Graham, "Gruesome, isn't he? He fumbles at your head like a freshman pulling at a panty girdle" (Ratner, *Red Dragon*; the jibe originally appears at Harris, *Dragon*, p. 60). It is, as so many of the best lines in Harris's novels and the films are, recycled in the television series—where, however, it is taken out of Lecter's mouth and put into Chilton's own: "The irony is that [Will Graham] is my patient, but he refuses to speak to me. It makes me feel like I'm fumbling with his head, like a freshman pulling at a panty girdle" (*Hannibal*, Season 2, "Kaiseki"). Of course, once it is Chilton himself making the "panty girdle" reference, it isn't really mockery any longer—Chilton isn't mocking anyone, he's making a self-deprecating confession about the difficulty of treating Will Graham. What was once an indication of Lecter's disdain for Chilton, and which helped the reader and moviegoer to cultivate some Lecter-like disdain for Chilton, as well, becomes instead one of Dr. Chilton's most human moments—and helps us to see him in a more sympathetic light.

The transformation of the sense of the joke—from *Red Dragon* to *Hannibal*—is characteristic of the differences in the way humor is used in the books and films, on the one hand, and the television series on the other, although not always by way of changing the point of view from which the joke is told. As we'll continue to see, Lecter's humor is treated by Thomas Harris and the filmmakers typically as one of his many persuasive and destructive instruments. It is, it seems, a means to an end for Dr. Lecter more than anything else, and becomes indicative primarily of his disdain for the weak, dull, and rude. It is more than this in the television series, however: in Bryan Fuller's *Hannibal*, Lecter is hardly ever mocking. Mockery is more often than not a weapon wielded by the weak. In *Hannibal*, humor is power.

Are You Setting a New Standard of Care?

Although the second type of humor I've identified differs, I think, in some substantial ways from the first type, the jokes themselves are often in fact quite similar. While mockery is frequently used by the genuinely powerless to bring their enemies down—in the manner of a schoolyard bully—this second type of joke, humor as an expression of power, is told from a position of ostensible weakness but as a reminder of the "real" balance of power. A few such witticisms occur throughout the films. In *Hannibal*, for example, when captured by Mason Verger's Sardinian henchmen, Lecter finds himself in the company of Carlo, whose brother, Matteo, Lecter killed in Florence. Carlo is understandably upset with Lecter, but by ordinary standards, Carlo is the one with power in this situation: he is unbound, an agent of the man who has masterminded the capture and planned torture of Hannibal Lecter.

Lecter, on the other hand, is bound, barefoot so that Verger's specially raised pigs can eat his feet. Thus, it is important that, in this scene, Lecter is the apparently calm and collected one; Carlo is the agitated one. And to this combustible situation, Dr. Lecter adds the observation, "Your little brother must smell almost as badly as you do by now" (Scott, *Hannibal*). There is of course something mocking about such a joke—Lecter is exploiting Carlo's weakness, the death of his brother, for his own personal and comedic gain. But at the same time, in making *this* joke in *this* situation, Dr. Lecter reminds Carlo and the viewers that, despite appearances, he is always in control. The joke appears again in the television series, when under the same circumstances, Lecter tells Carlo, "I take it Matteo didn't make it. Did he foul himself? I imagine he smells worse than you by now" (*Hannibal*, Season 2, "Tome-wan"). Not only in wording but in the difference in tone the actors bring to their performances can we see that Hopkins's Lecter is a bit more taunting, a bit more mocking, than Mikkelsen's. But this difference—that Mikkelsen's Lecter is apparently even more in control than Hopkins's—seems to lend the televisual Dr. Lecter even more power. (The joke under discussion originally appears in the novel, where Lecter says to Carlo, "Your brother, Matteo, must smell worse than you by now. He shit when I cut him" [Harris, *Hannibal*, p. 403].)

An excellent example of this sort of humor also occurs in Peter Webber's *Hannibal Rising*. In that film, the young Hannibal Lecter is being questioned about his possible involvement in the murder of a butcher who had, during the Second World War, been a supporter of the Vichy government. The French police inspector, Pascal Popil, observes that Lecter might have motive, identifying the butcher with Vichy and the Nazis. Lecter asks Inspector Popil whether he, too, suffered as a victim of war crimes perpetrated by Vichy—which Popil admits. "Then we're both suspects," Lecter notes. "I can say you were fishing with me, if you like" (Webber, *Hannibal Rising*). Here, again, we see that in an externally powerless situation—in police custody, being questioned about a murder he did in fact commit—Lecter reasserts his power, and does so through humor.

In one final example of Hannibal Lecter's humorous power, at one point in the second season of *Hannibal*, Will Graham asks an orderly at the Baltimore State Hospital, where he is being kept, to kill Hannibal Lecter. The orderly—Matthew

Brown—finds and captures Lecter at a swimming pool. After rendering the good doctor unconscious, Brown suspends him from a noose around his neck. He has slit both of Lecter's wrists, and stands Lecter atop a wobbly bucket. At any time, Lecter could give up, kick the bucket (*haha!*), and allow himself to be hanged. If he doesn't, he'll bleed out. Brown then engages Lecter in conversation. As the young man speaks, Dr. Lecter recognizes him: "You're a nurse at the hospital." Following a brief, non-verbal acknowledgment by Brown, Lecter then asks: "Are you setting a new standard of care?" (*Hannibal*, Season 2, "Mukōzuke"). Lecter has a noose tightening around his neck, and is literally fighting for his life. His question is not snide or condescending; it is reminiscent of Hopkins's Lecter in almost no way. And yet . . . it's exceedingly funny, not *in spite of* but *because of* its lack of a mocking tone. That Dr. Lecter can make a joke in such dire circumstances is, again, a strong reminder of how powerful he really is. One need only compare such quiet mastery of himself and his situation to the frequent belittling threats made by Dr. Chilton to see the power differential in stark contrast. Lecter, hanging and bleeding to death, demonstrates more power than Chilton—keeper of the keys—will ever have.

It's Nice to Have an Old Friend for Dinner

The last type of humor employed by Hannibal Lecter—the "inside joke"—is admittedly more characteristic of the television series than it is any of the films. It is almost totally absent from the novels. And the reason for this difference is not difficult to discern: one of the things that a good in-joke requires is that all parties involved be sufficiently familiar with the matter at hand to understand the references and get the joke. Harris's novels lay the groundwork for the entire Hannibal Lecter phenomenon, and each introduces something new about the character to readers. As a novelist, Harris does not presume the same cultural familiarity of his audience that, say, Bryan Fuller does of his own. But some of Lecter's in-jokes are humorous, or meant to be humorous, to other characters in his fictional world, as well. As such, we find ourselves with two sorts of inside jokes.

The first sort of in-joke that has become characteristic of Hannibal Lecter is the joke that makes sense to some characters in the fictional world Lecter inhabits but not to others. This is the sort of joke, say, that you share with your friends but not with acquaintances; when you're in a mixed gathering and a certain sort of reference is made, only you and your friends are going to think it's funny (everyone else is likely to be confused). The first and most famous of these occurs as the very last line of the film version of *Silence*: on the telephone with Clarice Starling from an undisclosed South American country, Dr. Lecter sees the oblivious Dr. Chilton disembark a small aircraft. Lecter sees Chilton, and so do we; obviously, Starling does not. Nevertheless, she is "in" on the joke, aware as she is of Lecter's cannibalism, when he bids her farewell: "I'm having an old friend for dinner." This may be the oldest cannibal pun there is, and it recurs in the television series on a few occasions—occasions I'll mention again shortly.

There are a couple of other instances of in-jokes that Dr. Lecter shares with other characters in the television series. At dinner, again with Jack Crawford, Lecter presents his guest with kholodets, an incredible fish aspic that depicts a nature scene suspended in gelatin: in this case, fish pursuing each other, which Crawford dubs "the eternal chase," wherein pursuer and pursuant are ever unclear. At this point in the story, Jack knows Lecter is a cannibal, and Lecter knows that Jack knows. And so, Dr. Lecter responds, "Whomever is pursuing whom in this very moment, I intend to eat them" (*Hannibal*, Season 2, "Tome-wan"). The humor in this moment is lost on neither man, but both see its humor only because both are aware of the fact that, given the opportunity, Hannibal Lecter would readily kill and eat Jack Crawford.

A final example of the in-character in-joke occurs earlier in the second season, after Freddie Lounds, the voluminously redheaded journalist, has gone missing—presumably murdered by Will Graham (a presumption Hannibal Lecter appears to share). Will arrives in Lecter's kitchen with a bag of groceries, offering to provide the ingredients if Lecter decides how to prepare them. And the first thing Will removes from the bag is a paper-wrapped packet of meat. Both men quietly acknowledge that the meat they are about to prepare is not only human flesh (which it probably is), but also that it is specifically the product of butchering Freddie Lounds (which it isn't—but Lecter doesn't know that). Lecter determines that they will make lomo saltado, a Peruvian stir fry, hands a knife to Will, and says, "Will, you slice the ginger" (*Hannibal*, Season 2, "Naka-Choko"). *Hannibal*'s food stylist, Janice Poon, notes on her blog that, in an earlier draft of the script, Will responds, "I already have"—making explicit the much-funnier-when-merely-implied joke, that their meal is the result of Will's having killed and butchered ("sliced") the red-haired Lounds ("the ginger"). Will gets the joke, but no one else—no one without knowledge of Will's involvement in Lounds's "death"—would.

The other sort of in-joke, however—the sort which none of the characters, except perhaps Hannibal Lecter himself, would understand as humor—is in some ways the specialty of *Hannibal*'s dark humor. Only one such joke really stands out in the films, and it occurs in the prologue written for *Red Dragon*, depicting events only mentioned but not described in the novel. There, hosting a dinner party for the Baltimore Symphony Board of Directors, Dr. Lecter is asked what is in the "divine-looking" amuse-bouche. Of course, once Hannibal Lecter aficionados learn that the people gathered for dinner are the symphony board, we know what—or, more accurately, *who*—is on the menu: Benjamin Raspail, former flutist of the symphony, whose playing apparently left something to be desired. Lecter—played perfectly in this scene by Anthony Hopkins—notes, almost wistfully, "If I tell you, I'm afraid you won't even try it" (Ratner, *Red Dragon*). Naturally, the humor here is lost on everyone else in the room (otherwise, as Lecter rightly notes, they wouldn't eat; they would leave as quickly as possible, presuming Lecter didn't do something to insure that he could savor their presence at his table whenever he wanted—*teehee!*). The joke is for *our* benefit, and Hannibal Lecter's. Nobody else gets to partake of this one.

As early as the second episode of the first season of *Hannibal*, however, we begin to see these sorts of jokes dominate the humor landscape of the series. Dining with Jack Crawford, Dr. Lecter suggests, "Next time, bring your wife. I'd love to have you both for dinner" (*Hannibal*, Season 1, "Amuse-Bouche"). Two episodes later, at another meal with Jack, Lecter chastises him: "You promised to deliver your wife to my dinner table" (*Hannibal*, Season 1, "Œuf"). Later in the season—again over dinner, although this time while dining with the serial killer, Tobias Budge—Lecter makes perhaps the most sophisticated version of this joke yet. Tobias has confessed his intention to murder Lecter, and Lecter has admitted he was similarly murderously inclined toward Tobias. Tobias then glances warily at the plate from which he has been eating, to which Lecter casually but meaningfully responds, "I didn't poison you, Tobias. I wouldn't do that to the food" (*Hannibal*, Season 1, "Fromage"). This joke functions on two levels, only one of which is accessible to Tobias himself: Lecter is a famed gourmand, and it is funny to think that, although he is willing to murder someone, he is unwilling to spoil a meal. (This element of the joke works on the incongruity theory of humor I mentioned earlier.) At the same time, however, and unbeknownst to Tobias, Lecter probably intends not merely to kill—but afterwards, to eat—Tobias Budge. And knowing this is the case, "I wouldn't do that to the food" takes on a second, deeper, darker, much more humorous meaning. No one willingly poisons an animal they intend for slaughter.

The best instance of this sort of humor in *Hannibal*, however, occurs in an earlier episode in the first season. Lecter is having dinner with Frederick Chilton and Alana Bloom; he has prepared for them what he claims is lamb's tongue. Chilton, in his arrogant and studied way, notes that, "The Romans used to kill flamingos, just to eat their tongues." Dr. Lecter smiles, looks Chilton in the eye, and responds, "Don't give me ideas. Your tongue is very feisty. And as this evening has already proven, it's nice to have an old friend for dinner" (*Hannibal*, Season 1, "Entrée"). This in-joke works on two levels, both of which are accessible (at this point in the series, at least) only to Hannibal Lecter and his loyal viewers. On the one hand, like the other jokes I've just mentioned, Lecter is making a joke about cannibalizing Chilton. He makes the joke overtly—it is not secretly about cannibalism—but only Lecter knows that he is actually willing to make the joke a gruesome reality. On the other hand, as we've seen, this is an old joke for Fannibals (and an even older joke for cannibals). It is perhaps the most famous joke Hannibal Lecter makes in *The Silence of the Lambs*. And, like so many other jokes from the novels and films, it finds its way beautifully—and quite humorously—onto the small screen.

Following this trend, of bringing the audience closer and closer to Dr. Lecter (and Dr. Lecter, closer and closer to us) through humor, we see him interacting ever more frequently with the audience. Although this is never done in the extremely explicit manner of such characters as Frank Underwood in Netflix's *House of Cards* or Deadpool of the eponymous Marvel Comics series, where the anti-heroic character addresses the viewing audience or readers directly ("breaking the fourth wall," as they say in the theater), there are subtle hints in this direction, one of the most obvious being the closing lines of the seventh episode of Season 1. There, hosting a dinner party, Lecter announces: "Before we begin, you must all be warned: nothing here is vegetarian." The gathered diners laugh and raise their glasses, to which Lecter responds by looking into the camera, raising his own glass, smiling, and saying—to us?— "*Bon appétit*" (*Hannibal*, Season 1, "Sorbet"). In making jokes only he and we can be expected to understand, Hannibal Lecter comes closer to us than ever before. And that—as in the cases of Frank Underwood and Deadpool, and even less diabolical comic characters, like Alvy Singer in Woody Allen's *Annie Hall* and Groucho Marx's Captain Spaulding in *Animal Crackers* (both of whom address the cinema audience directly from the screen)—is not only indicative of a very modern understanding of the relationship between the character and the audience. It's an expression of power.

Humorous Power

Hannibal Lecter has appeared before us now in five different guises: as a character in Thomas Harris's novels, and in the performances of Brian Cox, Anthony Hopkins, Gaspard Ulliel, and Mads Mikkelsen. I think the realization that humor, *telling a joke*, can be a demonstration of power that bridges the gap between the fiction of Hannibal Lecter and our reality helps us to see why we might think Mads Mikkelsen's Dr. Lecter is the funniest of the five. This is of course a controversial claim. Mikkelsen plays Lecter with an equanimity and lack of expression that is far from Hopkins's snide, glaring, sometimes even ravenous interpretation. One of the first criticisms of Mikkelsen's take on the character (and, after Hopkins's inspired performance, there were bound to be criticisms) was that he is humorless: "Attempting, perhaps, to distance this version from the iconic portrayal by Anthony Hopkins, Mikkelsen plays Lecter almost completely devoid of humor.

Which is a huge problem" (McNamara). Naturally, I don't want to get into a debate about whose portrayal is superior: both Hopkins and Mikkelsen bring a great deal to Harris's character. But what they bring is different. And, for whatever reason, Mikkelsen's Lecter tells more jokes, and more jokes of a different kind, than Hopkins's—more inside jokes, even, than Thomas Harris's Hannibal Lecter. Which helps to make Mikkelsen's Lecter a somewhat more powerful character than Hopkins's Lecter was or could be.

Perhaps this is due to the nature of television as a medium, with the greater intimacy and more extended storylines it affords us. Perhaps this has to do with the fact that the pre-*Red Dragon* Lecter we see in *Hannibal* is genuinely more free, and thus able to exercise his power more freely, than the mostly imprisoned Lecter of the Hopkins films. I don't know. What I do know is that Hannibal Lecter is a funny guy—and he is more so in the television series than he has ever been before. Which isn't to say that Hopkins's Lecter isn't funny, just that his jokes are less frequent and of a different sort. It's almost as if Hopkins's Lecter and Mikkelsen's Lecter are a comedy duo, with Hopkins as the straight man. Hopkins gives us the set-up in *Silence*: "A census taker once tried to test me. I ate his liver with some fava beans and a nice Chianti" (Demme, *Silence*). In 1991? Just terror, and the thrill of terror. But let the set-up percolate for twenty-two years . . . and then Mikkelsen's Lecter can respond, in bed with Alana Bloom after the doorbell rings: "Last time someone rang my doorbell this early, it was a census taker" (*Hannibal*, Season 2, "Futamono"). No explanation, no explicit references, no mentioning of livers or fava beans or Chiantis, definitely no vampire-inspired sucking of the teeth. Just Hannibal "The Cannibal" Lecter—and us—bound together in the memory of something that, from Mikkelsen's Lecter's fictional perspective, hasn't happened yet.

Now, that's funny.

15
The Art of Killing

Andrea Zanin

John Douglas—a former special agent with the U.S. Federal Bureau of Investigation (FBI), one of the world's first criminal profilers, criminal psychology author, and the man who inspired the literary birth of Jack Crawford, top gun at the Behavioral Science Unit of the FBI in Thomas Harris's monstrous Hannibal Lecter mythology—says of serial killers: "If you want to understand the artist, you have to look at the painting" (Douglas and Olshaker, p. 32). Seriously? It's sort of sick, this art and murder business. Douglas's metaphor evokes ideas so disturbing, so repulsive, that the brain revolts with revolutionary fervor. And yet it was Douglas's pioneering work that inspired a villain so vile that society's inherent-but-mostly-repressed deviance lurches to know more, to understand and even to bask in the latent ambiance of Hannibal Lecter's dark incandescence. We want to know him; we want him to know us. *And yet we don't.* Saturated in contradiction, Harris's man-eating monster dines on the rude with a helping of fava beans and a glass of nice Chianti, an absentminded hand rising and falling in time with the cadence of Bach's Goldberg Variations. It's a mish-mash of "high culture" and debased immorality, and it's utterly diabolical. To the tune of which, Douglas would have us believe that a successful serial killer is much like Picasso, working as carefully as a painter planning a canvas. These killers consider what they do their "art" and they keep refining it as they go along (Douglas and Olshaker, p. 6).

Just as one might admire a work of art, it's not so difficult to imagine a serial killer reveling in blood spatter and body part assemblage; the scene likely embellished with a prop or two—a stained knife, a reddened axe, a bouquet of flowers, some fruit, a trendy hat, a collection of bullet casings, maybe a designer bag or Jimmy Choo heel—for effect. It's easy because it's a subjective experience. And murderers are deviants anyway, which allows us to view their weirdo fetish-type behavior with a judging eye. But what is not so easy is appreciating the aesthetic value of a murder scene as an objective work of art. Disembowelment, decapitation, facial reconstruction, a masticated tongue . . . how is this art? *Oh but it is!* Forget classic notions of aestheticism proposed by the likes of Georg Hegel and his cronies, or at least be prepared to *imagine* with a postmodernist perspective, one that gives you license to open your mind to the notion that an invoked sense of revulsion is as much a symptom of the aesthetic as is gushing glorification.

The best way to understand Hannibal, popular culture's favorite cannibal, is to go all "Jack Crawford" on the guy and investigate the aesthetic of Lecter's crimes with the savvy of an FBI agent. By probing Harris's novels with CSI-type precision, the way in which art has informed Lecter's upbringing and permeated every aspect of his existence, murder included, will materialize. And although our minds will writhe and reel with the effort, the dark Disturbia that lurks in the recesses of our very-human consciousness will relish the ride. *Welcome to horror* . . . equivocal in its ability to both repel and seduce. Like Pablo Picasso. Like Hannibal Lecter.

Carving the Canvas: Horror IS Art

On the face of it, a marriage of Horror (ugly) and Aestheticism (pretty) might seem like an oxymoronic assimilation, but the art of the twentieth century (in particular) has altered the principles of the aesthetic, proposing a definition amended by context and social change. Italian idealist philosopher and sometime politician Benedetto Croce was a proponent of the idea that "expression" is central to the definition of an artistic aesthetic in the way that beauty was once thought to be a fundamental component thereof. Art reflects the society of which it is a part, and it only makes sense that the terms used to define art evolve along with that which influences its character. So, what then? The world only became ugly in the last fifty years—at least, if the movies are anything to go by? Not at all. The world's always been partially dismal but modern society, governed by a new set of social conventions, has stopped going all Pollyanna on the pain. The "glad game" is dead and buried. These days, we like to "keep it real," also known as "freedom of expression."

But let's backtrack a bit. Before rampaging against the so-called implications of traditionally defined aestheticism, what is it—*aestheticism*—and what do classical thinkers say about it? In philosophy, "aesthetics" deals with the nature of art, beauty, and creation—the appreciation of beauty, in other words. And so aesthetics and art are invariably linked—one cannot be without the other, kind of like Lecter and his muzzle, Jason and his mask, Freddy and his razors, Jigsaw and his bicycle, Leatherface and his chainsaw. Right? The problem with aesthetics is that it gets complicated when trying to understand the character of "appreciation": what denotes "beauty" and thus what defines art. Philosopher David Novitz, acclaimed for his theories on the connection between art and everyday life, has argued that the typical hoity-toity brawl over what is and isn't art (you'd be surprised to know what academics are willing to lose teeth over) is rooted in the subjective understanding of whatever trend so happens to be society's "value of the day," rather than an objective set of criteria. Novitz would agree that the deeply offensive manifestation of Hannibal Lecter's morose immorality does not preclude his "work" from being defined as art, which is a radical concept in light of traditional aestheticism.

Hegel, a classical philosopher famous for his lectures on aesthetics, would definitely not be endeared to Novitz's notes on art. But Hegel has some good points. He admits that "aesthetic" means, more precisely, the science of sensation or feeling—how the world perceives or reflects on art (culture and nature). What Hegel alludes to is that beauty invokes a plethora of positive emotions (joy, friendliness, confidence, revelation) and it is the presence of this response that defines art as *art*, which, naturally, excludes any sort of *anything* that might invoke terror, angst, melancholy, repugnance, fear or any number of other negative emotions on the spectrum. The thing with Hegel's reasoning is that it just *ain't real*—art, classic or modern, is not just about charming cherubs or nice nature scenes: it's John the Baptist's head on a platter, it's a man without a face, it's a shark resting in formaldehyde. Art isn't always obvious and it's not required to be pleasant. Which is where the thinking of American philosopher, poet and founder of Aesthetic Realism, Eli Siegel, comes in.

An important philosophy to emerge in the twentieth century, as articulated by Siegel, is that reality itself is aesthetic. *And reality isn't always pretty.* Neither is expression, as per Croce. Novitz reminds us that the traditionalism that has defined "high art" for centuries and its accompanying exclusivity has been eradicated by contemporary thought, which has transposed great freedom onto the individual, freedom to express and to be real in doing it. Art that was once frowned upon for its mass appeal has gained in stature thanks to the vista of modern thinking, thinking that allows the value of "realism" and "expressionism" to reveal both the ethic and the aesthetic of Hannibal Lecter's crimes.

In the novel, *Hannibal*, Thomas Harris describes Lecter as a connoisseur of the worst in mankind. Lecter, attuned to man's evil, says that ". . . the essence of the worst, the true asafoetida of the human spirit, is not found in the Iron Maiden or the whetted edge; Elemental Ugliness is found in the faces of the crowd" (Harris, *Hannibal*, p. 128). Moral perversity is not something that escapes the human race; it is the condition of being human. But if you happen to let that perversity slip whilst under the gaze of the ever-observant Hannibal the Cannibal Lecter, then *sayonara,* see you in the next life. Lecter notices immorality (ironic!) and it disgusts him, so much so that those who contravene Lecter's code of politeness end up on his dinner plate. Miggs, the poor bastard, swallows his own tongue at the behest of Hannibal Lecter, as punishment for assaulting Clarice Starling with his semen. Lecter also kills: Paul the fat butcher boy, *for insulting Lady Murasaki;* an untalented flutist who is served to the symphony board members post-mortem; an obnoxious census taker whose liver Hannibal eats; and all the men who murdered his sister, Mischa. Lecter metes out punishment on corrupt officials (Krendler, Pazzi, and Chilton), and then there's Mason Verger, a convicted child molester who carves up his own face and feeds it to his dogs because Lecter told him to. But before we high-five the good doctor for his well-intended vigilantism, Lecter is, of course, not so noble in his murderous intent. His extermination of the rude is not an altruistic endeavor but something that is entirely self-gratifying, to the exclusion of all nobility and magnanimity—neither of which are a prerequisite for aesthetic prowess if we're talking "modern art."

Where Hegel's philosophy of art supports horror as an art form, like aesthetic realism and aesthetic expressionism, is in its preoccupation with the character of the aesthetic and how "true beauty" is informed by the notion of freedom—that art, at its best, presents us with the ideal of *freedom*. And "freedom," according to Hegel, is something that can only be achieved by the mind through intelligent thought and will. So, take blood, for example. It is a natural entity and is necessary to the function of life but is quite indifferent to its own purpose or value; this lack of self-conscious awareness is what shackles it. Blood, however, can be freed through art; an artist's rendition of blood (through paint, words . . . *murder*) imbues it with consciousness, thus destroying the shackles of its ignorance. Not only does Lecter force his consciousness onto *blood* but death, too, justifying it with an ethic. And as unpleasant as being killed and eaten might be, in death there is an element of freedom. Lecter liberates the rude from the shackles of their own immorality and he attributes death, which is unaware of its function, with purpose. In death, Lecter's victims are freed—reinterpreted on the canvas of a dinner plate.

Blood and Charcoal: Symbolic Horror and the Skill of the Kill

Horror, as a genre, is permeated by symbolism. Horror offers insight into a fractured psyche, a broken world, and serial killers function as symbols for, and expressions of, human pathology. Lecter's murders represent his detestation of the frailty of the human condition. It was man's weakness and overall ignobility that led to his sister's death, which, arguably, awakened the evil that lay dormant in Hannibal into a monstrous, mythical being. And so Hannibal, as myth and monster, functions symbolically on two different planes: Hannibal as art (created by Thomas Harris) and Hannibal as artist (imposing his expression onto the world at large). Lecter is thrust into art by virtue of his being—he exists in fiction, his lifeblood is fueled by the art of the written word. He is thus art personified, subject to the aesthetic values that define his very existence. Harris amplifies Hannibal's literary predisposition to art by making it something inescapably essential to his character. And it makes sense to suppose that if an individual is artistic by nature, art is an intrinsic part of a person's character—it's genetic. Art will then bleed into all aspects of that individual's living, breathing existence. Murder included.

In *Red Dragon*, the first of the Lecter novels, Harris regularly draws on John Douglas's "serial killers are artists" reference in having characters think of and refer to the Tooth Fairy as an "artist," the crime scenes as "tableaux," and so on. In so doing Harris challenges his reader to acknowledge the artistry inherent in that, which on the face of it, is morally abhorrent. It's a difficult pill to swallow but unpacking the concept releases an objectivity that helps the mind rationalize the heart's reaction. The word "artistry" presupposes the notion of "skill," which, when applied in the context of traditional aesthetics, constructs "art" as a productive skill or a set of skills used to achieve an end (paintings, sculptures, operas, novels, and the like): Aristotle called it *techne*. But Novitz destabilizes classical thinking by proposing that the arts are not a set of skills that supervene on our lives with no more purpose than decorating our existence. Novitz says that the arts are a fundamental, indispensable part of life because they are the skills by which we live—the skills that one must possess in order to lead, and so have, a life. Murder is the skill by which Hannibal Lecter lives; it is an artistry permeated with symbolic value, beautifully constructed and inescapable in its drastic implications.

In *Silence of the Lambs*, Harris points at Lecter's artistic inclination when Clarice Starling notices the drawings on the walls of Lecter's cell in the asylum, including a drawing of the Palazzo Vecchio and the Duomo in Florence which Hannibal has sketched from memory, as well as an interpretation of Golgotha after the Deposition. Not only is Lecter's skill emphasized but also the fact that his art is important to him; Lecter's drawings (along with his toilet seat) are confiscated as punishment for killing Miggs, and Clarice, understanding the value they hold as an extension of Lecter's life essence, later offers him his drawings (not the toilet seat) back in exchange for information on Buffalo Bill. The symbiotic relationship between horror and art is further emphasized when Starling, upon one of her visits to Lecter in the asylum, finds Lecter sketching: "He was sketching on butcher paper, using his hand for a model. As she watched he turned his hand over and, flexing his fingers to great tension, drew the inside of the forearm. He used his little finger as a shading stump to modify a charcoal line" (Harris, *Silence*, p. 131). The juxtapositions in this passage are just insane with innuendo. The word "butcher," the deathly implications of which lurk under the guise of kraft paper, and "stump," innocent in its function as a make-shift shading tool, are anything but virtuous when used in reference to Hannibal Lecter—the ultimate butcher, carving his victims for the purpose of consumption with the same hands that sketch with a delicacy that hints at genius. The butcher and the artist; one and the same. As Clarice and Lecter engage in conversation about the "remains" of Buffalo Bill's (supposed) latest victim, Lecter sketches, rubbing "his charcoal on the edge of his butcher paper to refine the point"—again, "butcher" and "charcoal" mingle like old friends. The interplay is darkly comical and accentuates the relationship between death and aesthetics.

He Picked Up Two Flowers and the Knife

The hints that Harris drops in his first two novels undergo significant development in *Hannibal Rising*, series prequel, and *Hannibal*, series conclusion. The reader is transported back to the beginning in *Hannibal Rising*, which is a journey of discovery that sheds light on all the things we wonder about Lecter—it tells us *why* by offering insight into Lecter's past. The book positions Lecter not only as an artist by virtue of his action and passion, but because he was born that way. Hannibal Lecter's uncle, Robert Lecter, is a great artist; his paintings are, in fact, sequestered in Goering and Hitler's private collections after they had been seized for being "decadent," "subversive," and "Slavic" (Harris, *Rising*, p. 67). Lecter inherits his uncle's artistic aptitude and is described as being inherently talented from a young age.

Lecter's "promising eye" (Harris, *Rising*, p. 77) is revealed by an "excellent chalk and pencil drawing of a baby's hand and arm . . ." (Harris, *Rising*, p. 59) that is stuck above his bed in the orphanage that overtakes Lecter Castle in the aftermath of war. As a young man living in Paris (home to the Louvre and many other grand artistic pleasures), Lecter makes money by selling his sketches to art dealers and, attending medical school, is revered for his anatomical drawings. In fact, it's his artistic talent (a school-boy drawing of a frog) that wins him a scholarship to medical school in the first place. Hannibal's pre-occupation with art is emphasized by the amount of time he spends sketching—at the back of class, especially. He also immerses himself in contemplations relating to the technicali-ties of art, such as the intricacies of bringing nature to life in artistic media, marveling at "Turner's mist and his colors, impossible to emulate" (Harris, *Rising*, p. 139) after an after-noon of sketching boats on the pond.

Lecter proves his artistry in Lady Murasaki's presence when he arranges a vase of blossoms to feng shui perfection: "Hannibal considered. He picked up two flowers and the knife. He saw the arch of the windows, the curve of the fireplace where the tea vessel hung over the fire. He cut the stems of the flowers off shorter and placed them in the vase, creating a vec-tor harmonious to the arrangement and to the room. He put the cut stems on the table" (Harris, *Rising*, p. 77). The artistry of Hannibal's display would be futile without the knife to cor-rect the stems. Harris nurtures the notion that there is noth-ing haphazard about Hannibal Lecter, who acts with purpose and precision—every word he utters and every move he makes is done with thought, with intent. Even when a samurai sword is the weapon in play and a body is the flower. Paul the butcher boy ends up *sans* head as punishment for insulting Lady Murasaki. Hannibal sketches as he waits upon his victim and as the murder progresses to a climax, Hannibal looks into Paul the butcher's face, the moment before he takes his life, and offers him a glimpse at his artwork: a sketch of Paul the butcher's head on a platter with a name tag attached to the hair. The tag reads *Paul Mormund, Fine Meats*. The drawing is rendered into reality when Lady Murasaki finds Paul's head:

> A dark object stood on the altar before the armor. She saw it in sil-
> houette against the candles. She set her candle lamp on a crate near
> the altar and looked steadily at the head of Paul the Butcher standing

in a shallow suiban flower vessel. Paul's face is clean and pale, his lips are intact, but his cheeks are missing and a little blood has leaked from his mouth into the flower vessel, where blood stands like the water beneath a flower arrangement. A tag is attached to Paul's hair. On the tag in a copperplate hand: *Momund, Boucherie de Qualité.* (Harris, *Rising*, p. 110)

It's almost beautiful. No, it *is* beautiful, and certainly expressive and equally superb in its evocative symbolism. The reticent motif: the butcher drawing on butcher paper as Clarice Starling looks on—Hannibal's first victim a butcher's son. *Omg!* And the flowers—arranged with care and calculation just a couple pages back; a courtesy extended to Lady Murasaki's ancestors, illustrating Hannibal's exacting purpose and sense of artistry, whether it is placing a flower arrangement or placing a severed head. Later in the novel, Hannibal offers up Dortlich's head "on a tree stump"—remember the stump that modified the charcoal line? *Double omg!* And check this out: "Dortlich's cheeks were missing, excised cleanly, and his teeth were visible at the sides. His mouth was held open by his dog tag, wedged between his teeth" (Harris, *Rising*, p. 228), punished for cannibalizing Lecter's sister. Like Paul the unfortunate butcher-boy, Dortlich is also imagined in art (a portrait) before he is zapped by our favorite cannibal. The artistry of these murders is further enhanced by a reference to Caravaggio's "Judith Beheading Holofernes," which is a bloody depiction of the murder of the Assyrian general, blurring the lines between art and murder. Interestingly, just before Hannibal and Lady Murasaki come across this painting in the Jeu de Paume Museum, she greets Hannibal by kissing his forehead and touching his cheek, a familiar gesture between the two, as observed by Inspector Popil—an extension of the link between murder and the cheeks that Hannibal consumed (Paul the Butcher) and is yet to consume (Dortlich), and art. Triple *omg.*

A Superior Artist: He Cooks as Well as He Kills

Hannibal's innate sense of artistry bleeds into everything he does, it cannot be helped; it is just who he is. As a consequence, Lecter defines himself in terms of the artistic construct that prescribes his world and has done so since he was a child. Lecter contextualizes himself in terms of the aesthetic that surrounds him—literature, music, art, and history. His aspirations to artistic superiority are remembered in *Hannibal* when finally Lecter finds himself (after years of imagining) in Florence, a wanted man: hated, hunted, feared, and perhaps even venerated. Florence is the epicenter of European art, the heart of the Renaissance, and is yet imbued with a history of murder, exemplified in Harris's novel by Francesco Pazzi, who was thrown naked with a noose around his neck, to die writhing and spinning against the rough wall.

The continued juxtaposition of murder and art, as posed by the contradiction of a cultured beast, is recognized in Hannibal Lecter's relationship with Chief Investigator Rinaldo Pazzi (his death foretold by his name), who finds Hannibal living under the identity of Dr. Fell. Pazzi remembers a picture of Florence in the Behavioral Science Unit at Quantico—a pencil drawing with shaded charcoal of a view of Florence as seen from the Belvedere . . . it was a drawing in a photograph—a photograph of Hannibal Lecter. Deducing, with the instinct of a good cop, that Dr. Fell is *the* Hannibal Lecter, Pazzi gives him up—not to the authorities but to Mason Verger, to molest with man-eating hogs. Pazzi pays for his dubiousness, his betrayal; Lecter reenacts the original Pazzi disembowelment. As the hanging body of Rinaldo Pazzi reaches the upstretched arms of those on the ground, Dr. Fell's tableau is likened to "the great Deposition paintings" (Harris, *Hannibal*, p. 211). Art, violence, death, pain. It's all synonymous. In an earlier reference, Lecter recalls that avarice and hanging have been linked "since antiquity, the image appearing again and again in art" (Harris, *Hannibal*, p. 195). Florence is the concrete embodiment of Lecter's artistry— it inspires him to play the clavier, to compose, to cook . . . *to kill*.

Beware the Man Who Sits in the Black, Painting Colors on the Dark

Like the folk stories of old, horror is a cautionary tale, a warning: divert from the proverbial path (whatever it may be) and trouble will follow. Stay away from the monster, who "sits in the black library, his mind painting colors on the dark and a medieval air running in his head" (Harris, *Hannibal*, p. 137).

What Thomas Harris wishes to expose in his novels is the nature of "the monster" and in so doing brings to the fore an irony so great that it has grabbed the mind of the masses with resilience unparalleled. How can a man so cultured, an artist, be barbaric in such extreme measure? It's the conundrum of human existence—how we have the potential for great good but also the knack for being total dickheads. Hannibal is the hyperbole of this very fact. Horror, which thrives on exaggeration, uses Hannibal Lecter to reflect the human condition by offering an ironic representation of reality. Benedetto Croce called reality the aesthetic oneness of opposites; a theory that runs rampant through all four of Thomas Harris's Lecter novels. Hannibal Lecter leads a life infused with artistic process, a life characterized by experience—suffering, grieving, enjoying—of the reality that is his own. By alluding to Hannibal Lecter as the embodiment of the aesthetic (opposites), his psychopathology, when contrasted with his traumatic past and his love of art and associated skill, is undermined and presented as something recognizable. There is something about Lecter that we see in ourselves.

Does this mean that it's okay to go out and eat those who piss us off—for the sake of art, at least? Well, if it's for *art's* sake . . .

VI.

The Beauty and Art and Horror of Everything This World Has to Offer

16
Empathy for the Devil

DAN SHAW

> Hannibal: We will absorb this experience. It will change us.
> We are all Nietzschean fish in that regard.
> Will: Makes us tastier.

> —*Hannibal*, Season 2, "Su-zakana"

Hannibal Lecter is one of the most fascinating evil geniuses in the history of the moving image. His legend grows in the contemporary television series *Hannibal*, where our fascination with the title character is clearly greater than with the far more sympathetic Will Graham, who is relentlessly manipulated and tormented by Lecter throughout the first two seasons. This essay will explore several reasons that explain our perplexing identification with such a diabolical individual, and conclude that the most important factor is Lecter's unrelenting Will to Power, in the sense that Friedrich Nietzsche made the centerpiece of his philosophy. Like Nietzsche's Overman, Lecter exhibits almost superhuman power in all three senses of the term that Nietzsche stressed: he is in complete control of himself, his environment, and all of the inferior individuals that surround him.

Mirror Neurons and Close-ups

Let me begin by focusing on how Lecter has been depicted on both the big and small screens. In the television series, and in all of the Lecter films, his visage is often framed in close-up. This is the first crucial element in my account of why we feel empathy for this particular devil; as Carl Plantinga, a pioneer in the recent upsurge of interest in philosophy of the emotions, has argued at some length (Plantinga, pp. 239–56), the human face is the primal scene of empathy in films. The facial expressions of filmic characters have a profound effect on us, even to the point of moving us to mimic their expressions ourselves. This, in turn, causes us to feel with the characters we are mimicking, infecting us with their emotions. Recent developments in neuroscience provide an intriguing explanation for why this is the case (see Bruun Vaage).

In the early 1990s, neuroscientists in Parma, Italy were doing research on the brains of Macaque monkeys with electrode implants. The team, headed by Dr. Giacomo Rizzolati, was seeking information on how the brain exerts motor control over the hand, in hopes of finding ways that humans with brain damage could recover at least some degree of hand function. In the process, they made an astonishing discovery: certain brain cells of the macaque fired the same way if the monkey was watching another grasp an object or if it was grasping it itself. The idea that such cells would fire at the mere perception of another animal's action identically to when the animal itself engaged in the action was totally unexpected and had profound implications. To their surprise, the researchers found that twenty percent of the cells in the motor cortex of the brain of the macaque were such mirror neurons.

The discovery of such neurons shattered the cognitivist paradigm of brain function that had been widely accepted for decades. On that view, perception and action were governed by separate brain areas, and cognition was somehow the "go-between" that leads us to select and engage in the appropriate motor behavior that is warranted by the circumstances. The startling implication of the existence of mirror neurons was that the brain responds to the world in a far more immediate and holistic fashion. Interestingly, Hannibal himself explains Will Graham's extreme empathic abilities to Jack Crawford as resulting from "too many mirror neurons" (*Hannibal*, Season 1, "Buffet Froid").

The close-up is the signature shot distance in the movie that made Hannibal Lecter a household name, *The Silence of the Lambs*. One-on-one exchanges between Lecter and Clarice Starling are the dramatic highlights of the film, and Jonathan

Demme made the canny decision to depict these in a series of shot-reverse shot extreme close-ups. Both Anthony Hopkins and Jodie Foster delivered Oscar-winning performances, and I contend that one of the crucial differences between good and bad actors is that the latter are unable to set off infectious triggerings of our mirror neurons. Hopkins, on the other hand, made Lecter completely credible, and in so doing helped secure our empathy for his monstrous character. To appreciate the extent to which mirror neurons trigger affective mimicry, one need only reflect on how often entertainers have offered their impressions of the "fava beans" sequence in *Silence*.

The use of extreme close-ups of Lecter continued in the feature film version of Harris's next novel, *Hannibal*, especially in two of the most violent scenes. As Lecter prepares to hang and disembowel his nemesis, Rinaldo Pazzi, Ridley Scott provides us with a series of such close-ups, which convey his infectious glee. Then, when he is about to slit the throat of Matteo (one of Mason Verger's henchmen), we get another vivid close-up, as he looms out of the darkness to fill the screen with his expression of eager anticipation.

In his television incarnation, played with cool intensity by Mads Mikkelsen, Lecter is once again granted a significant number of close-ups. These occur mainly in the dialogues between Lecter and Graham, Lecter and Jack Crawford, and Lecter and his analyst, Dr. Du Maurier (which are held over dinner or during psychoanalytic sessions). One of the most complex and perplexing sequences occurs in Season 1, after Graham has been arrested (the result of Lecter's frame job) for the murder of Abigail Hobbs. In a session with his analyst, Lecter sheds a tear as he apparently laments being unable to save Abigail or help Will. Despite knowing that Hannibal had framed Will for the murder of Abigail, I felt his sorrow, which (in light of subsequent events) proves to be real and not feigned. This indicates that close-ups of Hannibal help to secure our empathy for his character independently of our cognitive evaluations of his actions.

Aesthetic and Culinary Taste

As the philosopher Cynthia Freeland has noted, another of the crucial elements that allow us to enjoy this morally heinous character is that "he has developed his own kind of refined standards of taste" (Freeland, *The Naked and the Undead*, p. 207). As Friedrich Nietzsche might have put it, Lecter gives a distinctive sense of style to his character, which permeates all of his actions. His impeccable taste is displayed throughout the films, and in every episode of the television series. It is expressed in his sartorial choices, in his love for the arts (especially music), in the striking spectacles of his murdered victims, and in his cannibalistic relish for fine cuisine.

Hannibal is a music aficionado, whose grisly crimes are almost always accompanied by a classical soundtrack. The most violent set piece in *The Silence of the Lambs* is his brutal slaughter of the two guards in Memphis, which is counterpointed (until its climax) by the Goldberg Variation of Johann Sebastian Bach that has become a leitmotif associated with Hannibal thereafter. While on the directing board of the Baltimore Symphony Orchestra in *Red Dragon*, Lecter chooses to slay one of its musicians because of the poor fellow's subpar performances.

In *Hannibal*, he attends a fictional opera in Florence, which featured an original song called "Vide cor Meum" (an exquisite piece based on Dante's poem "La Vita Nuova") that was composed specifically for the film by Patrick Cassidy. Its theme recurs in the final episode of Season 1 of the TV series, as Lecter triumphantly confronts Will Graham locked up in the asylum and permits himself a subtle smile. The Goldberg Variation discussed above appears several times in Season 2, and accompanies Lecter's escape on an Air France jet at its end.

Lecter's artistic taste is also in evidence in several of the striking tableaux that he creates out of his victims. Most famously, he mounts one of his guards in *Silence* on the outside of his cage, where the poor fellow is made to appear like the figurehead of a ship. He kills Rinaldo Pazzi in a fashion that mirrors the fate of the detective's Renaissance ancestor, who was hanged and disemboweled from the same building in Florence for colluding in an assassination attempt on Lorenzo de Medici. In *Hannibal Rising*, Young Hannibal guts the butcher who insulted Lady Murasaki in the French marketplace, by slicing him horizontally in a way that parallels his original disparaging remark about the configuration of her genitalia.

Surprisingly, the television series ups the ante on both the grisly and aesthetic nature of Hannibal's crime scenes. In a brilliant conceit, Lecter commits a series of copycat crimes that are even more gruesome, and executed with greater style, than the originals after which they are modeled. Garret Jacob Hobbs impales his victims on antlers hanging on walls, but Lecter splays his quarry out horizontally in an outdoor tableau that resembles a sacrificial altar. Georgia Madchen killed her friend by slicing the corners of the girl's mouth all the way back (and leaving her on the floor). Hannibal breaks Dr. Sutcliffe's jaw and leaves him sitting in his desk chair with a maw even more gapingly fixed in what has come to be called a Glasgow Grin (the same mutilation that was visited upon the Joker prior to the action in Christopher Nolan's film, *The Dark Knight*).

The second season is unrelenting. Hannibal hangs a judge up in his own courtroom like a beef carcass. He fashions body parts into a statue of Shiva, the destroyer. But most impressively, in the finale of Season 2, he leaves all of the characters that we care about (Will Graham, Jack Crawford, Abigail Hobbs, and Alana Bloom) writhing on the floor (or street) as they slowly bleed out, the defeated victims of savage confrontations poetically orchestrated (with segments in slow motion) by director David Slade.

The aestheticization of violence has long been recognized by Freudian critics like Robin Wood as crucial to our ability to enjoy such gruesome scenes (it is also important to note that we are often shown only the stylish results of Lecter's crimes, especially in the television series). This goes a long way towards explaining why, as Steven Schneider has observed, there has been a striking trend in horror movies since the 1960s toward depicting the monster as a corrupt artist (Schneider and Shaw, pp. 274– 97).[1] In his view, it is because doing so facilitates our identification with evil perpetrators who evidence real flair in the staging of their crimes. But that doesn't tell us the whole story. As I will show in the final section of this essay, this aestheticization of violence is also a factor in our admiration for the degree of control that Lecter's grisly craftsmanship exhibits.

---

[1] For a different approach to Hannibal Lecter as an artist in the medium of murder, see Chapter 15 of this volume.—Ed.

Lecter's artistic tastes and stylized murders go hand in hand with his love of fine cuisine. Most serial killers keep souvenirs of their victims; he usually eats part of them, cooked to perfection in classic dishes. In *Red Dragon*, he incorporates the innards of the untalented flutist he murdered, serving them up to the Symphony Board in a delightful *amuse-bouche*. Young Hannibal makes a brochette with the cheeks of his first quarry in the revenge vendetta in *Hannibal Rising*, and no one can forget how Lecter tells Clarice in *The Silence of the Lambs* that he ate a census taker's liver "with some fava beans and a nice Chianti" because of his demanding questions.

Lecter shares the internal organs of his victims with most of the primary characters in the TV series, where he is shown to be a consummate chef who produces a remarkable dish in virtually every episode (including an exotic version of chicken soup for Will Graham when the detective is hospitalized). Writer-producer Bryan Fuller invests this aspect of Hannibal's character with genuine authority by bringing in James Beard award-winning chef José Andrés as an expert consultant. Scenes of conspicuous consumption are lingered over, to the point where one can almost taste the fare being served, and the fine wines that accompany it. We relish these scenes despite knowing that several of them involve the consumption of human body parts. To underscore the importance of this culinary theme, the episodes of each season are named after courses in a gourmet dinner service (the episodes of Season 1 take their titles from French haute cuisine, those of Season 2 from Japanese haute cuisine, the first half of Season 3 from Italian cuisine).

I have always believed that our sense of taste reveals a great deal about us. In Hannibal's case, it marks him as a totally unique individual and a member of the elite upper class. In tandem, his remarkable aesthetic and culinary sensibilities attract us to him as a man of enviable discernment. We want to feel with a man of such taste, to experience the delicate sensations that only someone with such a degree of discernment can appreciate; as Nietzsche observed, "The happiness of those who can recognize [beauty] augments the beauty of the world, bathing everything that exists in a sunnier light; discernment not only envelops all things in its own beauty, but in the long run permeates the things themselves with its beauty"

(Nietzsche, *Dawn* §550). In this precise sense, Hannibal's artistic and culinary proclivities appeal to us emotionally, drawing us ever further under his spell.

Evil Genius

Evil geniuses like Dr. Mabuse, Professor Moriarty, Lord Voldemort, Simon Gruber (in John McTiernan's *Die Hard: With a Vengeance*), the Joker, Jigsaw (in the seven *Saw* movies), and Lex Luthor are the driving forces in many of our most popular action, suspense, and horror films. Yet most of them exist only to be thwarted by the good protagonist, while often contributing to their own demise: we love such wily villains for the intricacy and ingenuity of their diabolical plans, and for their black humor, and there is no greater genius in the history of the moving image than Hannibal Lecter. Seldom boastful, and often witty, he contributes to his own capture only when he gets sentimental. As Nietzsche put it in *The Dawn of Day*: "So long as genius dwells within us, we are courageous, as if mad, indeed, and are heedless of life, health and honour; we fly through the day freer than an eagle and in the dark we are more certain than the owl" (Nietzsche, *Dawn* §538).

Reputed to have an IQ of 200, Lecter's brilliance is flabbergasting. In *Red Dragon*, we learn that he was a model prisoner after his capture by Will Graham, until, having lulled his captors into a false sense of security, he bit the face off of one of his nurses. From his prison cell, Lecter manages to get in touch with Francis Dolarhyde, the serial killer dubbed "the Tooth Fairy," and sends him on a revenge mission to kill Graham at the detective's Florida home. In *The Silence of the Lambs*, Hannibal somehow kills his fellow inmate, Miggs, by getting the man to swallow his tongue, escapes by opening his handcuffs with a ball point pen nib, and masquerades as one of the guards by donning the victim's amputated face. He then tracks down his adversary Frederick Chilton at a medical conference held in the tropics, leaving no doubt that he will be dining on the criminal psychologist's remains after the film ends.

In *Hannibal*, he neatly slices the femoral artery of Pazzi's henchman, Gnocco, does away with Pazzi himself, and with Matteo as well. Lecter manages to get himself caught by dropping off a birthday gift to Starling, who saves him from being fed to Mason Verger's man-eating pigs. But he ultimately extricates them both from that mess, and (in the film version only) convinces Mason's right hand man Cordell to push his adversary into the pigs' pen (in the novel, Mason is killed by his sister, Margot). Finally, he captures Starling's antagonist, Paul Krendler, and (in the novel only) feeds her the FBI man's brains—which are so delicious she requests a second helping: "See if I sound like Oliver Twist when I ask for *MORE*" (Harris, *Hannibal*, p. 474).

Even young Hannibal is extremely crafty in *Hannibal Rising*. Bent on revenge against the foragers who ate his sister, he returns to the summer house where the siblings were held prisoner and unearths the Nazi dogtags of his captors. He methodically does them in one by one, finishing the job in the Canadian wilderness. While doing so, he manages to evade prosecution at the hands of Inspector Popil, who suspects young Lecter but can never amass the evidence necessary for a conviction.

But Hannibal's machinations are even more brilliant in the television series. He befriends Will Graham, and helps him catch a couple of early serial killers, while executing several copycat crimes that are attributed to various other people. He skillfully and subtly leads Jack Crawford to eventually suspect that Will committed the murders, revealing incriminating evidence slowly and reluctantly (as a supposed friend would). Lecter enlists the aid of Will's neurologist in covering up the investigator's encephalitic illness (which Lecter may have infected him with), convincing Graham that there is nothing physically wrong with him, and that he is suffering from a profound mental illness. By the time Will comes to realize Lecter's guilt, it is too late; the frame is complete, and Season 1 ends with Will in an institution for the criminally insane.

Season 2 begins with intense hand-to-hand combat between Jack Crawford and Hannibal, with each nearly killing the other and the outcome left in doubt. The show then flashes back to weeks earlier, tracing Will's fight for freedom, as he attempts to convince Jack Crawford, Alana Bloom, and the legal system itself of his innocence. It ends with Jack and an exonerated Will trying to take Hannibal out on their own, with no FBI backup. Hannibal is one step ahead of them, however, and leaves them both cut deeply and bleeding profusely.

The television series is designed as a prequel to *Red Dragon* (whose plot line was always planned to unspool in its third season). Our knowledge (as fans of the films) that Lecter's triumph is only temporary does not temper our admiration for his skillful execution of a "long con" (which only a season of episodes made possible). We are meant to delight in his remarkable ingenuity, and I did so unreservedly. His knowing smile in seeing Graham behind bars is positively exhilarating, and his sigh of relief as he downs a glass of champagne in first class while making his escape unscathed brings glee to Hannibal aficionados like myself.

"Free Range Rude" and Sympathetic Acquaintances

A fourth element in the saga of Hannibal Lecter that allows us to care for him is his choice of victims, and of acquaintances. His role in *Red Dragon*, *The Silence of the Lambs*, and the initial episodes of the *Hannibal* TV series is as helpmate to the detective protagonist. His insights help Will Graham track down the Tooth Fairy, and Clarice Starling capture Buffalo Bill. He is of great value to both of them, and to society, which has two less serial killers to worry about.

The Silence of the Lambs of course remains the locus of our empathy for Hannibal as a fictional creation. Once again Cynthia Freeland's account of his appeal is excellent: "Lecter functions primarily as both a suitor and a mentor for Clarice . . . he, like we, appreciates something very fine, and in doing so he manifests just plain good taste . . . Lecter really does function to help Clarice grow up and reconcile herself to her bad childhood memories" (Freeland, p. 204). We believe him when he observes that it would be something to know her in private life, and he confirms his suspicion in the next novel, *Hannibal*.

Many fans of the series (myself included) thought that author Thomas Harris went too far in having them become romantically involved at the end of that book. Despite Lecter's extensive use of hypnotic drugs, such an unlikely development simply strains our credulity.[2] Ridley Scott corrected the mistake

---

[2] For a reading of *Hannibal* that suggests their romance is both believable and important to both of their stories, see Chapter 18 of this volume.—Ed.

in the film version: near its end, Lecter asks, "Tell me Clarice, would you ever say to me stop . . . if you loved me you'd stop." Her response is unequivocal: "Not in a thousand years." Hannibal acknowledges that this reply is what he expected: "That's my girl." In a vulnerable moment while he is kissing her, she handcuffs the two of them together as the FBI closes in.

What he does next cements our identification with him. An unfeeling psychopath would simply sever her hand to extricate himself, and he threatens to do so ("This is really going to hurt"). But we see that she remains intact as the FBI arrives, and learn on the airplane that Lecter (like a trapped fox) has amputated his own hand to secure his escape. This confirms our belief that he indeed had genuine feelings for Starling, which textbook serial killers are supposed to be unable to sustain.

Who Hannibal chooses to murder, and the manner in which he does so, is also crucial to our empathic connection, which increases as the series of movies unfolds. Prison orderly Barney tells Clarice Starling that Lecter had a preference for killing "free range rude," and only poses a danger to people he respects if they stand in his way (and sometimes not even then). In *Silence*, he slays his guards, the ambulance attendants and the hotel guest he impersonates, which he had to do in order to escape. At the end of the film, he is preparing to kill and eat his other captor, Dr. Frederick Chilton, who had been portrayed in a totally unsympathetic fashion. We naturally revel in the prospect, especially given Lecter's witty observation to Clarice on the phone that he is planning to have an old friend for dinner. The film ends with him tracking his quarry and blending invisibly in with a tropical crowd, a scene that elicited a hearty round of applause from the audience in the initial screening I attended more than twenty years ago.

Lecter leaves a substantial trail of victims in *Hannibal*, all of them bounty hunters who seek his life for money; by this time he has been transformed from antagonist to protagonist. We root for him as he fends off Gnocco, Pazzi, and Matteo, and despite the fact that Lecter had caused Mason Verger to cut off parts of his own face and feed them to his dogs, Verger's repugnant child molestation (in the book) and insatiable thirst for revenge have ensured our antipathy towards him. Hannibal's stylish preparation of Krendler's brain, and Clarice's enthusiastic reception thereof (more so in the book than in the film), put the cap on his triumphs.

Young Hannibal is also the sole protagonist in *Hannibal Rising*, and, as noted above, the men he targets in his vendetta all deserve what they get. His murder of the butcher is somewhat disproportionate to the crime of suggestively insulting Lady Murasaki, but this is mitigated by the fact that, in the novel, his uncle dies of a heart attack trying to defend the lady's honor.

While Hannibal's evil is unmotivated and unexplained in *The Silence of the Lambs*, where the good doctor himself refuses to be psychoanalyzed and is proud of his choice to do evil, the later novels provide us with a pat Freudian etiology for his psychosis. His cannibalism is seen as resulting from childhood trauma, when his beloved younger sister Mischa was killed by a group of starving *Hilfswillige* (Russian POWs serving in the German army) and eaten in a stew that may or may not have been forced upon him as well. This trauma resulted in his losing his voice for years, and repressing the tragic memory, recovering it only with the help of truth serum in *Hannibal Rising*.

We have thus far discussed several factors that mitigate Lecter's evil and make it palatable for us. Primary among them are his selective decisions of who to kill, his black humor, and the caring relationships that he forms with Clarice and Lady Murasaki. This pattern has been broken, however, in the *Hannibal* television series.

Much has been made of the relationship between Hannibal and Will Graham, especially in Season 2, with some critics claiming that the series is really about the love between the two of them. Skeptical at the end of the first season myself, I have come to believe (after reading several end-of-season interviews with creator Bryan Fuller) that Hannibal did long for a friend (shades of *Dexter*) and sincerely hoped Will would take Lecter's side, embrace his murderous nature and run away. There is something very Nietzschean about that. A true friend, in Nietzsche's estimation, wishes above all else to make you stronger.[3] As a contributor to the website *Faustian Europe* put it:

---

[3] For a discussion of the possibility of friendship between Hannibal and Will, including discussion of Nietzsche's thoughts on friendship as they apply to *Hannibal*, see Chapter 10 of this volume.—Ed.

what is for Nietzsche the difference between friend and enemy? One can easily derive from the above mentioned that there is no difference at all. Both friend and enemy is someone who you consider your equal. It is someone who you think is worth fighting against. From the fight, you both learn and ultimately strengthen your resolve. In fact, it might be said that "your best friend is also your best enemy, and your best enemy is your best friend." Similarly, Nietzsche mentions Christ's "love thy enemy" as a commendable principle to follow, but not in the "Christian sense." For Nietzsche, since love and hate are almost inseparable, the enemy, your antithesis, is also someone to be truly admired, because this enemy inevitably forms a part of "who you are," the enemy shows you a different side of the coin, and thus makes you stronger in the end.

Lecter did consider Graham a potential equal, was certainly tested by him, and is eventually caught and brought into custody by Will.

In the first season of the series, Lecter relates details of his personal history and reflections only to his psychotherapist, and even then is admittedly less than candid with her. He weaves an inescapable web of lies around Will Graham (with whom we are clearly meant to sympathize), and the victims he chooses are largely innocent, mere extensions of the serial killers he is copying and one-upping (or, at worst, unmannerly individuals he has encountered in the business world). Graham seems briefly to turn the tables on Hannibal in Season 2, and Lecter reveals part of who he is in the process of trying to woo him over to the dark side. But Will is eventually overwhelmed, and Lecter remains the most compelling character in the show. The key to understanding why is his complete mastery over every person and situation that he faces, and this brings us to the most crucial piece of the puzzle, my Nietzschean theory of horror pleasure.

Hannibal and the Will to Power

The foregoing should not mislead anyone into thinking that I believe we only empathize with the monster in horror films. In my view, we empathize with *both* the powerful monsters in horror movies *and* with the "good guys" who eventually subdue them and, in so doing, we feel a shared sense of heightened power in seeing great resistance overcome. Beyond the factors I have identified above, the key to Hannibal's fascination for us is that his power—in Friedrich Nietzsche's sense of the term—is unmatched.

Nietzsche notoriously contended that, for good or ill, we all seek to exercise our will upon others. As he puts it in *The Gay Science*:

> *On the doctrine of the feeling of power.* Benefiting and hurting others are ways of exercising one's power upon others: that is all one desires in such cases . . . Whether benefiting or hurting others involves sacrifices for us does not affect the ultimate value of our actions. Even if we offer our lives, as martyrs do for their church, this is a sacrifice that is offered for our desire for power or for the purpose of preserving our feeling of power. . . . Certainly the state in which we hurt others is rarely as agreeable, in an unadulterated way, as that in which we benefit others; it is a sign that we are still lacking power, or it shows a sense of frustration in the face of this poverty . . . (Nietzsche, *Gay Science* §13)

Crucially, Nietzsche not only claims that we benefit others for the way it makes us feel (substituting an unapologetic egoism for a spurious altruism), but in this passage he affirms his belief that benefiting others, presumably by increasing their feeling of power, is (all other things being equal) more enjoyable than harming them. Harming others who are weaker than us simply for the sake of doing so is a sign that (like the typical class bully) we lack power.

By the beginning of *The Antichrist*, Nietzsche had formulated his value theory succinctly:

"What is good? —All that heightens the feeling of power, the will to power, power itself in man. What is bad? —All that proceeds from weakness. What is happiness? —The feeling that power increases, that resistance is overcome" (Nietzsche, *Antichrist* §2). The feeling of power is the feeling of being in control of yourself, the environment that surrounds you, and those who are your inferiors. In doing so, one should adopt "the conviction that one has duties only to one's equals; towards the others one acts as one thinks best" (Nietzsche, *Will to Power* §937). As Lecter has yet to meet anyone he considers his equal, he has done pretty much as he sees fit. In the films, he aimed the Tooth Fairy at Will Graham, served up Buffalo Bill to Starling, killed Rinaldo Pazzi, most of Mason Verger's henchmen, and all of the cannibalistic murderers of his beloved sister.

But this essay was provoked by my enthusiasm for the television series. The artistic success of the series stems in part from several ways that the depiction of Hannibal differs there from the classic films. I believe that those differences serve to confirm my theory more convincingly than the films ever did.

As noted above, there are many extenuating circumstances in the cinematic depictions of Lecter that facilitate our approval of this chilling serial killer. His relationships with Clarice Starling and Lady Murasaki mitigate his inhumanity by providing him with love interests whom he cares for and helps. His choice of victims that either deserve to die, are totally unsympathetic, or are trying to kill or incarcerate him, tempers our outrage. His dark humor gives birth to a number of amusing one-liners, and once a character has made us laugh we are well on the way to approving of him.[4]

Several of these elements are absent in the television series. Hannibal's apparent romantic interest in Alana Bloom in Season Two was clearly feigned, and (with some regret) he ends up having Abigail push her out a third-story window. Lecter murders innocent and anonymous figures throughout the TV series (with the exception of Dr. Sutcliffe, who deserves his fate for conspiring with Lecter to conceal Will Graham's encephalitis), and there are no comedic taglines to enter into popular culture. The remarkable culinary and aesthetic tastes are still present, and he does help the FBI catch other serial killers, but he is not in love, his victims are (by and large) sympathetic innocents, and his black humor is held to a minimum. Yet I believe that Lecter has been even more compelling on the small screen, because his power is even greater and more impressive.

Early critics of the series were troubled by the fact that, despite its title, Will Graham figured more prominently in the first half dozen episodes than Hannibal himself. Yet this was the case in the first two movies as well. Following their template, Hannibal began the series as a consultant to Graham, helping him capture other serial killers. Graham, deeply troubled by his

---

[4] For more on Hannibal Lecter's humor, especially as an expression of power, see Chapter 14 of this volume.—Ed.

ability to empathize with such murderers, had quit his job as an FBI homicide investigator, only to be brought back into such a psychologically unsettling position by Jack Crawford. Hannibal is brought in as a consultant in Graham's psychotherapy, and initially seems to be trying to help this troubled profiler (who can feel with serial killers to a disturbing degree). As the first season unfolds, Will's psychological and physical condition degenerates, and while we sympathize with his worsening plight, we do not empathize with him (in the sense of wanting to *be* him and share his feelings of powerlessness).

Hannibal slowly becomes the central figure of the show, in both a dramatic and an empathetic sense. Other serial killers become almost an afterthought, eclipsed by Hannibal's ability to easily outstrip them in a series of copycat crimes. The battle of wills between Graham and Lecter takes center stage, and it is no contest. Hannibal reduces Will to a virtual puppet, convincing the investigator that he is experiencing a purely mental collapse, and framing him for the murders that Lecter was perpetrating.

His ruthlessness is also demonstrated in his treatment of Abigail Hobbs, the daughter and accomplice of Garret Jacob Hobbs, the serial killer who Graham guns down to save Abigail's life. Lecter seems to take Abigail under his wing, helping her to conceal a murder she commits in his home, and to deal with her role in her father's crimes. Yet he eventually cuts her throat as well, a surrogate father who tries to kill her just like her real father did. The best efforts of Will, Jack, and Alana to end his reign of terror are all in vain, and after their climactic confrontation, a bloody Hannibal walks out into a bracing rainstorm in total triumph. As he tells Alana Bloom in Episode 10 of Season 2, he has played them all like his beloved Theremin ("a very psychological instrument," as she describes it). He is the virtual embodiment of Nietzsche's vision of the master of power, the Overman.

Entertainment Weekly critic Jeff Jensen picked up on this theme in his review of the finale of Season 1:

> How about that smirk that rippled across Hannibal's lips? I would like to think that Lecter's show of delight meant something more than just relished triumph, as I also would like to think that the ubermenchy mastermind sincerely wanted to help Will gain mastery over his

chaotic internal world and transform his guilt-wracked pathology into the same kind of liberating, Nietzschian beyond-good-and-evil moral code he has for himself. Or maybe I'm just suffering from dementia. Will would certainly think so: His theory was that Hannibal was just conducting a mad scientist psych experiment in the wild, that Hannibal merely wanted to wind him up and see what would happen. (Jensen)

It may well be a combination of both, and Will emphasizes the experimental element when he mimics Hannibal's own words in explaining that he told Mason Verger the good doctor was going to kill Mason because he was curious to see what would happen.

Lecter conspires with Dr. Sutcliffe to conceal Graham's illness for nefarious reasons. They agree to jointly study Graham like a lab rat, Sutcliffe for the physical effects of encephalitis, Lecter for its psychological effects, noting what a "rare occasion" it was to be able to do so. Lecter had the added motive of wanting to exercise his power over the FBI, by eluding their dragnet and tormenting their crack investigator in the process.

The framing of Will for Hannibal's string of murders is nothing less than a masterpiece of engineering. Not only does Lecter plant Abigail's DNA on Will, but he also kills Sutcliffe right after Will had been in for further tests. The comb which sparks the conflagration that incinerates Georgia Madchen appears right after Will visits her; bits of flesh from earlier victims are tied into the fly-fishing flies that Will fashions; Will spits up an amputated ear into his sink; and the list goes on. In the final episode of Season 1, Hannibal is triumphant and Will appears doomed.

Meanwhile, Lecter has slowly (and apparently reluctantly) revealed Will's supposed mental illness to Jack Crawford. He brilliantly plants the seeds of doubt in Jack's mind, implicating Will and setting the stage for the season's climax, when Crawford (convinced of his guilt) shoots Graham for threatening Hannibal. In short, Hannibal does precisely what he wants to do with all of the primary figures in the drama. Corresponding to how Harold Alderman outlined the traits of Nietzsche's *Übermensch*, Lecter expresses his anger directly, is ingeniously creative, self-directed and this-worldly, remarkably self-aware, experimental and proudly egoistic, while being both unashamedly aristocratic and discretely masked (Alderman, p. 66). Hiding in their midst, Hannibal was (in Nietzsche's words), "always disguised: the higher the type, the more a man requires an incognito" (Nietzsche, *Will to Power* §490).

In several ways, then, the Lecter persona has been stripped of its black humor and romantic interest, pared down to a pure and immensely powerful figure. He exercises complete control over himself, his environment, and every other character with whom he comes in contact. He kills and eats his victims with impunity, manipulates those around him mercilessly (his psychoanalyst may be an exception), and leaves little doubt of his intellectual and strategic superiority. Dr. Du Maurier's warning to Jack Crawford in the penultimate episode of Season 2 proves to be prophetic: "If you think you are about to catch Hannibal it is because he wants you to think so. Don't fool yourself into thinking he's not in control of what's happening" (*Hannibal*, Season 2, "Tome-wan"). I can't remember another season-ending episode of a series where the "bad guy" triumphed as completely.

For Nietzsche, in the absence of a perfect Creator, we are called upon to be god-like creatures, to create meaning and value in an inherently meaningless world. Libby Hill, in her review of the series for NPR, captured the divine aura of Hannibal:

> Intentional or otherwise, Hannibal Lecter is not the devil; he is god. He is that force in his universe that exists in concert with but still wholly outside the world at large. He is something unnatural. Uncanny. He is the danger. He is the unknowable presence lurking in the shadows. He is omnipotent. He is omniscient. And he will beguile. He will persuade. He will manipulate. He will undermine your fear with fascination and your seduction will be your undoing. (Hill)

What I have been arguing is that we empathize with Lecter for a number of reasons, the most prominent of which is this god-like power. The many close-ups he is featured in, his culinary and aesthetic tastes, his evil genius, and his discriminating choice of both victims and acquaintances, all of these factors play important roles in allowing us to enjoy Lecter's escapades.

But, in my view, it is his absolute control over every person and situation which he confronts that is the fundamental ground of our empathy with him. Those of us who love horror identify with monsters, and the one with whom I most enjoy doing so is Dr. Hannibal Lecter.

17

The Beguiling Horror of Hannibal Lecter

WILLIAM J. DEVLIN AND SHAI BIDERMAN

In Jonathan Demme's *The Silence of the Lambs*, FBI trainee Clarice Starling is assigned to conduct interviews with, and develop a psychological profile on, the infamous psychiatrist and serial killer, Dr. Hannibal Lecter. Her supervisor, Special Agent Jack Crawford, advises her to be very careful with Hannibal and suggests the mental dangers she'll face on this assignment. He warns her, "Believe me, you don't want Hannibal Lecter in your head." Meanwhile, at the asylum, Dr. Frederick Chilton warns her of the physical dangers she'll face as he shows her photos of a nurse Hannibal attacked, pointing out that, though the doctors were able to re-set her jaw and save one eye, Hannibal's pulse "never got above eighty-five, even when he ate her tongue." Together, Crawford and Chilton aim to let Starling know the gravity of her assignment and who the subject really is. As Chilton points out, "Oh, he's a monster. Pure psychopath. It's so rare to capture one alive."

Even before we, the audience, meet "Hannibal the Cannibal," his reputation precedes him. He is a monster—a living, breathing, captured, but still highly dangerous (both mentally and physically) monster. His path of horror incites fear in both the characters and the audience alike, and yet we are *still* drawn to him—anxiously awaiting our first glimpse of the monster "in chains" as Starling makes her way down the cold, dark prison hallway to meet Dr. Lecter. But this raises an interesting philosophical question: Given how fearful Hannibal the monster is, why are we so interested in watching him? In this chapter, we explore this question and address why it is that, despite the horror this iconic monster instills in us, we are still so drawn towards him, watching his every move.

Hannibal and Monster Movies

As suggested, both Crawford and Chilton startlingly warn Starling that Hannibal is a monster. But Hannibal is not alone in this regard: the gruesome depiction of Hannibal as a monster is a common trait of the cinematic horror genre. As such, he is one among many famous monsters in the cinematic history of the horror genre. In the first half of the twentieth century, audiences saw various monsters from literature brought to the moving image. In 1910, we find the Frankenstein monster from Mary Shelley's novel, *Frankenstein: or, The Modern Prometheus* (1818), portrayed in J. Searle Dawley's short film *Frankenstein*. In 1920, we encounter the monster, Edward Hyde, in John S. Robertson's *Dr. Jekyll and Mr. Hyde*, drawn from Robert Louis Stevenson's novella, *The Strange Case of Dr. Jekyll and Mr. Hyde* (1886). In 1922, audiences were introduced to the vampire, Count Orlok, in F.W. Murnau's *Nosferatu*, a film that adapted (and paved the way for many more film adaptations of) Bram Stoker's *Dracula* (1897). In 1932, the world saw the first cinematic introduction of zombies in Victor and Edward Halperin's *White Zombie*, adapted from William Seabrook's book, *The Magic Island* (1929); meanwhile, the zombie phenomenon was later catapulted by George Romero's *Night of the Living Dead* (1968).

In the latter half of the twentieth century, while those same monsters of literature continued to frighten audiences, other monsters were introduced. Alfred Hitchcock's *Psycho* (1960) offered the psychotic character, Norman Bates, a psychologically disturbed man who, dressed as his mother, would kill his victims at the Bates Motel. This film helped to inspire the sub-genre in horror known as "slasher films" that followed. There, we find a new series of famous monsters in cinema. We meet the chainsaw wielding Leatherface in Tobe Hooper's *The Texas Chainsaw Massacre* (1974). In 1978, the monster Michael Myers begins his decades of terror in John Carpenter's *Halloween*. Three years later, Jason Voorhees comes to life in Steven Miner's *Friday the 13th Part 2* (1981). In 1984, Freddy Krueger haunted us in our dreams in Wes Craven's *A Nightmare on Elm Street*.

It is during this era that author Thomas Harris creates the monster, Hannibal the Cannibal, through the series of horror novels, *Red Dragon* (1981), *Silence of the Lambs* (1988), *Hannibal* (1999), and *Hannibal Rising* (2006). While Dr. Hannibal Lecter (or Lecktor) first hit the big screen in Michael Mann's *Manhunter* in 1986, based on Harris's *Red Dragon*, it wasn't until Anthony Hopkins's Oscar-winning performance as Hannibal in Demme's *Silence of the Lambs* (1991) that the monster became embedded in popular culture. From there, Hannibal's journey on the big screen continued with the sequel, Ridley Scott's *Hannibal* (2001), and the prequels, Peter Webber's *Hannibal Rising* (2007) and Brett Ratner's *Red Dragon* (2002). All of these films are notable, not simply for including Hannibal as a character, but for focusing on Hannibal *as a monster*.

The fascination (to the point of obsession) of moviegoers with monsters and the personification of monstrosity has thus furnished the cinematic culture of horror from the dawn of cinema to the contemporary age. This rather unique (and definitely strange) phenomenon raises an interesting philosophical question: given how fearful the monster is, why are we so interested in watching him? What is it in the cinematic appearance of the monster—an appearance that, for lack of better words, involves an unpleasant experience, and negative emotions like fear, dread, and disgust—that anxiously draws us to sneak the excruciating peek? Moreover, and to the extent that Hannibal helps to make a new breed of "realistic" monsters (who exist "in the flesh," so to speak, as integral to the human race), how should we treat Hannibal, as we compare him to those which inhabit the fictitious (and highly improbable) world of zombies, vampires, and the like? And what, if anything, is cinematically unique in the monstrosity of Hannibal Lecter?

The Monster and Paradox of Horror

These questions about monsters and horror films take us into the philosophy of horror, a renewed branch of the philosophical interest in film and cinema. One of the proponents of such philosophy, the contemporary philosopher Noël Carroll, offers a significant and influential account of the horror genre. According to Carroll, the horror genre is determined by its engagement with the inexplicable (and thus revolting) existence of *the monster*. Accordingly, the centrality of the monster in the plotline of a film is a precondition for a film to be considered a horror film. Carroll's definition of a horror film thus spreads in three consecutive steps. First, a work of cinematic horror is that which attempts to raise fear and disgust. Second, these stirred emotional responses are directed at the monster. Third, the monster is a threatening creature beyond the realms of scientific possibility. For Carroll, "a work should be classified as horror if it attempts to arouse fear and disgust directed at a monster. . . . a threatening creature not thought to exist by current science" (Carroll, *The Philosophy of Horror*, p. 27). So, for example, we can clearly see that Frankenstein is a monster insofar as, via a combination of chemistry and alchemy, a new hideous inhuman creature is created that threatens and terrifies us all. Likewise, Count Orlok and Count Dracula are dangerous immortal monsters that live by sucking the blood, and life, of their human prey. Meanwhile, Freddy is not only already dead, but also only "lives" in the dream world, insofar as he is able to be a non-physical dream-like being that can physically harm and kill his victims in their nightmares. Clearly, these monsters are both threatening creatures and not explainable or posited to exist by current science.

But, following Carroll, notice two striking features about how the audience relates to the cinematic monster. While these monsters do not exist in real life, we are horrified by them (like the boogeyman that lays await under our beds) and yet we are *still* drawn in to watching them on the big screen. That is, we, the audience, have two different but seemingly simultaneous emotional responses to the monster. First, we are *horrified* by the monster. From Frankenstein to Dracula to Michael to Freddy to Jason: each one of them terrifies us, making us cower away in fear. Second, we are also, as awkward as it may seem, equally *attracted* to the monster. Although we may cower in fear, we *want* to see the monster on the prowl, attacking, and taking his next victim. Many movie-goers seeing *A Nightmare on Elm Street* watched intently and maybe even covered their eyes (while peeking past their fingers) as Glen Lantz screamed and struggled while Freddy sucked him into the bed and released a geyser of blood upon the ceiling. Or, if you were like this co-author, Bill, you were a kid who hid behind his couch in fear, but still poked his head out, watching Jason stalk Chris Higgins until Chris bravely swings an axe into Jason's head, apparently killing him in Steve Miner's *Friday the 13th Part 3*.

This strange set of feelings we hold of being scared of, but attracted to, the monster (and its centrality to the definition of horror films) raises a problem. How is it that we can be both horrified by and attracted to the monster at the same time? Is it a case of Stockholm syndrome? Is the monster our captor, and we the captive audience, as we follow him and develop a traumatic bonding to him? Is there a way for us to resolve, or at least explain, this tension that we have towards monsters in cinema? Carroll calls this *the paradox of horror*. If horror films present us with monsters, and if the sole purpose of this presentation is to disgust and to stir unpleasant emotions while doing so—why is it that we seek this mental anguish to begin with? This becomes all the more important, when we recall that in real life we are typically keen to avoid such painful emotions. In cinema, on the other hand, while encountering the monster in horror, we seem to be attracted to that which is fundamentally repulsive. How is it, then, that we routinely seek out the horror monsters, knowing that they will raise painful emotions of fear and disgust? This behavior seems to be paradoxical.

Carroll provides an answer to the apparent paradox of conflicting feelings we hold towards the monster. The reason why audiences seek out horror films, knowing full well that we will experience fear and disgust, is for the pleasures we'll gain from them. Despite the terror instilled in us, we watch the fictional Frankenstein's monster terrorize the villages on the big screen, or Dracula draw blood from his prey, or Michael murder his innocent victims, because the experience of horror is the "price we are willing to pay" for the pleasures of discovering and learning about the horrific being (Carroll, *The Philosophy of Horror*, p. 186).

The Paradox of Hannibal

At first glance, Hannibal appears to fit the model of Carroll's analysis of the monster and the paradox of horror. First, as mentioned, Hannibal is a monster who threatens us, similar to the classic monsters in cinematic history. In *The Silence of the Lambs*, we hear of, and witness, Hannibal's sadistic infatuation with human flesh, as he eats a nurse's tongue, tears at a guard's flesh, and proceeds to wear his facial skin as a mask to escape imprisonment. In *Red Dragon*, we see how vengeful Hannibal can be as he agrees to work with FBI Agent Will Graham to help him catch the serial killer, Francis Dolarhyde, known as the "Tooth Fairy." However, Hannibal's agreement is just a clever ruse, as Hannibal uses his resources to provide Dolarhyde with Graham's home address through a coded message in a tabloid. Although Graham and his family survive the Tooth Fairy's subsequent attack, he is left "disfigured." Aware of this, Hannibal sends Graham a chilling letter, saying "I hope you're not too ugly. What a collection of scars you have! Never forget who gave you the best of them" (Ratner, *Red Dragon*). Meanwhile, in *Hannibal*, Hannibal continues his lineage of sadistic homicides. He publicly hangs and disembowels Chief Inspector Rinaldo Pazzi in Florence. He lobotomizes Justice Department Agent Paul Krendler and forces Starling to watch as he cuts out Krendler's prefrontal cortex, sautées it, and feeds it to him. Later, as Hannibal makes his escape on a commercial plane, he offers a piece of Krendler's cortex to a young boy, teaching him, "it is important to always try new things" (Scott, *Hannibal*). Lastly, in *Hannibal Rising*, we witness the development, growth, and unleashing of the monster within, as Hannibal kills his first victim (via beheading) as a teenager and then carries out and completes his crusade of revenge as he murders those who killed his sister, Mischa. Thus, the series of films in the Hannibal Lecter franchise depicts Hannibal as a monster and puts him with the famous cast of Frankenstein, Dracula, Leatherface, Jason, and others.

Furthermore, when we examine Hannibal as a cinematic monster and consider the audience's relationship to such a character, we notice the paradox is raised. First, we, the audience, are *horrified* by him! Hannibal the Cannibal terrifies us. Though he is small in stature, well-spoken, and deceptively polite, we know there is a dark and ferocious monster just beneath the surface. While Dr. Lecter is a well-read, aristocratic socialite and patron of the arts who charms his guests as he hosts soirées, we know that, given even a moment's opportunity, he'll savagely lunge at Graham, threatening to eat his heart first, or chillingly serve a victim's body as an amuse-bouche for all of his guests to eat. And so, he repulses us. Just like with Jason, who wears a hockey mask and hunts his victims with a machete, or Freddy who haunts us in our nightmares with his razor-blade glove, or Michael who stalks teenagers with a knife while wearing a Halloween mask, we are utterly terrified by Hannibal. Even when he is standing, bound to a hand-truck and wearing a restraining mask, we are petrified by his searching eyes, fearful that the monster within will somehow break through his chains and devour another victim.

Second, at the same time, we are *attracted* to Hannibal. Even though he incites fear, we are drawn to him. We anxiously await every move the monster will make. Audiences enjoyed *Silence of the Lambs* because we became mesmerized by Hannibal the Cannibal. It was Hopkins's portrayal of the cold, detached monster that led him to win the Oscar for Best Actor. Fans fell in love with the character and eagerly anticipated the subsequent films to see the monster return. We are intrigued by his odd tenderness towards Starling. We smile when he tells Starling that he is about to have an old friend, the arrogant and condescending Dr. Chilton, "for dinner." Furthermore, we even grow to root for Hannibal. Just as we were excited to see Jason and Michael's bodies disappear at the end of their films (thereby indicating they are alive) or to see Freddy return at the end of his films (indicating he will continue to haunt us), we are excited when we see Hannibal capture and kill his victims and escape the authorities. Simultaneously, then, Hannibal is both the villain and the hero of the franchise.

The Mythos of Hannibal

Nevertheless, upon closer inspection, Hannibal is *not* the classic monster. Hannibal resists Carroll's definition of the monster, in at least two ways. First, unlike Dracula or Frankenstein's monster or zombies or Freddy, Hannibal is realistic—he is *not* a "creature not thought to exist by current science." In fact, he *is* a creature thought to exist by current science. While we cannot imagine vampires or re-animated corpses or a dead man who can literally kill us in our dreams, we can recognize Hannibal as a person who could very well be alive today. He is an intelligent and persuasive human being, who attended Johns Hopkins University, developed a career and practice in psychiatry, enjoyed the arts, and became a well-known socialite in the Baltimore area. In this sense, Hannibal is, more or less, like us. Or, at the very least, we can imagine living a life similar to his. Here, Hannibal deviates from one of the central attributes of the cinematic monster: Hannibal is human. He does not have super-human powers that can help him to overcome his fights with human beings. While a bullet to the head would not kill Dracula, it would likely kill Hannibal. While stabbing Jason in the chest with a pitchfork would only slow him down, it would surely end Hannibal's reign of terror. Even further, as we saw in *Red Dragon*, Hannibal can be caught and captured, as he was by Graham. When Hannibal prods Graham as to how he thinks he caught him, Graham admits, "You had disadvantages . . . you're insane." Soon after, Hannibal responds, "Don't you understand, Will? You caught me because we're very much alike. Without our imaginations, we'd be like all those other poor dullards" (Ratner, *Red Dragon*).

And yet it is these human attributes of Hannibal that make him so threatening and terrifying. His heightened sense of smell suggests he is above average as he recognizes Starling uses Evyan skin cream and sometimes wears L'Air du Temps ("but not today"), and he detects Graham by the fact that he is wearing "the same atrocious aftershave" that he "wore in court." His social charm allows him to woo his victims into a false sense of security, just as he did with Graham and Pazzi. His appeal to the arts allows him to develop culinary skills for cooking and eating his victims (and even serving them to his unknowing dinner guests).

His developed ability at the gentle art of persuasiveness allows him to prey upon others. At the asylum, in response to Miggs's assault on Starling, guards "heard Lecter whispering to him all afternoon and Miggs crying" and later found Miggs had committed suicide by swallowing his tongue (Demme, *Silence*). At an earlier point, Hannibal gives the man who would become his only surviving victim, Mason Verger, amyl nitrate and convinces him to cut his face off with broken glass. Later, when Verger seeks revenge by having Hannibal eaten by wild boars, Hannibal convinces Dr. Cordell, Verger's physician, that he can feed Verger to the boars, and "always say it was just me," to which Cordell agrees (Scott, *Hannibal*).

Likewise, his natural but well-developed intelligence makes him menacing. On the one hand, he is able to outsmart others.

As a prisoner, he uses both Graham and Starling: the former, to attempt to kill him in revenge; the latter, to set up the opportunity to escape from the asylum, which is proven successful as he wears the skin of a dead guard to be escorted towards his freedom. On the other hand, he cleverly outsmarts those who are trying to stop him. He becomes aware of the Bureau's attempt to cover up their knowledge of his correspondence with Dolarhyde (by noticing the rubber gloves in the back pocket of the agent pretending to be a janitor), and is able to continue his plan to have Graham killed. He also becomes privy to Pazzi's plan to capture him for a reward and subsequently kills both the street thief hired to secure his fingerprints and Pazzi himself.

Thus, unlike Carroll's monster, who is a creature beyond scientific thought and existence, it is Hannibal's *human* attributes and demonstration of scientific *plausibility* that make him so threatening and terrifying to us. Carroll does acknowledge that Lecter does not seem to fit his definition of a monster. Instead, he suggests that Lecter "is arguably only a psychotic—albeit one unprecedented in the annals of psychiatry—rather than a monster." However, Carroll offers a way around this problem—namely to recognize that Lecter is an example of science fiction, not contemporary psychology. He writes that examples like Lecter and Norman Bates "are actually creatures of science fiction, though in these cases we are dealing with science fictions of the mind, not the body" (Carroll, "Horror and Humor," p. 148). We, however, offer an alternative response. Rather than emphasize Lecter's unrealistic, or "science fiction" characteristics, we focus—and think audiences generally focus—on Lecter's more human qualities. Rather than trying to force Lecter into a restricted definition of the monster, we think a widening of the definition to account for anomalous examples of monsters such as Lecter is in order.

Moreover, unlike the human Leatherface or even the semi-human Jason or Michael (ignoring their apparently supernatural ability to withstand scientifically plausible ways of being killed), Hannibal has a *mythos* that enhances our fear and attraction towards him. Leatherface, Jason, Michael, and other similar monsters are too simple. These monsters are silent, hide behind masks, and have very brief backstories: Leatherface is child-like and under the thumb of his family and kills others out of fear; Jason drowned at Camp Crystal Lake, his mother sought revenge and now he does, too; Michael, as a child, kills his sister and then fifteen years later breaks out of the asylum to return to his hometown to kill more teenagers. Meanwhile, Hannibal is a far more complex character and monster. The mythology that the Hannibal Lecter movie franchise created for their monster shows that Hannibal is a multi-layered character, which makes him all the more *realistically human*, *horrifying*, and *attractive*.

If we watch the films in the order that chronicles the life of Hannibal, we witness the complex layers of the character more clearly. In *Hannibal Rising*, Hannibal, an innocent boy, is raised in a seemingly good family in Lithuania during World War II. Fleeing the Nazis, his family retreats to their mountain lodge. However, several soldiers kill Hannibal's parents and hole up with Hannibal and Mischa over the cold harsh winter. In order to survive, the soldiers kill and eat Mischa, and unbeknownst to Hannibal at that time he, too, eats her. After escape, Hannibal is later raised by his widowed aunt, Lady Murasaki. Though his love for Murasaki is clear (he even kills his first victim to defend her), he is ultimately driven by revenge, as he seeks vengeance from the men who killed and cannibalized his sister. There, by torturing and mutilating his former captors, Hannibal loses his humanity, even leaving Murasaki to ask him, "What is left in you to love?" (Webber, *Hannibal Rising*).

In *Red Dragon*, we find Hannibal years older, settled in the states, but still carrying on his disregard for human beings, as he is a psychopathic murderer who eats his victims. He attempts to kill, mutilate, and eat Graham when Graham catches on that he is the serial killer he was trying to find, and only assists in the effort to catch the Tooth Fairy (in *Manhunter* and *Red Dragon*) as a means of exacting further revenge on Graham. While Hannibal would like to see Graham dead, in *The Silence of the Lambs*, he meets Starling. Though the monster seems to be ready to kill anyone in any way, shape, or form (Verger, a classical musician, Graham, a nurse, Miggs, guards, Chilton, Pazzi, Krendler, etc.), he clearly has no intention of harming her. Instead, they play their game of *quid pro quo* and, while he earlier sent Graham a rather spiteful letter, when he later escapes, he calls Starling to tell her, "I have no plans to call on you, Clarice. The world's more interesting with you in it." In *Hannibal*, when Starling handcuffs her wrist to

Hannibal's with FBI agents in pursuit, Hannibal even cuts off his own hand as opposed to hers. All of this suggests that, given Hannibal's love for his sister, he treats Starling as if she were Mischa grown up. Thus, given the mythos that expands the character of Dr. Lecter from his life after escaping from prison, to his early youth that shapes the monster we see today, we find that Hannibal is a multi-layered character that explains his behavior and yet horrifies us further.

Hannibal the Monster

Thus, while Carroll's account of the monster partially helps us to understand Hannibal as a monster, it has its limitations. While Hannibal does, indeed, threaten us, given his complex and multi-layered (but realistic and human) character, Hannibal is a person that can exist according to current science. As this limitation goes against our initial impression of Hannibal, we need to broaden the scope of Carroll's otherwise accurate definition. An attempt to do just that was made famous by the philosopher Cynthia Freeland. According to Freeland, the monster is, and definitely can be, a true-to-life being rather than a supernatural one. The guiding principle, for Freeland, should not be scientific but, alternatively, conventional (or ethical). A monster, according to Freeland, is therefore a creature (of any kind) which exhibits and embodies a social or moral perversion and deviancy. In other words, a monster is a manifestation of evil (see "Realist Horror" and *The Naked and the Undead* by Freeland). This definition fits Hannibal rather well. In fact, it is due to the very fact that Hannibal *is* human, but has lost his humanity and is morally and socially deviant, that makes him the threatening monster. This is why he tells Graham, "We live in a primitive time, don't we, Will? Neither savage nor wise. Half measures are the curse of it. A rational society would either kill me or put me to some use" (Ratner, *Red Dragon*). Hannibal recognizes that he is a unique monster, not because he is beyond scientific possibility, but rather because he is, indeed, a *human* monster, whose cold, calculating, detached mental and physical behaviors make him all the more threatening.

Finally, Freeland's account of the monster helps to further enhance, and explain, Carroll's paradox of horror that we, the audience, face when we watch Hannibal on the big screen. We are, as Carroll would say, both horrified by and attracted towards Hannibal. We are attracted to him, even though we find him fundamentally repulsive. But not in the same exact way we are repulsed by and attracted to Frankenstein or Dracula. Hannibal's humanness makes him a unique cinematic monster. As we find that Hannibal is a multi-layered character, and as much as we are still horrified by him, we nevertheless find a way to identify (and maybe even sympathize) with him. Yet, as Hannibal explains his behavior (to the point that we see the human and not the monster), he horrifies us further. Following an alteration of Carroll, we thus pay the price of intensified repulsion for the deeper reward of sympathizing, discovering, and getting to know the human behind the monster. The mythos of Hannibal thus intensifies, and enhances, the paradoxical feelings of fascination and revulsion, thereby making the payoff all the more rewarding. Thus, despite the fact that he is a cannibal and his nature as a monster exists in many dimensions, he raises sympathy.[1] He's in a way a combination of a monster and a tragic figure. As such, his existence as a character in cinematic horror helps to change the way we look at the nature of the horror genre, how we define a monster, and how we discuss the contradictory feelings of repulsion and attraction known as the paradox of horror.

---

[1] For two alternative accounts of the empathy (or sympathy) we feel for Hannibal Lecter, see Chapters 12 and 16 of this volume.—Ed.

18
Doctor, Heal Thyself

RICHARD MCCLELLAND

Hannibal Lecter is like many other animals found in nature: adept at hiding in plain view. We think of the praying mantis, the North American walking stick, chameleon lizards, the patterns of coloration on caterpillars, butterflies, moths, and birds. All often enable these creatures to hide from their predators while remaining in the open. Lecter hides his deepest motivations while practicing psychiatry in Baltimore for many years, only to be found out and captured more or less by accident. He hides in plain view when he has escaped from the authorities in Tennessee by the simple expedient of checking into a hotel near a major plastic surgery unit in St. Louis, where large bandages obscuring his face are not exceptional. He hides in plain view in Florence, Italy, as Dr. Fell, again in part by obscuring his true face and having had his extra finger removed from his left hand, and also by speaking a very pure and fluent Tuscan dialect of Italian, and possessing encyclopedic knowledge of Florentine culture and history. When we last see him, living in Buenos Aires, he is once again living in luxury and in the open, but disguised from his predators.

He is in all these respects, the master of illusion. We know that illusions are often worked by means of misdirection. I think Lecter works as an illusionist at a much deeper level than these would suggest, a level so deep as to reveal many of his own otherwise hidden psychological depths (and their underlying biology, which Harris renders with extraordinary realism and insight). To discover those depths we must look more closely at the history of Clarice Starling. Lecter begins to interact with her in *The Silence of the Lambs*, at the beginning of her FBI career. The interaction continues off and on for seven years, culminating in *Hannibal*, at the end of that career. Aristotle once observed that "choice reveals character more than actions do" (Aristotle, *Nicomachean Ethics* 1111b5). And it is arguable that choices, especially momentous choices, arise very often in our social relationships. Both Starling and Lecter make momentous choices in the course of their relationship, especially in the final stages that we see in the novels. We will misjudge the moral values of these choices until we look more deeply into their interaction and especially the transformation that it effects in both of them. Nor will we know why we do not like Hannibal Lecter—or we may dislike him for the wrong reasons.

Starling's Early Encounter with Lecter

Clarice Starling first encounters Dr. Hannibal Lecter in the asylum for the criminally insane in Baltimore. Lecter chooses to talk with her, when he has already refused to talk with many others. Evidently he finds her attractive, later saying, "I think it would be quite something to know you in private life" (Harris, *Silence*, p. 137). In the course of their conversations he gives her many insights into her own personality. These ring so true that Thomas Harris writes: "Here she had heard things about herself so terribly true her heart resounded like a great deep bell" (Harris, *Hannibal*, p. 78). Late in one of their talks, Lecter produces a pair of metaphors that foreshadows a much later and more profound interaction: the metaphor of the change a grub undergoes in its chrysalis (metamorphosis) and the metaphor of the *imago*, "an image of the parent buried in the unconscious from infancy and bound with infantile affect" (Harris, *Silence*, p. 149). It will be important to recall later that one of the strongest of the infantile emotions is rage. For both Starling and Lecter himself harbor important *imagoes* that are bound by rage and which in turn have bound them from free and adaptive action. The binding power of the imago is not released without dealing with its associated rage. The deep psychological exploration required to reach Starling's rage (primarily directed at her dead father) will require all of Lecter's medical (and especially pharmacological) skill, all of his psychotherapeutic insight, and a great deal of courage from both of them. He will also have to act as the consummate illusionist. However, before we see how this happens, there is further preparation for Starling's metamorphosis.

Starling's Social Exclusion: Stations on the Way

The novel *Hannibal* is as much the story of Starling's gradual disillusionment with the FBI as it is the story of Lecter's life in Florence, his capture by Mason Verger's Sardinian kidnappers, and his eventual rescue by Starling. We meet her after some seven years in federal service, years that have resulted in her career "flatlining." Starling has lived her life since childhood in institutional settings, following their constitutive rules with diligence and success until she encounters the rageful envy of Paul Krendler and others in the institutional hierarchy of the FBI, envy aroused by her early success in finding the serial killer Jame Gumb, ahead of and in spite of Krendler's machinations. Harris notes several times that Starling has no gift for or insight into institutional politics. At the same time, she is tempted by the corrosive responses of Krendler (and others) to doubt herself, rather than them: "The worm that destroys you is the temptation to agree with your critics, to get their approval" (Harris, *Hannibal*, p. 29). Both she and Jack Crawford, her mentor in the FBI, are substantially disillusioned by their experience of corrupt higher-ups. So strong is this commonality between them that Starling once falls out of her role as protégé and calls Crawford by his first name. Starling herself is aware that disillusionment is one of Dr. Lecter's surest sources of amusement and that he seeks to foster her "loss of faith." But such loss is also an objectively valid response to her situation. And things get worse.

Following the gunfight at the Feliciana Fish Market, a firefight in which John Brigham is killed and for which Starling is made to take the fall, we read: "Her coworkers had caution in their faces when they dealt with her, as though she had something contagious. Starling was young enough for this behavior to surprise and disappoint her" (Harris, *Hannibal*, p. 223). This is social exclusion, one of the most powerful forms of human behavior for the encouragement of social conformity and cooperation. We know from recent scientific studies that social exclusion tends to decrease a person's ability to inhibit socially unacceptable behavior, tends to increase, accordingly, aggressive responses to the exclusion, and tends to heighten a person's awareness of conflicts and errors, especially in the social behaviors of others. Social exclusion can also result in efforts to seek affiliation with new partners. The pain of social exclusion and these behavioral responses have well-known and distinctive bases in neural circuits of the brain. One thing social exclusion does not do, according to these studies, is tend to erode the self-esteem of the excluded person. Indeed, in Starling's case, her sense of confidence in herself is heightened by her exclusion, which is one element in the complex dynamic that exclusion causes in her.

Starling's "Sea Change"

There are three things notable about Starling's response to her social exclusion at the FBI. The first is her loss of faith in technique, in her forensic and FBI training in particular. The alternative is for Starling to turn to her own judgments, and especially her aesthetic judgments, her sense of taste. In doing so, she also begins to track the tastes of Dr. Lecter, as these are revealed by the patterns of his past purchases of exotic wines, foods, and cars. This trust in her own taste and judgment is the second element of Starling's dynamic response to exclusion.

The third is a certain kind of "letting go." She visits the grave of John Brigham, and while there she is reminded of her father's grave in Texas, which she thinks of visiting. Like her father, Brigham is now more firmly than ever something in the past (she thinks). About this time we also read that Starling, aware that Jack Crawford is about to retire, understands that his counsel will not always be available to her. This causes her "flashes of panic," but she carries on in her hunt for Lecter nonetheless, more confident in her own judgment than she has a right to be. She has taken a small step away from her dependence on Crawford also. She is learning to do without mentors. But Starling's pilgrim's progress has yet another stage to go through, one that is far more perilous.

Later in *Hannibal*, while on suspension from duty at the FBI, Starling defies the authorities in several ways. The first is to pursue Lecter's kidnappers to Verger's farm, despite her suspension—a pursuit which eventuates in Lecter's escape. She deliberately equips herself to impersonate an active FBI agent on her own authority, and while doing so, shoots and kills a (corrupt) off-duty sheriff's deputy in Verger's employ. With these actions, she distances herself immensely from her previous loyalty to the Bureau. In sum, she has finally "exited" from the institutional framework that has primarily shaped her early adulthood.

Later still, towards the close of the famous dinner Starling has with Paul Krendler, she finally kills the "worm" that used to destroy her. She says to Krendler: "Every time you wrote something negative in my personnel folder, I resented it, but I still searched myself. I doubted myself for a moment, and tried to scratch this tiny itch that said Daddy knows best" (Harris, *Hannibal*, p. 471). But no longer will she scratch that itch. No longer is it the case that "Daddy knows best." This turning marks an even deeper transition in Starling. This is the product of her metamorphosis, a deep-seated psychological change that is the product of her treatment at the hands of Dr. Lecter, to which treatment and its biological basis, I now turn.

What Happens Inside a Chrysalis

Metamorphosis, literally "change of form," is what some insects undergo to reach their mature form and structure (together with the causal powers that define that structure). The chrysalis itself is the body of the insect that emerges with its last molt or casting aside of its skin. Inside the chrysalis a set of powerful enzymes partially dissolve the tissues and organs of that body. The result is a largely undifferentiated "soup" which serves as culture medium for change. Several small cells (called "imaginal disks") start to grow and become new structures (rather like stem cells), such things as wings, legs, antennae and other organs. Most of the old organism is rebuilt, even its heart and much (though not all) of its nervous system. The whole process can take days, weeks, or months, depending on species and external conditions. It can use up as much as half of the original body weight of the insect, so much energy does it require. But not all the original structure is lost, else there would be nothing on which the rebuilding and reshaping process could work. Perhaps most startling of all is the survival in some insects of memories from its earlier experience as a grub. Some moths, for example, are known to preserve across the gulf of metamorphosis memories of food sources (plants) that were especially attractive or repulsive. These memories are postulated to reside in small clumps of neurons known as "mushroom bodies." They shape the later behavior and choices of the adult in these species.

Starling is rendered unconscious during her attempted rescue of Dr. Lecter, by the injection of a massive dose of the drug acepromazine. Lecter makes good his escape and takes her unconscious body with him, later to revive her with great care and to shepherd her through a long and arduous "treatment" which is the basis for her psychological metamorphosis. The changes she undergoes during that treatment constitute a restructuring of basic elements of her personality akin to what happens to the grub in its chrysalis. And, as we will see, Lecter himself is not unaffected by these changes.

Lecter first helps Starling to revive from the effects of acepromazine, taking care to do so gradually and safely. He then makes use of a combination of hypnotic/sedative drugs and "deep hypnosis" to engage her in a psychotherapeutic investigation aimed primarily at altering the parental *imago* he has hinted at in *The Silence of the Lambs*. He had already obtained the drugs in his raid on the dispensary at the Baltimore hospital where he used to work. The drugs Harris names here are noted for their sedative/hypnotic, sleep inducing powers, and also their capacity to relieve anxiety. The latter is probably the main reason Lecter wants them. It is notable that he secures these drugs well in advance of his capture by Verger's men. Clearly, Lecter is already planning some form of psychological intervention with Starling. His treatment of her is not merely fortuitous. Moreover, we learn what motivates that treatment, and with it uncover one of his major flaws as a therapist.

Replacing Mischa

The evening before his raid on the hospital drug supply, Lecter revisits a film about the work of the cosmologist Stephen Hawking. Hawking once thought that time could be reversed and the universe run backwards. Lecter hopes to follow

Hawking's thinking in this regard and imagines "the expanding universe to stop, for entropy to mend itself, for Mischa, eaten, to be whole again" (Harris, *Hannibal*, p. 363). Reminded by the more pedestrian evening news reports about Starling's disgrace and suspension from the FBI, and fueled by his desire for her, Lecter's imagination goes further:

> He held her countenance whole and perfect in his mind long after she was gone from the screen, and pressed her with another image, Mischa, pressed them together until, from the red plasma core of their fusion, the sparks flew upward, carrying their single image to the east, into the night sky to wheel with the stars above the sea. Now, should the universe contract, should time reverse . . . a place could be made for Mischa in the world. The worthiest place that Dr. Lecter knew: Starling's place. (Harris, *Hannibal*, p. 364)

Of course, such replacement may require the death of Starling herself. This possibility is not fully discounted until near the very end of her treatment with Lecter. It is already a grave flaw in him, as no responsible therapist would have such an agenda.[1]

I take his imaginings here to be a point of fixation in Lecter. At no time in Harris's novels is either Starling or Lecter (yet) assigned any adult sexual experience. Starling is fixated on her father, and thus prospective lovers like John Brigham inherit the incest taboo human culture places on parents. But something parallel has to be said about Lecter himself. Incest taboos also apply to siblings, and his fixation on reversing the fate of his beloved sister blocks him from complete intimacy with Lady Murasaki (otherwise freely offered to him by her). And it appears that such blockage has continued through his adulthood. It is perhaps his deepest flaw and at least partially responsible also for his eating of parts of some of his victims, as Mischa was murdered for food. He thereby seeks to reverse his earlier and traumatic inability to save Mischa from her fate. As we shall see, his fixation point is also relieved in the treatment with Starling, and thus she is not the only one to undergo metamorphosis.

---

[1] For a more wide-ranging study of the ethics of psychiatric practice as they apply to Dr. Lecter, see Chapter 5 of this volume.—Ed.

Hypnosis

Recent decades of scientific research have begun to uncover sound empirical bases for the practice of hypnosis. We have begun to see that hypnosis is a real phenomenon, that many of its characteristic features have real biological underpinnings, not least in the neural patterns of the brain during the different phases of the hypnotic experience. Much is disputed still, and much research remains to be done. But it is no longer possible to regard hypnosis and hypnotic therapy as a mere invention of folklore.

One real consequence of hypnosis is a relative lack of self-awareness while in the hypnotic state. Such awareness and thinking especially oriented to the self is supported by the default mode network of the brain (DMN), and we now know that important elements of the attentional system are negatively correlated with activity in the DMN, such that heightened activation of the attentional system lowers activation in the DMN. This appears now to be the objective basis for the subjective experience in hypnosis of lessened self-awareness. Harris repeatedly writes of Starling that, during hypnosis, she is "herself and not herself," "not yet herself," "awake and not awake" (Harris, *Hannibal*, pp. 440–41).

A further result of this condition is that the hypnotist, in this case Lecter, takes over the executive functions of the subject's brain. He does so by way of his suggestions. This is the basis for hallucinations under hypnosis: subjects can be made to see highly colored objects as lacking color, or the reverse. They can imagine complex scenes and psycho-dramas and take them for realities. Starling "visits" with her dead father, once in the person of Lecter himself (perhaps his greatest illusion), who dresses in his clothing and speaks in his voice. A subsequent "visit" is more realistic, as she views his skeleton and the hat he wore on the night he was killed. In the first of these visits, Starling is distinctly child-like in her behavior, and in the second is much more a grown person, closer to reality.

What Starling discovers, of course, was foreshadowed in Lecter's account of the parental imago in *Silence of the Lambs*: she discovers her enduring intense rage at her father for abandoning her and her family by his death. As her "treatment" progresses under Lecter's care, some of the tableaux she envisions involve her father, and some involve Paul Krendler:

> Her resentment of the very real injustices she had suffered at Krendler's hands was charged with the anger at her father that she could never, never acknowledge. She could not forgive her father for dying. He had left the family, he had stopped peeling oranges in the kitchen. He had doomed her mother to the commode brush and the pail. He had stopped holding Starling close . . . (Harris, *Hannibal*, p. 454)

Only now Starling is held close in the safety of the hypnotic state, under the care and watchfulness of Lecter (and with the aid of powerful anxiety-relieving drugs). And now she can revisit her hidden rage, draw it to the surface of her mind, metabolize it in the safety of the therapeutic setting. Only in this way can she achieve also a well-functioning and adaptive attitude towards her dead father, one that combines his best qualities with his worst in a mature representation that resides securely in her autobiographical memory. Only in this way can she achieve release from the fixation point that has been the mainspring of her life up to now. Only in this way can she expect to enjoy normal relationships with other men.

Metamorphosis

Lecter's treatment of Starling is like the action of a surgeon: he must dig deeply into her psyche to reach the abscess that threatens to poison her whole life. With success goes a whole restructuring of Starling's personality, a re-ordering of her emotional set, entertainment of a wider range of associations, discovery of new intentions and goals for action. The proof that she has gone this far lies in the closing stages of her treatment, especially during the dinner with Krendler. There she explicitly defies Krendler's authority to his face, as we have noted: "You *don't* know best, Mr. Krendler. In fact, you don't know anything . . . You are forever an . . . an *oaf*, and beneath notice" (Harris, *Hannibal*, p. 471). And there she asks for *more* of his brains to be served up in the opening course of the meal, "releasing in Dr. Lecter glee he could scarcely contain" (Harris, *Hannibal*, p. 474). Starling is also quite calm and accepting of Krendler's death by cross-bow. But there is more to her metamorphosis than this.

During the final course of the meal, Starling reverses the field on Lecter. He has confessed his desire to find a place in the world for Mischa and that Starling's place might suit. She responds, "If a prime place in the world is required for Mischa, and I'm not saying it isn't, what's the matter with *your* place? . . . if, as you say, there's room in me for my father, why is there not room in you for Mischa?" (Harris, *Hannibal*, p. 476). Lecter is discomfited by this move. But Starling is not finished with him, and there follows the famous scene where she offers him her own breast, drawing on her own experience to achieve a primary insight into Lecter himself: that he had resented his younger sister and having to give way to her at his mother's breast. This whole scene is pretty unrealistic, but emotionally and imaginatively satisfying. It seems to prove that Lecter has indeed suffered from a neurotic fixation on his sister (his denial here smacks of self-deception), as we have suspected all along since the story of his war-time experiences unfolded.

Lecter responds to Starling's invitation and they become lovers. And when we "see" them three years later, living in Buenos Aires, their love for one another, including adult sexuality, is thriving. Lecter has at that point not even dreamed of Mischa for several months. Better proof you could not have for the success of the treatment, as well as for the symmetry that is typical of deep psychotherapy, which changes both the patient and physician. Better proof you could not have for our hypothesis of a flaw in Lecter answering perfectly to the flaw in Starling. But have the illusions stopped?

A Concluding Challenge

I hope to have shown that Thomas Harris's imaginative intuition has discovered in Hannibal Lecter (and Clarice Starling) processes and dynamics that have a sound footing in our understanding of human biology and psychology. We can also see in both of them something that is common to the experience of social exclusion, namely the search for affiliation with new partners. Belonging is a fundamental human biological imperative, and both of these very unusual characters have that need as much as anyone else does. In finding each other and in forming what at least appears to be a successful partnership, they satisfy their common need.

It might be tempting to conclude that Lecter is a kind of "wounded healer," making use of a motif found widely in human cultures. It would be better, in my view, to say that he is a *flawed* healer. But, despite his flaws (his possibly murderous agenda, for example), it is finally the healing impulse that dominates in him. Lecter shares with Starling an inability to remain indifferent to the plight of innocent sufferers. This common characteristic may be largely responsible for the bond that has formed between them. The dominance in Lecter of the healing impulse also serves to order his motivational set. Out of that order emerges many of his most momentous choices.

And what of us? We may identify very strongly with Starling, especially. She has many very attractive qualities, after all. She is physically beautiful. She is intelligent. She is persistent and conscientious. She is brave, to a fault. She is strong, both physically and mentally. She is shown repeatedly to befriend others very well. Harris's portrait of her is such as to evoke our admiration and identification. We *pull* for Starling and for her success. This lays the ground for a challenge to us: perhaps the autonomy that Lecter thirsts for and that we see Starling begin to exercise might also be ours. Perhaps our institutional loyalties might be re-ordered in a similar fashion. Perhaps they need to be so re-ordered.

But can we really accept that Clarice Starling partners with Hannibal Lecter? Many of Harris's readers have refused to do so. And this is understandable. It is one reason for thinking that Lecter's "treatment" of Starling is itself immoral: delving too deeply into her personality results in a transformation into someone we do not recognize. True, both Starling and Lecter are released from their disabling incestuous fixations, and are able to undertake normal adult sexual relations. True, Starling is in need of release also from her "Daddy knows best" strategy with regard to major social institutions and their representatives. True, they seem, as we last see them, to be living a form of life that suits them and realizes many of their potentialities. They have established a well-functioning household. But she is now a fugitive along with Hannibal. And we do not know if their union will finally prove to be adaptive and a cause of their flourishing.

We also do not know, however, that it is an *impediment* to that flourishing. I take the view of any Aristotelian: whether the metamorphosis of Starling (and Lecter) is good or not depends on its long-term consequences. Especially important are the consequences with regard to their basic biology, given the constraints of their environment. And these we have not yet seen. Accordingly, it seems to me that the answer to the primary ethical question is that we do not know. And herein lies a standing challenge to us and to Harris.

The challenge to us is to take seriously the possibility of a similar metamorphosis in us, or at least in our imaginations. We see how far-reaching the results of Starling's "sea change" are. The incalculable consequences of such momentous changes are enough to frighten almost anyone. Think about what happens when people eschew religious belief, separate from an abusive spouse, leave their homeland, attempt a major career change, and so on. Indeed, fear of the results of such changes is one major reason why so many potential patients stay away from psychotherapy (as well they might). Such fear is, I submit, a sound basis for disliking Hannibal Lecter. And it is all very well to reject the outcome of *Hannibal* (as the filmmakers did). But it is quite another matter simply to burke the issues that Starling's history raises (as the filmmakers did, as well). The former is a difference of interpretation; the latter is a failure of courage.

Finally, there is implicit in the story of Hannibal Lecter a challenge for Thomas Harris himself. When we last see the couple at the end of *Hannibal*, they are living the life of wealthy individuals in Buenos Aires. But such a life may seem curiously empty. They dance, they go to the opera, they enjoy fine meals and talk to one another in many languages. But there are no children. There is no socially responsible work being done. Isn't this just another—albeit comfortable—"low-ceiling life?" (Harris, *Hannibal*, p. 454). What comes next? Can a 36-year old woman and a 68-year old man form a durable partnership? The challenge for Harris will be to return at least once more to Hannibal and Clarice, to explore his characters further, to see if their transformations allow for an autonomy that is genuinely worth having or if they are condemned to remain locked in some more profound illusion of human flourishing. Meanwhile, their temporary success may constitute a sharp-pointed poke at our own assumptions about what constitutes the good life.

*Whoever fights monsters should see to
it that in the process he does not become a
monster. And when you look long into an
abyss, the abyss also looks into you.*

— NIETZSCHE

Ingredients

The Hannibal Lecter Canon

Novels

Harris, Thomas. *Red Dragon*. New York: G.P. Putnam's Sons, 1981.
———. *The Silence of the Lambs*. New York: St. Martin's Press, 1988.
———. *Hannibal*. New York: Delacorte, 1999.
———. *Hannibal Rising*. New York: Delacorte, 2006.

Films

Mann, Michael, director. *Manhunter*. De Laurentiis Entertainment Group, 1986.
Demme, Jonathan, director. *The Silence of the Lambs*. Orion, 1991.
Scott, Ridley, director. *Hannibal*. Metro-Goldwyn-Mayer/Universal Pictures, 2001.
Ratner, Brett, director. *Red Dragon*. Metro-Goldwyn-Mayer, 2002.
Webber, Peter, director. *Hannibal Rising*. Dino de Laurentiis Company, 2007.

Television

Hannibal. Developed for television by Bryan Fuller. NBC, 2013–2015.

Stage

Red Dragon. Adapted for the stage by Christopher Johnson. Premiered at the Defiant Theatre, Chicago, 1996.
Silence! The Musical. Book by Hunter Bell. Music and lyrics by Jon and Al Kaplan. Premiered at the Lucille Lortel Theatre, New York, 2005.

Works about Hannibal Lecter

Bottai, Sean, and Kristine Peashock. "Movie Discussion: Michael Mann's *Manhunter* (1986)," *Girl Meets Freak: Rethinking Horror Movies* (blog), April 15, 2014.

Brown, Jennifer. *Cannibalism in Literature and Film*. Basinstoke, UK: Palgrave Macmillan, 2012.

Carroll, Noël. "Enjoying Horror Fictions: A Reply to Gaut." *British Journal of Aesthetics* 35 (1995): 67–72.

———. "Horror and Humor." *Journal of Aesthetics and Art Criticism* 57, no. 2 (1999): 145–60.

Conceição, Ricky da, Simon Howell, and Edgar Chaput. "Michael Mann's *Thief* and *Manhunter*." *Sordid Cinema Podcast*, no. 56 (audio recording), *Sound on Sight*, April 28, 2013.

DeLisi, Matt, Michael G. Vaughn, Kevin M. Beaver, and John Paul Wright. "The Hannibal Lecter Myth: Psychopathy and Verbal Intelligence in the MacArthur Violence Risk Assessment Study." *Journal of Psychopathology and Behavioral Assessment* 32, no. 2 (2010): 169–77.

Dery, Mark. "Eat the Rude: Hannibal Lecter Meets the 99%." *Boing Boing*, February 17, 2015.

Freeland, Cynthia A. *The Naked and the Undead: Evil and the Appeal of Horror*. Boulder, CO: Westview Press, 2000.

———. "Realist Horror." In *Aesthetics: The Big Questions*, ed. Carolyn Korsmeyer. Malden, MA & Oxford: Blackwell, 1998, 283–93.

Greggio, Ezio, director. *The Silence of the Hams*. Silvio Berlusconi Productions/30th Century Wolf, 1994.

Harris, Thomas. "Author's Note." In *The Silence of the Lambs*, 25th Anniversary Edition. London: Arrow Books, 2013.

———. "Foreword." In *Red Dragon*. New York: Berkley Books, 2000.

Hill, Libby. "God, the Devil and 'Hannibal'." *Monkey–See: Pop Culture News and Analysis from NPR* (blog), *National Public Radio*, May 23, 2014.

Jensen, Jeff. "Hannibal." *Entertainment Weekly*, June 20, 2013.

King, Stephen. "Hannibal the Cannibal." *New York Times*, June 13, 1999.

Lewis, Paul. *Cracking Up: American Humor in a Time of Conflict*. Chicago: University of Chicago Press, 2006.

McLean, Jesse. *The Art and Making of Hannibal: The Television Series*. London: Titan Books, 2015.

McNamara, Mary. "'Hannibal' Drains the Mirth Out of Lecter." *Los Angeles Times*, April 4, 2013.

Poon, Janice. "Episode 10 Naka choko," *Feeding Hannibal* (blog), May 7, 2014.

Robinson, Mike (mister X). "A Tale of Two Lecters: 'Red Dragon' vs. 'Manhunter'." *Film Threat*, October 10, 2002.

Schneider, Steven, and Daniel Shaw, editors. *Dark Thoughts: Philosophic Reflections on Cinematic Horror*. London: Scarecrow Press, 2003.

Seitz, Matt Zoller, and Aaron Aradillas. "Do You See?: Michael Mann's Reflections, Doubles, and Doppelgängers." *Zen Pulp*, Part 4 (video). *Moving Image Source*, July 15, 2009.

Shaw, Daniel. "The Birth of a Killer: *Hannibal Rising*." *Philosopher's Magazine*, no. 47 (2009).

———. "The Mastery of Hannibal Lecter." In *Dark Thoughts: Philosophic Reflections on Cinematic Horror*, edited by Steven Schneider and Daniel Shaw. London: Scarecrow Press, 2003, 10–24.

———. "Power, Horror and Ambivalence." *Film and Philosophy*, Special Edition on Horror, edited by Daniel Shaw (2001), 1–12.

Simpson, Philip L. *Making Murder: The Fiction of Thomas Harris*. Santa Barbara, CA: Praeger, 2010.

Stephenson, Cliff, director and producer. "A Taste for Killing" (commentary). *Hannibal: Season One* [Blu-ray]. Lions Gate Films, 2013.

———, director and producer. "This Is My Design" (commentary). *Hannibal: Season Two* [Blu-ray]. Lions Gate Films, 2014.

Szumskyj, Benjamin, editor. *Dissecting Hannibal Lecter: Essays on the Novels of Thomas Harris*. Jefferson, NC: McFarland & Company, 2008.

Ullyatt, Tony. "To Amuse the Mouth: Anthropophagy in Thomas Harris's Tetralogy of Hannibal Lecter Novels," *Journal of Literary Studies* 28 (2012): 4–20.

Walker, Doug. "Nostalgia Critic: Old vs New—*Manhunter* and *Red Dragon*" (video). *Channel Awesome*, April 10, 2012.

White, Mike, Rob St. Mary, and Mike Robinson (mister X). "*Manhunter*" (podcast). *The Projection Booth*, Episode 170. June 10, 2014.

Other Resources

Agamben, Giorgio. *Homo Sacer: Sovereign Power and Bare Life*. Translated by Daniel Heller-Roazen. Stanford: Stanford University Press, 1998.

———. *The Open: Man and Animal*. Translated by Kevin Attell. Stanford: Stanford University Press, 2003.

Alderman, Harold. *Nietzsche's Gift*. Athens, OH: Ohio University Press, 1977.

Aristotle. *The Nicomachean Ethics*. Translated by David Ross and Lesley Brown. Oxford: Oxford University Press, 2009.

Avramescu, Cătălin. *An Intellectual History of Cannibalism*. Translated by Alistair Ian Blyth. Princeton: Princeton University Press, 2009.

Bataille, Georges. *The Bataille Reader*. Edited by Fred Botting and Scott Wilson. Oxford, UK: Blackwell, 1997.

———. *Erotism: Death & Sensuality*. Translated by Mary Dalwood. San Francisco: City Lights, 1986.

Beam, Christopher. "Blood Loss: The Decline of the Serial Killer." *Slate*, January 5, 2011.

Berry-Dee, Christopher. *Cannibal Serial Killers: Profiles of Depraved Flesh-Eating Murderers*. Berkeley, CA: Ulysses Books, 2011.

Brillat-Savarin, Jean Anthelme. *The Physiology of Taste: or, Meditations on Transcendental Gastronomy*. Translated by M.F.K. Fisher. New York: Knopf, 2009.

Bruun Vaage, Margrethe. "The Empathic Film Spectator in Analytic Philosophy and Naturalized Phenomenology." *Film and Philosophy* 10 (2006): 21–38.

Bullough, Edward. "'Psychical Distance' as a Factor in Art and an Aesthetic Principle." *British Journal of Psychology* 5, no. 2 (1912): 87–118.

Buss, David. *The Murderer Next Door: Why the Mind is Designed to Kill*. New York: Penguin, 2005.

Carroll, Noël. *The Philosophy of Horror, or: Paradoxes of the Heart*. New York and London: Routledge, 1990.

Cleckley, Hervey. *The Mask of Sanity: An Attempt to Clarify Some Issues about the So-Called Psychopathic Personality,* 5th ed. Emily S. Cleckley (private printing), 1988.

Dolan, Maria. "The Gruesome History of Eating Corpses as Medicine." *Smithsonian.com*, May 6, 2012.

Douglas, John and Mark Olshaker. *Mindhunter: Inside the FBI Elite Serial Crime Unit*. London: Arrow Books, 2006.

Dumas, Alexandre. *Dictionary of Cuisine*, edited and translated by Louis Colman. London: Routledge, 2005.

Ellis, Brian. *Scientific Essentialism*. Cambridge: Cambridge University Press, 2001.

Egger, Steven. "The Less Dead." In *Encyclopedia of Murder and Violent Crime*, edited by Eric Hickey. London: Sage, 2003.

Everts, Sarah. "Europe's Hypocritical History of Cannibalism." *Smithsonian.com*, April 24, 2013.

Feeney, F.X. *Michael Mann*. Edited by Paul Duncan. Koln & London: Taschen, 2006.

Foucault, Michel. *The History of Madness*. Translated by Jonathan Murphy and Jean Khalfa. Abingdon, UK: Routledge, 2006.

Fox, James Alan, and Jack Levin. "A Surprising Truth about Serial Killings." *CNN*, October 24, 2014.

———. *Extreme Killing: Understanding Serial and Mass Murder*. 3rd ed. Thousand Oaks, CA: Sage, 2015.

Girard, René. *Deceit, Desire, and the Novel: Self and Other in Literary Structure*. Translated by Yvonne Freccero. Baltimore: Johns Hopkins, 1965.

Griswold, Eliza. "The truth behind the cannibals of Congo." *Independent*, March 26, 2004.

Hegel, Georg Wilhelm Friedrich. *Introductory Lectures on Aesthetics*. London: Penguin, 1993.

Herodotus. *The Histories*. Translated by Aubrey de Sélincourt. London: Penguin, 2003.

Hirschman, Albert. *Exit, Voice, and Loyalty: Responses to Decline in Firms, Organizations, and States*. Cambridge, MA: Harvard University Press, 1970.

Howe, David. *Empathy: What It Is and Why It Matters*. New York: Palgrave Macmillan, 2012.

Iacoboni, Marco. *Mirroring People: The Science of Empathy and How We Connect with Others*. New York: Picador, 2009.

Irvine, William B. "Cannibalism, Vegetarianism and Narcissism." *Between the Species* 5, no. 1 (1989): 11–17.

Jenkins, Philip. "Catch Me Before I Kill More: Seriality as Modern Monstrosity." *Cultural Analysis* 3 (2002): 1–17.

Logan, Caroline. "Cannibal Warlords of Liberia." *Borgen Magazine*, July 3, 2014.

Lu, Matthew. "Explaining the Wrongness of Cannibalism." *American Catholic Philosophical Quarterly* 87, no. 3 (2013): 433–58.

Maibom, Heidi, and James Harold. "Without Taste: Psychopaths and the Appreciation of Art," *La Nouvelle Revue Française d'Esthétique* 6 (2010): 71–84.

Mauss, Marcel. *The Gift: The Form and Reason for Exchange in Archaic Societies*. Translated by W.D. Halls. New York: W.W. Norton, 1990.

Mearns, Dave, and Brian Thorne. *Person-Centered Counselling in Action*. 4th ed. London: SAGE Publications Ltd, 2013.

Meloy, J. Reid, and Jessica Yakeley. "Antisocial Personality Disorder." In *Diagnostic and Statistical Manual of Mental Disorders*. 5th ed. (DSM-5). Arlington, VA: American Psychiatric Publishing, 2013.

Montaigne, Michel de. "On the Cannibals." In *The Complete Essays*, translated by M.A. Screech. New York: Penguin, 2003.

Neiman, Susan. *Evil in Modern Thought: An Alternative History of Philosophy*. Princeton: Princeton University Press, 2002.

Nietzsche, Friedrich. *Twilight of the Idols and The Anti-Christ*. Translated by R. J. Hollingdale. New York: Penguin, 1968.

———. *The Dawn of Day*. Translated by John M. Kennedy. New York: The MacMillan Company, 1911.

———. *The Gay Science*. Translated by Walter Kaufmann. New York: Vintage, 1968.

———. *Thus Spoke Zarathustra*. In *The Portable Nietzsche*, edited and translated by Walter Kaufmann. New York: Penguin, 1954.

———. *The Will to Power*. Translated by Dragan Nikolic. Chicago: Aristeus Books, 2012.

Novitz, David. *The Boundaries of Art: A Philosophical Inquiry into the Place of Art in Everyday Life*. Rev. ed. Rochester, MN: Cybereditions, 2001.

Plantinga, Carl. "The Scene of Empathy and the Human Face in Film." In *Passionate Views: Film, Cognition and Emotion*, edited by Carl Plantinga and Greg M. Smith. Baltimore: Johns Hopkins University Press, 1999.

Plato. *Phaedrus*. Translated by Alexander Nehamas and Paul Woodruff. Indianapolis: Hackett Publishing, 1995.

Proctor, Robert N., and Londa Schiebinger, eds. *Agnotology: The Making and Unmaking of Ignorance*. Palo Alto: Stanford University Press, 2008.

Rifkin, Jeremy. *The Empathic Civilization: The Race to Global Consciousness in a World in Crisis*. New York: Penguin, 2009.

Rogers, Carl. *Client-Centered Therapy: Its Current Practice, Implications, and Theory*. London: Constable and Robinson Limited, 2003.

Sanday, Peggy Reeves. *Divine Hunger: Cannibalism as a Cultural System*. Cambridge: Cambridge University Press, 1986.

Schmall, Emily, and Wade Williams. "Liberia's Elections, Ritual Killings and Cannibalism." *GlobalPost*, August 1, 2011.

Sedgwick, Eve Kosofsky. *Between Men: English Literature and Male Homosocial Desire*. New York: Columbia University Press, 1985.

Siegel, Eli. *Self and World: An Explanation of Aesthetic Realism*. New York: Definition Press, 1981.

Sugg, Richard. *Mummies, Cannibals and Vampires: The History of Corpse Medicine from the Renaissance to the Victorians*. London: Routledge, 2011.

Thompson, Andrea. "Neanderthals Were Cannibals, Study Confirms." *LiveScience*, December 4, 2006.

Travis-Henikoff, Carole A. *Dinner with a Cannibal: The Complete History of Mankind's Oldest Taboo*. Santa Monica, CA: Santa Monica Press, 2008.

Ungar, Michael. *The Social Ecology of Resilience: A Handbook of Theory and Practice*. New York: Springer, 2012.

Vronsky, Peter. *Serial Killers: The Method and Madness of Monsters*. New York: Berkley Books, 2004.

Wilde, Oscar. *The Picture of Dorian Gray*. Mineola, NY: Dover, 1993.

Wittgenstein, Ludwig. *Notebooks, 1914–1916*. 2nd ed. Translated by G.E.M. Anscombe. Chicago: University of Chicago Press, 1979.

The Psychopaths

Here we are: a bunch of psychopaths, helping each other out.

—Freddie Lounds in *Hannibal*, Season 1, "Entrée"

Shai Biderman holds a PhD in philosophy from Boston University, and teaches film and philosophy at Tel Aviv University and at Beit-Berl College, Israel. He is the co-editor of *The Philosophy of David Lynch* (2011), and has published articles and book chapters in philosophy of film, film analysis, and film-philosophy, in journals such as *Film and Philosophy* and *Cinema*, and in edited volumes such as *The Philosophy of the Western* (2010), *The Philosophy of Science Fiction Film* (2008), *Lost and Philosophy* (2008), and *Movies and the Meaning of Life* (2005). He enjoys writing papers with his co-author, Will, not because of Will's writing style or the fact that he can interpret the evidence of psychopathic monsters, but because his liver will more than likely taste good with some fava beans and a nice Chianti.

Selena K.L. Breikss is a graduate student at Washington State University, pursuing a PhD in American studies. Her broad academic interests are in gender, race, and class in film and television. After seeing *The Silence of the Lambs* at a young age, she dreamed of being the next Clarice Starling and has continued to be an avid Fannibal (complete with themed tattoos and a bearded dragon named Mason Verger). When she is not being gorged, drowned, plucked, and roasted by graduate school, she spends her free time crafting, reading, baking, and cooking—often having friends for dinner.

When the body of **Jason Davis** was eventually found, the fact that some of his organs had been removed post-mortem was not made public. Crime writers and bloggers covering his murder had already made cheap irony of how he had been a contributor to *Dexter and Philosophy* (2011). But should anyone caring to uncover more about his death at Macquarie University where he worked, a hastily obscured copy on his desk of *Planet of the Apes and Philosophy* (2013), which he'd also contributed to, hides something much more telling. Waiting in its pages is a torn and creased photo of an immaculately dressed, balding yet ponytailed man Jason had been tailing as a mysterious donor to the university. And on the other side, in elegant handwriting, half of a recipe for devilled kidneys.

WILLIAM J. DEVLIN holds a PhD in philosophy from Boston University, and is Associate Professor at Bridgewater State University and Summer Lecturer at University of Wyoming. He is the co-editor of *The Philosophy of David Lynch* (2011), and has published articles and book chapters in philosophy of film and philosophy of popular culture concerning such topics as time-travel, ethics, Nietzsche, and selfhood. He is published in edited volumes such as *The Philosophy of Steven Soderbergh* (2011), *The Philosophy of the Western* (2010), *The Philosophy of Science Fiction Film* (2008), and *Lost and Philosophy* (2008). He also publishes in the field of philosophy of science and is co-editor of the volume, *Kuhn's Structure of Scientific Revolutions: 50 Years On* (2015). As much as he enjoys writing papers with his friend and co-author, Dr. Biderman, he is just now beginning to grow suspicious that the good Doctor is trying to eat him.

DERRICK HASSERT is Professor of Psychology, Chair of the Department of Psychology, and Chair of the Division of Social and Behavioral Science at Trinity College in Palos Heights, Illinois. He teaches courses in neuropsychology, cognitive neuroscience, and ethics, and has published in the areas of cognitive and behavioral neuroscience, neuroethics, and philosophy of mind. While he has served edible brains to his students, they have all been made of gelatin—and none of them were Paul Krendler's.

JASON HOLT is Professor at Acadia University, where he teaches courses in philosophy and communication for the School of Kinesiology. His principal research area is aesthetics. His books include *Blindsight and the Nature of Consciousness* (2003), various edited volumes, and literary works, most recently a book of poetry, *Inversed* (2014). He's more into Valpolicella than Chianti.

TIM JONES holds a PhD from the University of East Anglia in England, where he also teaches literature. He also holds a Diploma in

Counselling and Psychotherapy and so is pretty proficient at thinking about and working with the empathy discussed in his chapter. If you didn't enjoy reading it, you're objectively wrong and deserve to be eaten.

DANIEL P. MALLOY is a lecturer at Appalachian State University, where he teaches a wide variety of philosophy courses and cooks a wide variety of dishes. His research focuses on issues in ethics, broadly construed. He has published numerous chapters on the intersection of popular culture and philosophy. Daniel took up cooking as a serious endeavor about the same time that *Hannibal* hit the airwaves, which he assures us is pure coincidence. As of this writing, he has mastered many French and Japanese dishes, and plans to begin learning the art of Italian cuisine soon.

JOHN MCATEER is Assistant Professor at Ashford University, where he serves as Chair of the Liberal Arts program. Before receiving his PhD in philosophy from the University of California at Riverside, he earned a BA in film from Biola University and an MA in philosophy of religion and ethics from Talbot School of Theology. He probably has an empathy disorder, but he doesn't really care what you think about that. Like Hannibal, he never feels guilty eating anything.

RICHARD T. MCCLELLAND holds a PhD from the University of Cambridge. He also pursued post-graduate training in two psychoanalytic institutes in the Seattle area for some years. He retired as Professor of Philosophy from Gonzaga University in January 2014. His research is at the juncture of philosophy of mind, evolutionary psychology, and cognitive neuroscience. He is married, with three grown children and three grandchildren and lives in British Columbia, Canada. He continues to pursue a vigorous program of research and writing, and reports happily that the percentage of severe psychopathology (including psychopathy itself) in his near vicinity has declined markedly since his retirement; alas, his last chance to capture a pure psychopath alive was almost certainly while working among university faculty.

BENJAMIN W. MCCRAW teaches philosophy at the University of South Carolina Upstate. His research focuses on epistemology and philosophy of religion, and he has published articles recently in *Social Epistemology* and the *International Journal for Philosophy of Religion*. In addition, he's the co-editor of a forthcoming trilogy of books on really scary stuff on the devil, hell, and evil—but he's unlikely to be mistaken for Shaitan in the streets of Florence. He assures us his is not the least common form of polydactyly.

TRIP MCCROSSIN teaches in the Philosophy Department at Rutgers University, where he works on, among other things, the nature, history, and legacy of the Enlightenment. The present essay is part of a broader effort to view various forms of popular culture through the lens of Susan Neiman's understanding of the same. He's occasionally tempted in class to counsel, "Simplicity! Read Marcus Aurelius: Of each particular thing, ask what is it in itself, what is its particular nature?," but suspects that someone might just get the wrong idea. He's also occasionally hopeful that if in the end even Lecter can find love without computer dating, then there's got to be hope still for the rest of us!

ANDREW PAVELICH received his PhD from Tulane University in philosophy in 1999. He is now Associate Professor at the University of Houston-Downtown, where he teaches a wide variety of classes that may or may not appeal to Hannibal, including Ethics, World Religions, and the Philosophy of Death. He is a sometimes vegetarian, but would almost certainly jump at the chance to eat a drowned, plucked, and roasted songbird, bones and all.

DAN SHAW is a professor of philosophy at Lock Haven University, and Managing Editor of the journal *Film and Philosophy*. He first proposed his Nietzschean power-based theory of horror in a special edition of that journal on horror (2000). With Steven Schneider, he is the co-editor of *Dark Thoughts: Philosophic Reflections on Cinematic Horror* (2003), where he characterized Hannibal Lecter as exhibiting a mastery reminiscent of Nietzsche's Overman. He is also the author of a critical review of *Hannibal Rising* ("The Birth of a Killer," 2009), a book on ethics and film (*Morality and the Movies*, 2012), and a book on existentialism and film (*Movies with Meaning*, 2016). His relish of horror is complete, and he once said that he wouldn't mind being Hannibal Lecter for just one day, to feel what such amoral control would be like—especially at mealtimes.

JOSEPH WESTFALL is not a Pazzi of the Pazzi, but is a Westfall of the Westfalls (bowels in). He is Associate Professor of Philosophy at the University of Houston-Downtown, and the author of *The Kierkegaardian Author* (2007) as well as numerous articles and book chapters, including a contribution to *Curb Your Enthusiasm and Philosophy* (2012). His research interests are primarily in European philosophy, aesthetics, and the philosophy of literature and film. He is very likely someday soon to begin receiving aftershave for Christmas that smells like it has a ship on the bottle, and is perfectly happy responding to such criticism with the maniacally insightful retort, "Smell yourself!" He likes to think he eats well, and has no known victims.

MANDY-SUZANNE WONG is an independent scholar and writer. She holds a PhD in musicology from UCLA, and began her academic career as a musicologist. During her research on late-twentieth-century musical philosophies, she became fascinated by Dr. H. Lecter's unique approach to, shall we say, *taking in* classical music and musicians. (See the case of Benjamin Raspail: the juicy bits do surprisingly well in the fridge.) This predilection was unfortunate, for it did not sit well with her colleagues. Since they adamantly assured her that she was making it all up, she turned to writing fiction. And indeed, the company of homicidal trees, argumentative amphibians, and other maniacs of various degrees of nonexistence seemed to suit her well. To exacerbate her instability, she began to hang around philosophers: reckless individuals who cook up wild ideas to suit their dangerously adventurous palates. Her seizure of the editorship of *Evental Aesthetics,* a philosophical journal, testifies to her issues with control.

ANDREA ZANIN has always been partial to a little killer with her Chianti and her writing path, by natural inclination, has taken her on a journey through the moonstruck minds of the butchers and brutes that horror has spewed into society with diabolical delight. It all started in South Africa, a country all too familiar with scandalous crime and sociopathic tendencies but, as a *cum laude* English honors graduate (with a law degree to boot) from the University of Johannesburg, Andrea has used her "classical" education as a platform to pick apart the psyches of such offenders, translating man's dark heart into something . . . *more palatable.* Currently based in London, Andrea is a working writer/editor with expertise in discourse analysis; she is also the author of pop-culture blog Rantchick.com, and has contributed a chapter to *Sons of Anarchy and Philosophy* (2013).

Index

Lightning Source UK Ltd.
Milton Keynes UK
UKHW011033191218
334260UK00014B/1586/P